ADVANCE PRAISE FOR *POSTGATE*

"John O'Connor's *Postgate* is a welcome new piece of the Watergate puzzle. Part memoir as Deep Throat's attorney, part deep dive into overlooked aspects of the nation's greatest political scandal, *Postgate* is an investigation of the investigators–how the *Washington Post* crafted its coverage of Watergate, what was included and what was left out."

–Luke A. Nichter, Author of *The Nixon Tapes: 1973*

"In *Postgate*, Mark Felt's lawyer, John O'Connor, continues his masterful duel with Bob Woodward and the *Washington Post*. Having previously forced Woodward to name Felt as Deep Throat, O'Connor now uncovers in *Postgate* layer upon layer of deceit concealing the true story of Watergate and its journalism. It is a must-read for anyone interested in our country's most significant scandal."

–Len Colodny, Author of *Silent Coup: The Removal of a President*

"John O'Connor has done it again. The sleuthing attorney who uncovered the identity of the whistleblower of Watergate, Deep Throat–when every reporter, historian, and would-be detective failed–now sets his sights on the WHY of Watergate. More than forty-five years after the infamous break-in, pundits and politicians still cannot fathom the purpose of the botched political spy escapade. Building his case as the reader would expect from a brilliant courtroom lawyer, O'Connor takes us through the corridors of Washington power–including the *Washington Post*, the CIA, the FBI, and the White House–to discover the most probable answer–along with the episode's real instigators."

–Dan Lungren, Former US Representative
and Attorney Generalfor California

How the *Washington Post* Betrayed Deep Throat, Covered Up Watergate, and Began Today's Partisan Advocacy Journalism

JOHN O'CONNOR

A POST HILL PRESS BOOK
ISBN: 978-1-64293-259-1
ISBN (eBook): 978-1-64293-260-7

Postgate:
How the *Washington Post* Betrayed Deep Throat, Covered Up Watergate, and Began Today's Partisan Advocacy Journalism

Cover art by Cody Corcoran
Interior design and layout by Sarah Heneghan, sarah-heneghan.com

Post Hill Press
New York • Nashville
posthillpress.com

Published in the United States of America

To my first grandson, John Michael Kawaja (DOB 9/9/2018), in hopes that he will live in a society in which our news media attempt to report as objectively as possible all salient facts, varying opinions are encouraged, and the marketplace of ideas is truly open for business.

Table of Contents

Introduction xi

Chapter One: Calling Woodward 1
Chapter Two: The *Post* Uncovers Watergate 8
Chapter Three: Deep Throat 17
Chapter Four: Meeting Deep Throat 36
Chapter Five: Felt's Friend 43
Chapter Six: Mark to Kill 53
Chapter Seven: The Secret Man 66
Chapter Eight: The *Post*'s Publisher 82
Chapter Nine: Woodward And Bernstein Visit Deep Throat 99
Chapter Ten: The Epiphany 104
Chapter Eleven: The Unexplored Story 114
Chapter Twelve: Mullen And Hunt 126
Chapter Thirteen: The Hermès Notebooks,
The CIA Defense, And Dean 139
Chapter Fourteen: The Baldwin Cover-Up 153
Chapter Fifteen: The Burglary Trial Concealment 171
Chapter Sixteen: James McCord 183
Chapter Seventeen: Michael Stevens 200
Chapter Eighteen: Lou Russell 209
Chapter Nineteen: Eugenio Martinez and the Key to Watergate 219
Chapter Twenty: The Baker Report 235
Chapter Twenty-One: The *Post* Responds 246
Chapter Twenty-Two: G. Gordon Liddy 256
Chapter Twenty-Three: Final Argument 264

Acknowledgments 266
Cast of Characters 267
Index 275

INTRODUCTION

In April 2002, I began representing Mark Felt, a man I knew was Watergate's Deep Throat but who had not yet admitted that to his family or, of course, to me. I soon persuaded Mark to admit his identity in major part by promising him that I would tell the world his story and that of his beloved FBI. I would not leave him or his Bureau, I told him, at the mercy of description after death by Bob Woodward, the *Washington Post* reporter with whom he worked to end a successful cover-up of responsibility for the Watergate burglary.

As I will describe in this book, my precautionary advice about Woodward's postmortem depiction was prescient. My promise to him to tell his story widely and well, it turned out, took on far more significance than I could have predicted.

I wrote what I think was a decent article in *Vanity Fair* magazine in June 2005 ("I'm the Guy They Called Deep Throat") revealing Mark's role and recounting his motives, a piece I credit in no small part to my brilliant editor David Friend. But my later book, *A G-Man's Life*, traveled a much rockier path as I tried to fulfill in more depth my promise to Mark.

Because of interference from my publisher of *A G-Man's Life*, I was unable either to expound on the complex relationship between this omniscient source and the glorified journalist who was his outlet, nor upon Mark's investigative insights that Watergate was about far more than Nixonian evil.

To the contrary, I wished to detail that the churlish and unattractive Nixon may well have been a victim as much as a victimizer in Watergate—without, I hasten to add, offering excuse for his criminal behavior. Much of the Watergate story that Mark Felt wished to tell was, in short, not told at the time, and I was frustrated in my efforts to tell it later.

To top off my constrained authorial performance, the book was marketed seemingly so amateurishly that the publisher's promotional efforts likely suppressed sales rather than enhanced them.

However, some years after publication I realized I had been, and more importantly my client had been, victimized not by ineptitude but by fraud designed to suppress his important story. I needed to learn why. I needed to know the intent and motive behind this, which I now know involved a thuggish *Washington Post* acting in league with my not-so-amateur publisher.

I had spent over two years of my life in the mid-1970s sussing out the identity of the Deep Throat character depicted in *All the President's Men*. Now I vowed to determine why the *Post* would resort to extreme, childishly fraudulent measures to contain our story, no matter how long it took me. What was the paper hiding? The result is this book.

For the Watergate story, the *Washington Post* could not have found itself in a better place at a better time. Washington, DC, was still a bit of a backwater in 1972, and the *Post* faced only weak competition from the poorly funded *Star-News*. Because the burglary began as a local crime matter, the paper had a natural monopoly on the witnesses–most in government or local and federal law enforcement where the paper's crime reporters had long been firmly imbedded–thus putting the *Post* far ahead of major newspapers in other areas. Although cable television news and talk radio would come soon after, they weren't ubiquitous yet, and major networks did few original investigations. So the field was clear for the *Post*.

Like many other Americans, I had become a huge fan of the *Post* during Watergate, as it overcame the Nixon administration's initial charge of partisanship and was proven bull's-eye correct.

As Watergate was winding down, I looked forward to a new era of great investigative journalism modeled after that of Bob Woodward and Carl Bernstein. As a young assistant United States attorney, I saw that this in-depth reporting would not only inform the citizenry but would also assist white-collar law enforcement. But at each key juncture, I found myself disappointed in what followed.

In 1978, for instance, Mark Felt, whom I knew to be Deep Throat, was indicted for authorizing warrantless break-ins, or "black bag jobs," of the supporters of the Weather Underground, who were engaged in a widespread campaign of bombing government buildings. Even though warrantless searches for national security purposes have always been constitutional (Felt's case gave rise to the Foreign Intelligence Surveillance Act, better known as FISA, which authorizes searches for national security reasons that would not otherwise be compliant with the Bill of Rights), the *Post* was the loudest cheerleader for Felt's indictment and conviction.

But at almost the same time, Billy Carter–brother of then-president Jimmy Carter–broke the law as a dishonest and undeclared foreign agent for America's biggest terrorist enemy, Libya's Muammar Gaddafi, yet the *Post*[1] supported a corrupt deal letting Billy off with a civil case wrist slap, contrary to normal prosecutorial guidelines.

The *Post* supported Iran-Contra independent counsel Lawrence Walsh, in spite of his dismaying ethical abuses, such as the 1988 "October surprise" indictment of Reagan officials, clearly intended for electoral impact. But Independent Counsel Kenneth Starr was later subjected to unremitting *Post* criticism when he went after its boy Bill Clinton, even though Starr, compared with Walsh, was a teddy bear.

In 2004, after Vice President Dick Cheney's chief of staff Lewis "Scooter" Libby was indicted in a "perjury trap," where there was no possibility of a criminal violation (Valerie Plame did not qualify for protection of her identity as a foreign agent), the *Post* was silent on clear prosecutorial abuses perpetrated mainly by acting attorney general James Comey.

When facts needed to be molded to fit a preconceived narrative, as, for example, in the Duke Lacrosse, Covington Catholic High School, and Trayvon Martin cases, the *Post* complied, covering up exculpatory facts while distorting others in order to destroy the designated villain.

In all these cases, and many more, I saw these failings as simply a fall-off from the near perfection of Watergate, where a clearly guilty White House was no match for the *Post*'s energetic reporting, especially aided by a gold-plated source.

1 Richard Cohen, "Personalities Only Part of Billy Carter Affair," *Washington Post*, August 3, 1980. Cohen writes this about Billy Carter, an undeclared paid agent of America's then most dangerous terrorist enemy: "It is really the story of the inability of our nation to deal with a bandit regime because we have neither the will nor the capacity to say 'no' to oil. Beggars, after all, can't be choosers."

But, sadly to say, as I fought my publisher on writing the Felt book, I came to realize that the widely praised Watergate journalism was not an exception to the often dishonest reporting frequently put forth by respected outlets; it was the cause.

While conservatives attribute this biased reporting to the leftist bent of most journalists, there is a sound argument that conservative investigations are just as biased, albeit perhaps less numerous because of the liberal leanings of a great majority of journalists. Indeed, the only difference between the liberal bias of the *Post* outlined above and the conservative bias of the "birther" and Vince Foster conspiracies is the established mainstream reach and respectability of the *Post*. So I here do not limit deceptive journalism to the left. The two wildly differing media renditions of the recent *Mueller Report* serve to confirm this point.

Rather, in my view, the problem is inherent in the hunt-to-kill orientation of modern investigative journalism itself, as pioneered by the *Post*. By sticking to the "who, what, when, where, why, and how" of traditional journalism, a good reporter tends to tell all the facts regardless of which way they cut. But a modern investigative journalist (that is, one trying to prove someone or something wrong) is not successful if he or she tells both sides. It is as if a lawyer can speak to a jury to seek a verdict without an opponent and judge present. Is he going to tell *all* the facts and do so fairly? Probably not.

Let me explain for nonlawyers the concept of fraudulent concealment. If you are selling property and the prospective purchaser tells you he wants to drill a well, you have a duty to tell him all you know of a material nature about this subject. If you truthfully tell him he can hit water at twenty feet and accurately say that the water is plentiful but neglect the small detail that the water is contaminated with deadly toxins, you are committing fraud. Any deliberate concealment of a material fact is fraud. There may be instances where the *Post*'s failures were not intentionally fraudulent but deceptive nonetheless. In investigating a subject, the journalist needs to disclose all material facts, but he or she often will not in order to achieve a desired effect.

The result is journalism that seeks to indict, inflame, and anger as journalists seek their roadkill. As began with Watergate, the electronic media magnify and make viscerally disturbing any negative reporting. Journalists emulate Woodward and Bernstein not because they told both sides but because they did not—and they still slayed a powerful and hated political enemy. Wealth, fame, and professional acclaim were the rewards of Watergate reporting, all of which incentivize journalists today.

I hope to set the Watergate/Deep Throat record straight through this book, but not to slay any victim, whether the *Washington Post*, Woodward, or Bernstein. Neither Woodward nor Bernstein was an editor or a manager in 1972–1974, and present *Post* owner Jeff Bezos was still in grade school.

I sincerely hope we can use this material as a basis for public commentators to stop and reflect, to try to return to a time when we all could civilly discuss our differences. In other words, if the media would report without adversarial narrative embroidery all the pertinent facts as objectively as possible, the readers could decide for themselves with open minds what is true, and our democracy would be the better for it.

"Democracy dies in darkness" is the masthead the *Post* proclaims on a daily basis. Certainly, a prosecutor presenting his case against the president or any public official to the democratic jury of public opinion should not withhold potentially exculpatory evidence. Nor should such a prosecutor enflame the jury with excessively emotionally presented evidence. Our liberal Enlightenment values—of free speech and competition in the marketplace of ideas—are thereby threatened.

It will be difficult to wean ourselves from the hot, exciting, emotional, weaponized, and targeted thinking to which we have all become addicted because of Watergate-style journalism. But let's try.

Chapter One

CALLING WOODWARD

The date was May 2, 2002, and it promised to be one of the most exciting days of my life. I was about to call Bob Woodward, the esteemed reporter and editor of the world-renowned *Washington Post*.

Woodward, an important historical figure and a true modern celebrity, was by then known as perhaps the greatest investigative reporter of all time. It was Woodward who, together with his *Post* partner Carl Bernstein, won for the *Post* a Pulitzer Prize for their relentless reporting of the notorious Watergate debacle. Their journalism was instrumental in causing the demise of the powerful regime of Richard M. Nixon, thirty-seventh president of the United States, and the conviction of forty Nixon administration officials, proving Watergate to be the most significant political scandal in our nation's history.

And I wasn't calling Woodward on behalf of just anyone. I was representing W. Mark Felt, formerly the FBI second in command during the Watergate years and head of the FBI's Watergate investigation. I was certain that Woodward would immediately recognize Felt as having significance beyond my client's former prestigious job title. Indeed, I knew that Woodward would recognize Felt as "Deep Throat," his legendary anonymous source who had provided him the road map to breaking open a diabolical, wide-ranging, and nearly successful criminal conspiracy.

Since the 1976 release of the hit movie based on Woodward and Bernstein's bestselling book, *All the President's Men*, I had been convinced for very solid reasons that Felt was indeed Deep Throat. Through serendipity, I had met the aging former G-man and eventually was retained by him and his family to reach out to his former journalist friend.

Woodward had rendered Deep Throat an important, mysterious, and riveting character, both in the book *All the President's Men* and in the Academy Award-winning movie of the same name. Thus started a thirty-year parlor game among the world's political cognoscenti as Woodward steadfastly refused to name his source and Deep Throat stubbornly refused to reveal himself, despite the millions of dollars in book contracts and speaking engagements that awaited the public bow of this mysterious hero.

That I was calling Woodward on behalf of this storied source I assumed would, to put it mildly, greatly interest the reporter. But what I had to tell him I also knew would take away his breath: Deep Throat was ready, after his many years of hiding, to come in from the cold and announce himself to the public. And, to boot, he wanted to do so in collaboration with his friend Woodward! Finally, a thirty-year mystery would be solved and all the hidden details could finally be revealed to an eager public. I expected Woodward to exult when I explained my happy purpose and his major role in our plans.

Mark had done far more for Woodward than win his reporting a Pulitzer Prize and his movie an Academy Award. Indeed, he had enabled Woodward many successes beyond the sensational Watergate reporting, triumphs that could be traced directly to Deep Throat's courageous assistance during Watergate.

Woodward's very public refusals over the past thirty years to "out" his friend had made him the patron saint of journalistic source protection. Through worldwide recognition of his principled refusal to name Deep Throat, Woodward had developed the trust of every person whose conscience—or more calculated desire to talk—demanded publication of uncomfortable secrets but who also naturally feared the retribution that would ensue from being publicly named as a source. On the strength of his Deep Throat work, for example, Woodward was able, for the first time in American legal history, to persuade Supreme Court law clerks to reveal what had hitherto been inviolately secret: the inner deliberations of the court. Several of these key sources gave Woodward a blockbuster bestseller, *The Brethren*, chronicling the sometimes-vicious infighting, lobbying, and intellectual battles that underlie key modern Supreme Court decisions.

He, of course, had also written *The Final Days*, shortly following *All the President's Men*, detailing vividly the cartoonish dysfunction of the Nixon White House as it hurtled toward ignominy. Again, this book, with its unflattering portraits of President Nixon, his family, and administration figures, could only have been written with the no-holds-barred assistance of administration officials who could trust Woodward not to reveal their identities. The same analysis applies to later bestsellers of Woodward describing historical domestic and foreign tableaus, such as *Bush at War*.

These books proved to be highly informative behind-the-scenes portrayals of a variety of institutions and political figures, cementing Woodward's reputation as perhaps the Western world's greatest investigative journalist, living or dead.

Although Woodward became the very embodiment of the modern "investigative" journalist, these later books needed, ironically, little investigation beyond the reporter's access to principal characters and their knowledgeable assistants. In short, because these witnesses knew virtually everything within their bailiwick, albeit with differing opinions and analyses, the reporter needed to do little additional researching beyond the ken of his sources. Also, because the witnesses were generally intelligent, articulate policy makers or lawyers, the books in large part could write themselves. And–since these works were generally fact-laden–stylistic skills, for which Woodward was never known, were not crucial. English was, after all, Woodward's second language, as the joke in the *Washington Post* Watergate newsroom had it. His legacy of source protection with Deep Throat and his sincere, courtly manner, then, were about all that Woodward needed to engender the cooperation of these witnesses and create these bestselling blockbusters.

As these triumphs of insider access continued to mount, Woodward's status soared to that of journalistic rock star, commanding astronomical speaking fees, lucrative advances, and the highest celebrity treatment. Any Woodward question-and-answer session or media interview was sure to feature the inevitable fawning questions about Deep Throat. The continuing mystery of Deep Throat's identity only reinforced Woodward's nobility and became the prime example of the need for "shield" laws protecting against the forced disclosure of reporters' sources. As our nation reached consensus on the value of "whistleblowers" like Deep Throat, Woodward's status as their prime protector became legend.

But the Deep Throat story brought Woodward more than honor, celebrity, and money. It made him as well a huge *political* figure. President George W. Bush was likely not the only government official to rush through the latest Woodward offering on the war in Iraq with but one breathless question in mind: "How did Woodward treat me?" By subtly selecting, positioning, and slanting the narratives offered by his many, often conflicting, sources, Woodward could make a political figure look masterful (as President Bush appeared in *Bush at War*)[1] or inept (as Woodward portrayed Bush in *State of Denial*).[2] And if a potential source refused to cooperate at all, he risked his dismembering by those who did.

As thousands of young reporters, inspired by Woodward's success, poured out of journalism school, each sought fame and fortune from what he or she hoped would be the next iteration of Deep Throat. An irrefutable truth became embedded in journalistic stone as strong as any presidential monument: a successful reporter is more than a truth-telling journalist–he is a *political player*, able to make or break the most powerful politician, political group, or governmental policy. More than any other figure in journalism, Woodward elevated the *political power* of journalism. And none of this could have happened without the anonymous source that I was representing in May of 2002, Mark Felt, a.k.a. Deep Throat.

If Woodward was the role model for the individual reporter, the *Washington Post* emblemized both the prestige and the riches accruing to scoop-breaking publications. In 1972, at the beginning of the Watergate crisis, the *Post* was a sleepy, decidedly second-tier newspaper whose only importance was its status as the best of a mediocre group of dailies in our nation's capital. Its circulation was anemic and its political influence minimal. On its best day, it was little more than a Democratic gossip rag for the inside-the-Beltway players of that era. As a business, the total worth of the paper in early 1972 was likely in the seven figures.

But after the intervention of Deep Throat, this all changed. As a result of the electric surge of its Watergate reporting, the prestige of the *Post*

1 Bob Woodward, *Bush at War* (New York: Simon & Schuster, 2002).

2 Woodward, *State of Denial* (New York: Simon & Schuster, 2006).

skyrocketed. Editor Ben Bradlee was played by the great Jason Robards in *All the President's Men*; Woodward and Bernstein were portrayed by Oscar-winning actors Robert Redford and Dustin Hoffman. Renowned character actor Martin Balsam took the part of editor Howard Simons. Katharine Graham was featured not only in *All the President's Men* but in countless books, articles, and television features, becoming a role model for the emerging American woman business executive.

By 2002, the *Post* had a massive publishing empire worth billions, owning *Newsweek* magazine among other publications. Many of these purchases were made possible by soaring stock values after 1974 because of industry accolades, increased circulation, and premium advertising revenues.

Clearly the *Post*'s journalistic Watergate success had engendered dramatically increasing business success. Moreover, the *Post* had become, as a result of its Watergate reporting, a huge political power in America, and indeed throughout the world. The political imprimatur of the *Post*, whether in articles or editorials, became as valuable as *Post* disapproval could be disastrous.

The *Post* not only shaped the political landscape by the words on its own pages but also influenced other major media outlets. Many a Washington bureau reporter for both print and electronic media survived because of his or her *Post* connections, and many failed for lack of same. Media stalwarts Ted Koppel, Andrea Mitchell, and David Gergen assiduously courted the *Post*, knowing that it was a clearinghouse for the best and freshest of buzz. The *Post* reporters (and those of *Post*-owned outlets like *Newsweek*) became mainstays of Washington talk show journalism. All roads to Washington, DC, scoops and Washington power led to or from the *Washington Post*.

Given the prestige, power, and wealth that had flowed to both Woodward and the *Washington Post* as a direct result of Deep Throat's assistance, I was certain that both Woodward and his *Post* editors would embrace the opportunity to take a victory lap with their prize source, reliving the halcyon days of Watergate, evermore heightening the public perception of their power and glory. I could envision a Woodward speech before a packed black-tie crowd in Washington or New York, as Mark, seated in his wheelchair next to him, beamed at his buddy and protector. I saw the two on *Oprah*, on *Meet the Press*, on Leno or Letterman, perhaps with Mark on split-screen television. In short, I felt we could be kicking off, with my call to Woodard, a glorious and unprecedented celebration of that happy modern union between an inquiring journalist and his honest whistleblower. It would be an affirmation of the broad freedoms of America that foster individual journalistic and governmental heroes.

To be sure, I knew, as did Woodward, that Mark, then eighty-nine, suffered from the normal memory problems associated with aging. As all human beings age, arteries in the hippocampus area of the brain become hardened, and memories become difficult to encode or retrieve. This is the normal loss of memory with old age, suffered at clinical levels by 50 percent of the population at age eighty-five and 100 percent of those who might make it to 115, a natural process quite distinct from the terrible ravages of Alzheimer's or Parkinson's.

Because of these memory problems, I knew that there would be some discussion with Woodward about Mark's competence to make decisions, but at the same time I was quite comfortable that this was not an insuperable problem. So, while I did not expect Woodward to tumble immediately to my request for a collaborative outing, I assumed he would be eager to verify, formally or informally, Mark's willingness to have his identity revealed.

But I didn't anticipate that posing a problem. The family–Felt's children Joan and Mark Jr. most significantly–were all in favor and had acted for several years as Mark's informal guardians under valid powers of attorney. If Woodward insisted on the confidential approval of a doctor or judge, I could arrange that immediately. In any event, there appeared to be no legal obstacle to Mark's coming out, and certainly no practical problem. And we were confident that Woodward, for reasons I just stated, would jump at the chance.

This last assumption was one whose importance I did not recognize at the time. Mark, I should have told you, had put one condition on his permission to reveal his identity to the world: this revelation could be made with, and only with, his friend Bob Woodward.

I didn't emit one bead of perspiration over this requirement. After all, how could Bob Woodward possibly refuse the request of a man who had made his golden career, a man to whom Woodward had for thirty years publicly proclaimed his absolute fealty?

On that morning in 2002 when I was about to call Bob Woodward, I thought that the question of his cooperation was nothing but a formality and looked excitedly to an unprecedented public victory parade. I was nothing but a behind-the-scenes facilitator, as a lawyer so often is, but I was already proud of my bit part in what would surely be a jubilant historical celebration.

Chapter Two

THE *POST* UNCOVERS WATERGATE

The journey I was on, I realized, had begun in 1970, when I was an intern at the Department of Justice in Washington, DC. It had taken me through the key Watergate years of 1972 and 1973 as a young San Francisco lawyer, and then to meaningful places in my six years as a federal prosecutor from 1974 to 1980.

Now it was reaching a destination that I hadn't planned. Because my background played such an important part in my actions from April 2002 through the present, I should first go briefly back in time.

June 19, 1972, was an exciting day for me because I was about to start my first day of work in San Francisco as a freshly minted lawyer. That date was to take on much greater significance for me and millions of other Americans. June 18, 1972 was the day most of us learned, through wire service reports and our local papers, about the arrest of five burglars at the Democratic National Committee (DNC) headquarters in Washington, DC. For most, this was the beginning of a memorable, if troubling, historical epoch. For me, it also set in motion a weird set of coincidences and associations that would reach their culmination thirty years later.

The bylined report of Bob Woodward and Carl Bernstein of the *Washington Post*, or "Woodstein," as the two came to be known, was fascinating. At the outset of the scandal, Woodstein's reporting indirectly raised the intriguing questions of whether the CIA was in some way involved in the burglary. Burglar James McCord and his outside supervisor, Howard Hunt, were recently retired CIA agents. The four Cubans caught burglarizing with McCord were veterans of the CIA-backed Bay of Pigs Invasion, which Hunt had helped to supervise. A lawyer connected with Hunt's part-time employer Mullen and Company, Douglas Caddy, showed up at the next day's arraignment of the burglars.

So the first question presented to Woodward and Bernstein was whether the CIA was directly involved in Watergate.

Woodward was shocked and curious about Caddy's appearance in court because he knew from his local police sources that the burglars had not made a call after the arrest. How did Caddy know the burglars had been arrested? And what was his connection to the burglars? His coworker Hunt had not yet been identified. And who had arranged for lawyer Joseph Rafferty to appear on behalf of the burglars? When the judge asked McCord his last employment, McCord, as if telling the court in confidence, barely audibly intoned, "the CIA." Many in the courtroom gasped at this revelation. Speculation soon began that Mullen, Hunt's and Caddy's employer, may itself have ongoing CIA connections. The *Post* revealed, however, that the company had only a past, incidental connection with the CIA in its public relations work for Radio Free Cuba in the 1960s.

While initial *Post* reporting noted the many obvious connections of the burglary team to the CIA, as the days passed, the *Post* reports veered away from the CIA and began pointing solely to the White House, focusing on Hunt's undefined part-time job there. And the other alleged supervisor of the burglary, G. Gordon Liddy, was a lawyer at the Committee to Re-elect the President (CRP), where McCord also worked as a contract security consultant, thus pointing to the CRP as well as the White House. Mullen's president, Robert Bennett, the *Post* revealed, was heavily involved in Nixon campaign fundraising, further tying the burglars to both the White House and CRP.

Woodstein continued that summer to hammer on the connections of Hunt, Liddy, and McCord to the Nixon administration. But the administration scoffed at the idea that this "third-rate burglary," as White House spokesman Ron Ziegler called it, was worthy of either White House or public attention. Perhaps, it was suggested by administration supporters, this odd collection was off on their own venture for their own undisclosed purposes. Liddy, after all, was something of a nut, a wild card, and Hunt was known as a rogue adventurer. The question of whether this weird caper was authorized by higher White House officials remained open to the great curiosity of amateur political observers like me. And none of this made sense as a campaign operation, since the DNC was then not actively engaged in the campaign.

To be sure, aggressive reporting by the *Washington Post*'s young reporters linked Republican campaign contributions to the financing of the burglary, and possible campaign financing violations to boot. However, the lack of discernible campaign-related purpose kept the matter from having public impact.

I was therefore mildly disappointed that, as the summer progressed, Woodstein's reporting seemed to fade. Then, on September 15, 1972, the Department of Justice announced the indictments of the seven burglary suspects and stated, curiously, that "no more indictments are expected." This announcement was a letdown for me, given the apparent connection of the burglars to the White House and CRP, but was still quite consistent with the dead end that the Woodstein *Post* reporting had reached.

So the issue now presented was whether Watergate was limited to an odd, rogue, one-off operation or whether it was part of a broader plan or scheme, or at least directed by an undisclosed higher-up.

Then to my great surprise and delight, on October 10, 1972, Lazarus-like, the scandal was revived, with Woodstein reporting sensationally that, as the headline blared, "FBI Finds Nixon Aides Sabotaged Democrats." This bombshell article detailed a "massive campaign of spying and sabotage" directed by the White House through its operative Donald Segretti and aimed at its electoral opponents, all uncovered by the FBI investigation into Watergate. Fifty agents, the article declared, were engaged in such "dirty tricks" throughout the country. As Bernstein would later write, this article was the most important of all the pair's Watergate reporting, drastically changing public perceptions of the burglary.

A sensational series of articles followed that month, describing the large cash campaign "slush fund" used to finance these operations. The fund was controlled, it was reported, by high officials such as former attorney general and CRP director John Mitchell and White House chief of staff H. R. Haldeman.

One example of sabotage during the primary campaign was a phony letter, falsely attributed to the campaign of Maine senator Edmund Muskie, slurring "Canucks," or persons of French-Canadian ancestry, many of whom resided in New England. The letter, the *Post* reports claimed, was authored by White House press liaison Ken Clawson and was part of this program of spying and sabotage; this destroyed Muskie's once-promising candidacy.

The sum of these October 1972 reports was pivotal. The country was electrified. The television networks, which had paid scant attention to Watergate before October, now began to follow it closely. On October 15, 1972, the venerable Walter Cronkite devoted a section of his newscast to the burgeoning scandal.

Just prior to these dramatic reports, on October 4, 1972, an article from the theretofore silent *Los Angeles Times* gave the first hint of a motive for the burglary. The burglary team's wiretap monitor, ex-FBI agent Alfred Baldwin III, refused to talk about the contents of the calls he'd overheard. But he did offer to the *Times* that, when hot political gossip was overheard, he would take notes and, on one such occasion when McCord was out of town, he took the call logs to the CRP himself. So, one would reasonably infer from the article, political information from the DNC was the objective of the burglary, and this report now could be fit into the overall narrative of campaign spying and sabotage.

More ominously for the White House, after the electrifying Segretti article, Senator Edward Kennedy formed a special Watergate committee and eventually won subpoena power, the key component of any effective legislative investigation. Just days earlier, Representative Wright Patman's attempt to get the very same subpoena power for a House investigation had failed without the support of Republicans and conservative Democrats. But with the spotlight of publicity now on the scandal after the October 10 article, Republican senators were forced to assent to subpoena power. Kennedy wisely ceded the chairmanship to folksy North Carolina senator Sam Ervin, thereby avoiding comparisons to his Chappaquiddick skulduggery.

The heat from the judicial branch was also increasing. Chief Judge John Sirica was assigned the burglary prosecution and issued loud, demonstrative calls for the prosecution to delve into the motive for the burglary. Who authorized this, Sirica demanded to know, and for what purpose? Eventually, his insistent questioning led him to be named *Time* magazine's Man of the Year for 1973.

The burglary trial of January 1973, however, did no such thing–to Sirica's manifest frustration. No defendant testified, and the prosecution offered no coherent motive. Indeed, the only action of interest involved a quashed attempt by the prosecution to introduce evidence of the nature of the overheard calls. Claiming an intent to embarrass individuals associated with the Democratic National Committee, the DC Court of Appeals ordered that the content of the calls, and even their general subject matter, could not be placed in evidence. As a prosecutor, I found this ruling questionable. The basis for the ruling–that it was illegal to reveal the illegally overheard conversations–should not apply to a criminal prosecution. After all, if the prosecution were proving that crime, wouldn't it have to repeat the contents of the overheard conversations? By comparison, in a criminal libel trial, one must repeat the libel. Therefore, this restrictive ruling made little sense. In any case, the criminal trial ended with no revelations of White House involvement or motive and only continued to pique curiosity.

However, Sirica's strong comments raised the issue of whether there was a concerted effort to cover up any higher authorization for Watergate. The Senate confirmation hearing on interim director Patrick Gray's appointment as permanent director of the FBI, starting February 28, 1973, caused the first public cracks in the White House cover-up. The bumbling Gray admitted he had passed on FBI reports of the Watergate investigation to White House counsel John Dean. This was the first public implication of Dean, a young, obscure White House lawyer, in any suggestion of illegal cover-up. His exposure would soon drive him into the arms of prosecutors.

It was not until the burglars' sentencing hearing on March 21, 1973 that any direct accusations were made of higher involvement in the break-in. In a dramatic letter to Sirica, which he read in open court, burglary team leader McCord charged that perjury had been committed at trial (likely referring to CRP deputy director Jeb Magruder's denials of involvement), that his life had been threatened (presumably by the White House), that he had been offered clemency, and that higher-ups had been involved. Later *Post* reports of McCord's claims named John Mitchell as authorizing the burglaries, admittedly based only on McCord's hearsay knowledge from Liddy. But the case was now clearly heating to the boiling point.

Shortly after McCord's dramatic plea, the White House suffered another blow when Gray was forced to admit in early April 1973 that, at the behest of Dean, he had destroyed documents from Howard Hunt's White House safe, burning them in his home fireplace. Gray was, as John Ehrlichman famously said to Dean, "twisting slowly in the wind."

On April 30, 1973, another shocker came when the White House announced the resignations of Haldeman, Ehrlichman, and Dean. Around that same time were the resignations of Gray (April 27, widely expected) and Attorney General Richard Kleindienst (May 1, more surprising). The White House ship was taking even more water.

Although the McCord letter had generated headlines, he had little firsthand knowledge that could implicate higher officials. So, it was far more ominous for the White House when White House counsel John Dean and CRP deputy campaign director Jeb Magruder, a direct subordinate of former attorney general and CRP chairman John Mitchell, both turned prosecution witnesses.

Dean was prepared to recount the criminal cover-up in which the president and his aides were involved, including the payment of "hush money" to the seven burglary defendants, and falsely claiming interference with a CIA operation to keep the FBI from tracing the burglars' Mexican money trail. Magruder was to testify that Mitchell had authorized Gordon Liddy's "Operation Gemstone Plan," which included burglaries, wiretaps, and campaign sabotage directed against Democrats. According to Magruder, Mitchell specifically suggested a Watergate break-in as the first operation for Gemstone.

With Kleindienst's resignation, the Senate pressured new nominee Elliot Richardson to pledge to appoint a special prosecutor, which he promptly did, naming Harvard Law School professor Archibald Cox. This appointment, combined with the televised Ervin Committee hearings, would put a strong double whammy on the administration.

Dean, accompanied by his stunning blonde wife, Maureen, to the hearings, proved an impressive, detail-oriented witness against the president and his inner circle. Magruder, nervous and a weaker witness than Dean, nonetheless made an articulate–albeit questionable–case against Mitchell. A whole array of interesting witnesses, from Mitchell and Ehrlichman to McCord and colorful White House detective Tony Ulasewicz, made for riveting entertainment. The nation was transfixed.

With Dean's testimony, the reporting on Watergate now focused on Nixon's continued tenure in office. If his testimony proved credible, Nixon was in trouble.

The Ervin hearings also brought an unexpected twist. White House aide Colonel Alexander Butterfield testified that the president had installed a voice-activated taping system in the Oval Office, tapes of which Cox immediately subpoenaed. If Cox was successful, Dean's testimony about Nixon's complicity could now be subject to corroboration. Nine tapes were eventually turned over in late 1973. A year later, on July 24, 1974, and after much wrangling, the Supreme Court by a unanimous nine-to-zero ruling rejected the administration's contention that the remaining sixty-four tapes were protected by executive privilege.

At first the White House had been pressing Cox for compromise on his demands for the tapes, offering summaries of the tapes to be prepared by Senator John Stennis of Mississippi. When Cox refused to yield, President Nixon on Saturday night, October 20, 1973, ordered Attorney General Richardson to fire the special prosecutor. Richardson refused, and was fired himself. His deputy, William Ruckelshaus, also refused to fire Cox and was forced to resign. His successor, Robert Bork, fired Cox and then resigned. The "Saturday Night Massacre" turned sentiment strongly against the president, and calls for impeachment or resignation were widespread. The White House ship was taking more water.

Then, immediately following this debacle, in early November 1973, Woodstein exploded one of their biggest scoops: there was an extended eighteen-minute gap on one of the president's tapes and it was possibly the result of deliberate erasure. A number of White House sources confirmed the gap but claimed it occurred innocently. However, one of Woodstein's sources intelligently described the gap as having various indications of erasure, such as the "deliberate injection of background noise."

The eighteen-and-a-half minute gap captured headlines and late-night comedy routines. Presidential secretary Rose Mary Woods was pictured in an issue of *Time* magazine re-creating the acrobatic pose she claimed had innocently occurred to cause the erasure. Keeping her foot on the erasure pedal while grabbing for her phone several feet away, Woods was successful only in showing the absurdity of her explanation. Calls for impeachment grew.

Soon the Rodino Committee in the House convened to consider articles of impeachment against President Nixon. The nation was obsessed with the question of whether the president would be the first in our history to be removed from office.

Later, for the nationally televised 1974 impeachment hearings, a young Yale Law School graduate, Hillary Rodham, wrote a forceful brief arguing that impeachable offenses could implicate a wide range of bad presidential behavior and need not be limited to serious felonies. Her claims put her squarely at odds with the eminent law professor and legal scholar Charles Alan Wright. Her position was ultimately adopted by the Democratic-controlled House and was the basis for numerous articles of impeachment that went to the floor,[1] three of them passing in July 1974. Shortly after the release of the second group of tapes, on August 9, 1974, Nixon resigned his presidency.

Meanwhile, all the stars of Nixon's administration–indeed, virtually the president's entire inner circle and their associates–were tried and convicted on Watergate-related crimes, most dealing with the cover-up. Mitchell, Ehrlichman, and Haldeman were all convicted, along with thirty-seven other officials. Mitchell was convicted of authorizing the burglary.

All of these Watergate-related acts, however, paled in comparison to the explosive effect of a new bestselling book authored by Woodward and Bernstein, *All the President's Men*, released in April 1974. Generally, the book recounted step-by-step the excitement of their investigating, reporting, and eventually uncovering the Watergate scandal.

The book immediately shot to the top of bestseller lists. The pair of authors took readers through each step of the scandal, describing each piecemeal revelation that rocked the country and their key role as journal-

---

1 Years later, First Lady Hillary R. Clinton opposed her husband's impeachment by citing with approval the same opinions of Charles Alan Wright that she had scorned years earlier.

ists in affecting so profoundly the reversal of fortune experienced by the administration, one that theretofore had been one of our nation's historically most successful. The so-called fourth estate–journalists–were now a political force for all to reckon with.

The book elevated to an almost mythic level the new breed of "investigative reporter," represented by Woodward and Bernstein, who would actively dig into governmental and business wrongdoing.

As energetic as the reporting of Woodstein and the *Post* was, the book makes clear that its huge success could not have been achieved but for the extraordinary assistance of one man, an unnamed government official, an unusually effective source who insisted upon anonymity and on whom the reporters relied heavily to confirm key stories.

So, at bottom, the successful uncovering of presidential criminality would not likely have occurred but for the efforts of this one mysterious man. Because he would speak to Woodward only on "deep background"–that is, he could not be quoted or relied upon as a source–he drew the pressroom nickname "Deep Throat," a joking reference to the notorious pornography film of the same name.

Chapter Three

DEEP THROAT

The explosion of excited new interest in the scandal came mainly from this dramatic central figure in *All the President's Men*: Woodward's crucial anonymous source identified as an executive branch official known only as Deep Throat. Deep Throat took strenuous cloak-and-dagger precautions not to have his cooperation with Woodward discovered. When Woodward wanted a meeting with Deep Throat, always to occur at night, the reporter put a red flag in the flowerpot on his balcony. When his source wanted a meeting, he placed a circle on a certain page of the *New York Times* delivered to Woodward in the lobby of his apartment building. They would on all occasions but one meet in a parking garage, after Woodward took two separate cabs to ensure that he was not being followed. The description of these meeting protocols gave the sense of spycraft, suggesting a man with clandestine experience:

> *Woodward had a source in the Executive Branch who had access to information at CRP as well as at the White House. His identity was unknown to anyone else. He could be contacted only on very important occasions. Woodward had promised he would never identify him or his position to anyone. Further, he had agreed never to quote the man, even as an anonymous source. Their discussions would be only to confirm information that had been obtained elsewhere and to add some perspective...*
>
> *...At first Woodward and Deep Throat had talked by telephone, but as the tensions of Watergate increased, Deep*

> *Throat's nervousness grew. He didn't want to talk on the telephone, but had said they could meet somewhere on occasion...*
>
> *...When Woodward had an urgent inquiry to make, he would move the flower pot with the red flag to the rear of the balcony. During the day, Deep Throat would check to see if the pot had been moved. If it had, he and Woodward would meet at about 2:00 A.M. in a pre-designated underground parking garage. Woodward would leave his sixth-floor apartment and walk down the back stairs to an alley.*
>
> *Walking and taking two or more taxis to the garage, he could be reasonably sure that no one had followed him. In the garage, the two could talk for an hour or more without being seen. If taxis were hard to find, as they often were late at night, it might take Woodward almost two hours to get there on foot. On two occasions, a meeting had been set and the man had not shown up–a depressing and frightening experience, as Woodward had waited for more than an hour, alone in an underground garage in the middle of the night. Once he had thought he was being followed–two well-dressed men had stayed behind him for five or six blocks, but he had ducked into an alley and had not seen them again.*
>
> *If Deep Throat wanted a meeting–which was rare–there was a different procedure. Each morning, Woodward would check page 20 of his* New York Times*, delivered to his apartment house before 7:00 A.M. If a meeting was requested, the page number would be circled and the hands of a clock indicating the time of the rendezvous would appear in the lower corner of the page. Woodward did not know how Deep Throat got to his paper.*

Deep Throat was not so much a supplier of new facts for Woodward to print as much as a teacher and a guide to the reporter, steering him toward an understanding of the scandal, while nudging him away from false leads and inaccurate stories. Indeed, after their first garage meeting, an all-night affair ending at 6:00 a.m., Woodstein published the sizzling October 10,

1972, Segretti story and later sensational follow-up reports. This October 1972 journalism, relying heavily on Deep Throat's help, transformed Watergate from the strange story of a "third-rate burglary" into the earthshaking criminality of a widespread "campaign of spying and sabotage" against electoral opponents.

Woodward portrayed Deep Throat as a highly mysterious, deeply principled and astute veteran of Washington's wars. Woodward's descriptions of his source's mysterious methods made Deep Throat's identity a matter of intense curiosity:

> *The man's position in the Executive Branch was extremely sensitive. He had never told Woodward anything that was incorrect...*
>
> *...Woodward grabbed Deep Throat's arm. The time had come to press to the limit. Woodward found himself angry. He told Deep Throat that both of them were playing a chickenshit game–Deep Throat for pretending to himself that he never fed Woodward primary information, and Woodward for chewing up tidbits like a rat under a picnic table that didn't have the guts to go after the main dish...*
>
> *...Deep Throat was waiting. He looked worn, but was smiling. "What's up?" he asked mock-offhandedly, and took a deep drag on his cigarette. Just once, Woodward wished, Deep Throat would really tell him what was up–everything, no questions asked, no tug of wills, a full status report. The reporters had speculated on the reason for Deep Throat's piecemeal approach; they had several theories. If he told everything he knew all at once, a good Plumber might be able to find the leak. By making the reporters go elsewhere to fill out his information, he minimized his risk. Perhaps. But it was equally possible that he felt that the effect of one or two big stories, no matter how devastating, could be blunted by the White House. Or, by raising the stakes gradually, was he simply making the game more interesting for himself? The reporters tended to doubt that someone in the position*

> *would be so cavalier toward matters affecting Richard Nixon or the Presidency itself. More likely, they thought, Deep Throat was trying to protect the office, to effect a change in its conduct before all was lost. Each time Woodward had raised the question, Deep Throat had gravely insisted, "I have to do this my way."*[1]

While the "game" of not giving Woodward direct information befuddled many observers, as a prosecutor I knew that a law enforcement official would not want it to be known that he had given confidential file information to a reporter, an act that would perhaps endanger a future prosecution on the grounds of government misconduct or causation of prejudicial publicity.

Although fame and considerable fortune awaited Deep Throat if he revealed his identity, he steadfastly refused to come out, while Woodward dutifully and quite ostentatiously protected him. The upshot for the *Post* of its sterling Watergate reporting was prolonged financial success and a newly exalted reputation, while its use of Deep Throat only enhanced its prestige.

Immediately after the publication of *All the President's Men*, the country's media were alive with speculation about this mysterious figure's identity. One radio station broadcast, nonstop for several days, readings from *All the President's Men* relating to Deep Throat. At least among the country's educated elite, identifying Deep Throat became America's favorite parlor game.

I was at the time of the book's publication a newly minted prosecutor with authority to investigate white-collar crime, including election misconduct. I was also intensely interested in government's workings and their related politics, hoping, however idealistically and naively, to use the law to improve our society. So I began thinking of how to identify this historically and politically important figure. And perhaps an even more compelling motive for me was my newly discovered passion for using circumstantial evidence to resolve highly contentious and uncertain issues, a needed skill in white-collar prosecutors. His identity was important because it would

1 Carl Bernstein and Bob Woodward, *All the President's Men* (New York: Simon & Schuster, 1974), 71, 72, 135, 243, 317.

tell us whether the uncovering of Watergate was part of a self-curative design of the government or simply the lucky accident of a politician working against his own political interest.

I considered certain excerpts from *All the President's Men* especially telling because they expressed personality traits and attitudes of Deep Throat that could help me identify him:

> *Deep Throat was already there, smoking a cigarette. He was glad to see Woodward, shook his hand. Woodward told him that he and Bernstein needed help, really needed help on this one. His friendship with Deep Throat was genuine, not cultivated. Long before Watergate, they had spent many evenings talking about Washington, the government, power.*
>
> *On evenings such as those, Deep Throat had talked about how politics had infiltrated every corner of government–a strong-arm takeover of the agencies by the Nixon White House, junior White House aides were giving orders on the highest levels of the bureaucracy. He had once called it the "switchblade mentality"–and had referred to the willingness of the President's men to fight dirty and for keeps, regardless of what effect the slashing might have on the government and the nation. There was little bitterness on his part. Woodward sensed the resignation of a man whose fight had been worn out in too many battles. Deep Throat never tried to inflate his knowledge or show off his importance. He always told rather less than he knew. Woodward considered him a wise teacher. He was dispassionate and seemed committed to the best version of the obtainable truth.*
>
> *The Nixon White House worried him. "They are all underhanded and unknowable," he had said numerous times. He also distrusted the press. "I don't like newspapers," he had said flatly. He detested inexactitude and shallowness.*
>
> *Aware of his own weaknesses, he readily conceded his flaws. He was, incongruously, an incurable gossip, careful to label rumor for what it was, but fascinated by it. He knew too*

> *much literature too well and let the allurements of the past turn him away from his instincts. He could be rowdy, drink too much, overreach. He was not good at concealing his feelings, hardly ideal for a man in his position. Of late, he had expressed fear for the future of the Executive Branch, which he was in a unique position to observe. Watergate had taken its toll. Even in the shadows of the garage, Woodward saw that he was thinner and, when he drew on his cigarette, that his eyes were bloodshot.*

This description was consistent with a longtime civil servant, deeply concerned about presidential overreach. It also suggested someone whose job was in-depth fact finding, consistent with a law enforcement source. Many other passages revealed, directly or indirectly, his knowledge and experience, which for me were like mental fingerprints:

> *That night, Deep Throat seemed more talkative than usual... "Remember, you don't do those 1500 [FBI] interviews[2] and not have something on your hands other than a single break-in. But please be balanced and send out people to check everything, because a lot of the [CRP] intelligence-gathering was routine. They are not brilliant guys, and it got out of hand," Deep Throat said. "That is the key phrase, the feeling that it all got out of hand...much of the intelligence-gathering was on their own campaign contributors, and some to check on the Democratic contributors–to check people out and sort of semi-blackmail them if something was found...a very heavy-handed operation."*
>
> *Deep Throat had access to information from the White House, Justice, the FBI and CRP. What he knew represented an aggregate of hard information flowing in and out of many stations...*
>
> *...Deep Throat confirmed what the reporters' other sources had hinted. The FBI's and the grand jury's investigations*

2 The White House and the Justice Department had cited the number of interviews conducted by the FBI as evidence of the thoroughness of the Watergate investigation.

> *had been limited to the Watergate operation–and had ignored other espionage and sabotage. "None of the outside games were checked," he said. "If it wasn't limited to Watergate proper, they would never have finished, believe me. There was also non-corroborative testimony before the grand jury driving everyone wild, certain perjury."...*
>
> *...Though it wasn't true, Woodward told Deep Throat that he and Bernstein had a story for the following week saying that Haldeman was the fifth person in control of disbursements from the secret fund. "You'll have to do it on your own," Deep Throat said...*
>
> *...Deep Throat replied that failing to warn Woodward off a bad story "would be a misconception of our friendship." He would not name Haldeman himself. He shook hands with Woodward and left. Woodward was now more certain of two things: Haldeman was the correct name, and Haldeman had accumulated frightening power. Deep Throat did not scare easily...*

This man clearly had a position that would provide him a broad array of information about not just the burglary but other wrongdoing. This access pointed toward a White House lawyer, an FBI official, or a prosecutor, one with high-level responsibility for the big picture of the Watergate investigation. Other passages gave me clues as to which of the institutional cohorts likely employed Deep Throat:

> *Deep Throat stamped his foot. "A conspiracy like this...a conspiracy investigation...the rope has to tighten slowly around everyone's neck. You build convincingly from the outer edges in, you get ten times the evidence you need against Hunts and Liddys. They feel hopelessly finished–they may not talk right away, but the grip is on them. Then you move up and do the same thing at the next level. If you shoot too high and miss, then everybody feels more secure. Lawyers work this way. I'm sure smart reporters must, too. You've put the investigation back months. It puts everyone on the defensive–editors, FBI*

agents, everybody has to go into a crouch after this." Woodward swallowed hard. He deserved this lecture...

...He outlined four factors that might lead to the "inescapable conclusion" that Mitchell and Colson were conspirators: "One, the personalities and past performance of both. This way of life wasn't new to them. Two, there are meetings and phone calls at crucial times–all of which Colson and Mitchell claim involved other matters. Three, there's the tight control of the money, especially by Mitchell, who was getting details almost to the point of how much was spent on pencils and erasers. Four, there is the indisputable fact that the seven defendants believe they are going to be taken care of. That could only be done convincingly by someone high up, and somehow it has been done convincingly."...

"You've heard the Gray story?" Deep Throat asked. "Well it's true. On June 28, in a meeting with Ehrlichman and Dean, Gray was told the files were–quote–'political dynamite' and should–quote–'never see the light of day.' He was told, quote, 'they could do more damage than the Watergate bugging itself.' In fact, Ehrlichman had told Dean earlier in the day, 'You go across the river every day, John. Why don't you drop the goddamn fucking thing in the river?' Gray kept the files for about a week and then he says he threw them in a burn bag in his office. He says that he was not exactly told to destroy the files, but understood it was absolutely clear what Dean and Ehrlichman wanted."...[3]

These passages, more than any other in the book, suggested a prosecutor or FBI agent because Deep Throat understood how criminal conspiracies are successfully prosecuted. He was clearly analyzing in these passages the guilt of suspects on the basis of gathered evidence, not on the basis of firsthand knowledge of an insider. And he was largely wrong about Colson and Mitchell, understandable investigative conclusions given the positions of Hunt and Liddy as their underlings.

3 Bernstein and Woodward, *All the President's Men*, 130–131, 134, 173, 195, 196, 244–245, 306.

These passages in my view gave very meaningful clues pointing to a law enforcement official. Is this a bit too obvious? I asked. Why would Woodward do this to his "friend" who he was protecting?

Certainly, from on top of the world, it appeared that DOJ[4] employees would most likely form the center of the fertile field in which to find Deep Throat. After all, they were the individuals seeking to prosecute Nixon administration officials and had possession of investigative information, albeit necessarily incomplete factual findings. So, one possible role for Deep Throat would be that of a high-ranking official in the DOJ, probably not a political appointee, and not one who had political loyalty to the administration. This was just common sense.

But according to the facts laid out by Woodstein in *All the President's Men*, I could not focus solely on the DOJ just yet. That was because the book was replete with instances of knowledge that Deep Throat possessed that seemed to be gossip knowable only by White House insiders, and not by anyone in the far removes of the Justice Department.

If, then, I was to include Justice Department employees within my search, I had to explain these allusions by Deep Throat to intramural gossip in at least three very clear instances.

The first such incident related by Deep Throat was a Nixon Oval Office rant about leaks from the *Washington Post*:

> *Nixon was wild, shouting and hollering that "we can't have it and we're going to stop it, I don't care how much it costs." His theory is that the news media have gone way too far and the trend has to be stopped–almost like he was talking about federal spending. He's fixed on the subject and doesn't care how much time it takes; he wants it done. To him, the question is no less than the very integrity of government and basic loyalty. He thinks the press is out to get him and therefore is disloyal; people who talk to the press are even worse–the enemies within, or something like that.*[5]

---

4 Department of Justice, which includes both the FBI and federal prosecutors.

5 Bernstein and Woodward, *All the President's Men*, 269.

When I first read this account, like many other observers, I immediately formed the impression that Deep Throat had listened to the rant. If he had, of course, then logically Deep Throat was almost certainly a White House insider. Who else would be treated to such a letting down of presidential hair?

In fact, in the next few paragraphs, Deep Throat does not say directly, nor imply, that he was present. The account of the tantrum could have come from anyone in attendance and relayed to Deep Throat, who then described it to Woodward.

Shortly following this account, Woodward relates Nixon's stern direction to Gray, at their pre-confirmation Oval Office meeting, to stop the leaks from the FBI. No other Deep Throat sleuth I had read asked what I thought an obvious question: Was this part of the same rant Deep Throat described just a page earlier? Possibly. If so, Gray could have related the incident to any one of a host of DOJ employees, most likely another FBI official. Here is Woodstein's description of Gray's meeting with Nixon, not related by Deep Throat:

> *Stephen Sachs, the attorney for Gray, told Woodward in early 1974 that the suggestion that Gray had pressured or blackmailed the President was "outrageously false." "He [Gray] went to the White House expecting not to get the job," Sachs said. "Nixon told him that he should be as ruthless as Hoover in stopping leaks and be aggressive in the use of polygraphs [lie detectors]..." Sachs said that pressuring the White House was "not the way Gray handled himself with those guys. It was plain fear most of the time...Now it makes perfect sense that some of those guys down there would think he might be pressuring because that's the way they operate, but not Gray."*[6]

So it seemed that the Nixon-Gray meeting may have been the same as that of the first Nixon rant relayed by Deep Throat. At the very least, I decided that Nixon's Oval Office outburst did not disqualify Deep Throat as a DOJ/FBI employee. In fact, I concluded that these two passages described the same incident, suggesting that Deep Throat was someone close

6 Bernstein and Woodward, *All the President's Men*, 270.

to Gray, in whom he confided, with a slightly different description later provided by Gray's lawyer.

The second salient anecdote was Deep Throat's scoop that two important presidential advisors–Haldeman and Dean–would soon be resigning. Deep Throat shared this knowledge with Woodward in mid-April 1973, before seemingly any word of this had been heard elsewhere. Presumably only Dean, Haldeman, and their close aides (plus a few close to the innermost White House circles) would have known about the coming resignations at the time Deep Throat knew of them. The conclusion seemed ineluctable, then, that Deep Throat was a White House intimate.

But wait. Dean, unbeknownst to the White House, had been talking to the prosecutors and investigators throughout April, either directly or through his counsel Charles Shaffer. Any inside dope like this would have gone straight to the prosecution team negotiating with Dean for a deal. If Dean knew of pending resignations, so would certain DOJ officials, including some in the FBI.

Moreover, Gray at that same time was hanging onto his job by his fingernails. He had already been forced to disclose that, at Dean's behest, ostensibly on authority from Ehrlichman, he had destroyed documents he received from Dean that had been removed from Hunt's White House safe and not provided to regular FBI agents. Gray was then on borrowed time and likely talking to his White House contact, Ehrlichman, about the need to resign his interim post, which he did at the end of April, close in time to the other resignations.

Ehrlichman, logic would suggest, would have persuaded Gray to resign by citing the other pending resignations. If so, anyone close to Gray could have learned of these planned departures. Again, the conclusion I reached was that the resignation tidbit did not disqualify a Department of Justice source. More to the point, knowledge of these resignations affirmatively suggested a prosecution agent, a conclusion most analysts did not discern.

The third seemingly disqualifying piece of inside gossip was Deep Throat's knowledge of the presidential tape erasure resulting in the infamous eighteen-minute gap as described in *All the President's Men*:

> *Deep Throat's message was short and simple: one or more of the tapes contained deliberate erasures.*
>
> *Bernstein began calling sources at the White House. Four of them said they had learned that the tapes were of poor quality, that there were "gaps" in some conversations. But they did not know whether these had been caused by erasures...*
>
> *...The story quoted anonymously Deep Throat's remark that there were gaps of "a suspicious nature" which "could lead someone to conclude that the tapes have been tampered with."*[7]

Again, at first blush, this knowledge would appear to be limited to close presidential advisors. A few key trusted insiders were listening to the tapes, and the results were not yet being shared with Congress or law enforcement. But Woodward and Bernstein, we know, had *several* sources talking about the gap, as they here revealed. If these sources told reporters about the gap, why wouldn't one of them have told someone in the Department of Justice? After all, in November 1973, White House insiders were currying favor with whomever they could, hoping to hang on to the presidency, their jobs, and their freedom from indictment. Many DOJ officials had contacts at the White House and thus easily could have heard about the gap. I do admit that of the three "disqualifying" passages, this one bothered me the most and kept me thinking about it.

As in other passages where Woodward describes Deep Throat's conveyance of inside gossip, there is no assertion that Deep Throat *actually listened* to the tapes! He could have heard about the gap from anyone, including the reporters themselves. And Deep Throat's conclusion that erasures occurred sounded more like a law enforcement officer than a Nixon acolyte.

Later by happenstance, I had come across a quote of the pertinent *Post* article:

> *Of the five sources who confirmed that difficulties had arisen concerning the quality of the tapes, one said the problems*

---

7 Bernstein and Woodward, *All the President's Men*, 333.

> *"are of a suspicious nature" and "could lead someone to conclude that the tapes have been tampered with."*
>
> *According to this source, conversation on some of the tapes appears to have been erased—either inadvertently or otherwise—or obliterated by the injection of background noise. Such background noise could be the result of either poorly functioning equipment, erasure or purposeful injection, the same source said.*
>
> *The four other sources disputed that there is anything suspicious about the deficiencies and insisted the tapes are marred only by technical problems that can be satisfactorily explained in court.*[8]

Reading this article, one is left with a distinct impression that one of the sources was not inside the White House tent, and more significantly, that source appeared to have the technical knowledge of a criminal forensic lab. So, this reference pointed toward the DOJ or FBI. And nothing here suggested that Deep Throat actually heard the tapes, as opposed to learning secondhand of the odd sounds, then informally consulting with forensics experts he knew.

To my skeptical way of thinking, Woodward's inclusion of these items—each suggesting but not really proving that Deep Throat was a Nixon intimate—showed an attempt to throw analysts off the trail, whereas in fact they could well have pointed to a DOJ source. As a litigator, I had grown accustomed to the opposing party's attempts to fool my side. Put differently, if Deep Throat was a White House functionary, Woodward would not have included these bits, or at least would have disguised them.

Putting aside the issue of Deep Throat's seeming White House knowledge, I asked myself what confirmations Woodward sought from Deep Throat. Perhaps *Woodward's* state of mind would tell us how he viewed his source, which in turn would tell us where that source worked. One tableau that I could not get out of mind was the key inquiry as to whether Haldeman was implicated by CRP treasurer Hugh Sloan's grand jury testimony as having had access to the so-called "slush fund," which the report-

8 George Lardner Jr., "Tapes Have Puzzling 'Gap,'" *Washington Post*, November 8, 1973, A12.

ers then reported erroneously in the affirmative. Their biggest journalism blunder, it was featured prominently in the book and movie.

Recall that Woodstein had badgered an FBI agent about whether Sloan had confirmed Haldeman's access to the slush fund. This was an agent who apparently confused Ehrlichman with his Teutonic twin Haldeman, resulting in the embarrassing debacle. Deep Throat, though, would not confirm the story for Woodward, but the *Post* nevertheless published the bit. Later the chastened reporters confronted the FBI agent and his partner, accusing them of "setting up" the reporters by leading them into the error. The agents were, to put it mildly, not receptive to the accusations. What this tells us, of course, is that reporters had queried the FBI agents precisely because they would have had access to confidential grand jury testimony through *transcripts*.

I emphasize the word "transcripts" because the reporters were not inquiring into the underlying facts regarding the slush fund but rather into Hugh Sloan's *testimony* about them. While a White House functionary would not have had knowledge of what a transcript said, an FBI agent or Justice Department lawyer would. Thus, when Woodward also sought confirmation from Deep Throat about the same grand jury testimony, isn't Woodward telling us loud and clear that Deep Throat had access to such a transcript? Even though Deep Throat told Woodward that he could not help him, the question that Woodward insistently put to Deep Throat about this issue constituted a huge "tell." Thus, Deep Throat's failure to confirm this fact, which Woodward thought he should know, tells us that Deep Throat was likely a Department of Justice employee with knowledge of the transcripts. And, of course, it turns out that Deep Throat was not wrong, since he refused to confirm the naming of Haldeman. In any case, this tableau strongly supported DOJ/FBI employment for Deep Throat.

Everywhere I looked, I saw consistency between Deep Throat and a very high-ranking Justice Department/FBI source. For example, Woodward made much of the "game" that Deep Throat was playing with him, at least as Woodward saw it, wherein his source would not tell him facts anew but would only confirm or deny facts that the reporters gathered to keep them on the right track and presumably give Woodward confidence he could print those facts. This was a highly salient feature of their relationship, frustrating Woodward not only at the time but also years later, after Deep Throat's identity was revealed. Clearly, he never understood that an investigator or prosecutor could hurt his case by causing the publicizing of highly prejudicial and confidential facts about the defendant in a criminal prosecution.

In the same vein was the final garage meeting of May 16–17, 1973, in which an uncharacteristically panicked Deep Throat warned Woodward that "everyone's life is in danger!" This warning was of potential CIA skulduggery to conceal potential illegal activities of the Agency, whether committed during the Watergate episode itself or in operations that could be revealed in the Watergate investigation.[9] A high official in the Department of Justice or in the FBI may well have learned of this danger through an intelligence source, or through the CIA. But no one within the White House, perhaps apart from the Kissinger/Haig faction,[10] would likely have had access to the intelligence "street." Of the three possible entities that would have known of this threat–DOJ lawyers, FBI investigators, and Kissinger/Haig–the FBI would most likely have been the recipient. And others in the White House, apart from the Kissinger team, would have been highly unlikely to have learned of CIA skulduggery.

Finally, I would be remiss if I did not mention Deep Throat's revelation to Woodward in late February or early March 1973, at the roadside bar, of the so-called "Kissinger wiretaps." These taps targeted newsmen and national security officials after the 1969 Cambodia bombing was leaked to the media. Although Deep Throat ascribed these taps to an "out of channels vigilante group," they appear to have been authorized by FBI director J. Edgar Hoover himself or his top FBI aide, William Sullivan. Both the top-level connection to the FBI and the denial that regular agents were involved in these questionable incursions would tell us that Deep Throat was an FBI official who knew of the taps and who also wished to distance the agency from them, leaving only the deceased Hoover and the dismissed Sullivan as potentially implicated. These taps were so sensitive

9 The CIA was prohibited by its charter from engaging in domestic operations. Only the president's direct authorization could justify a domestic CIA operation, which is likely why Hunt sought so eagerly to gain White House "cover" via his Plumber's job.

10 Henry Kissinger, national security advisor, and his Chief of Staff Colonel Alexander Haig.

that the records were not kept in ordinary wiretap files. Only a select few knew–in the "main" Justice Department, Assistant Attorney General Robert Mardian, Mitchell, and Kleindienst, and only a few high FBI officials. So, knowledge of the Kissinger wiretaps pointed to Haig or a high FBI official, such as Hoover, Sullivan, Patrick Gray, or Mark Felt.

However, Hoover was dead and Sullivan retired at the time of the burglary arrests. All of Felt's subordinates had been transferred to other offices by Gray for, ironically, suspicion of leaking. But what was Felt's motive for morphing from Woodward's terse telephone source to an all-night "teacher" of Woodward in clandestine garage meetings?

The light went on in the fall of 1976 when as an Assistant US Attorney, I recommended fully investigating Jimmy Carter's presidential campaign for paying African-American ministers for their pulpit support, of which I had solid preliminary proof. However, I needed the permission of the main Justice Department, since this would be an election law inquiry.

I was turned down because, I sensed, Carter was ahead of Gerald Ford at the time by thirteen points and no DOJ supervisor wished to face potential demotion. Infuriated, I considered leaking so as to apply public pressure, but knew I would be the obvious suspect.

Then it hit me: Mark Felt wished to investigate Donald Segretti's "dirty tricks" campaign but was stymied by lack of permission from main Justice! The blockbuster *Post* article of October 10, 1972, the day after the first garage meeting, was about Donald Segretti's program, not yet allowed to be put before a Grand Jury.

So I had my man: Mark Felt was Deep Throat! Everything pointed to him, with no close second.

I would add that later I confirmed from the work of others (like Dean) that only eight officials had known of the Kissinger wiretaps before May of 1973, and only Haig and Felt were possible Deep Throat candidates. If Woodward really wanted and promised to protect his valued source, and if indeed Deep Throat really wished to evade detection, why did Woodward give us this rich vein of information, which I generally describe above, from which one could discern Felt's identity? And why would Woodward give us the highly specific information about Deep Throat's knowledge of the Kissinger wiretaps if he wished to protect Felt? And wouldn't Felt understand the key role in his detection that this information would yield? Weren't Woodward and his good "friend" Felt in constant, friendly contact? Did Felt approve of this key revelation by Woodward, a fingerprint of Felt's involvement?

Obviously, Woodward's book and movie were huge commercial successes due in large part to the compelling Deep Throat character. Presumably, Mark Felt, as his protected ward, would have needed to consent to these revelations. But why, if this clever man truly wished anonymity, would he ever do so?

I then concluded, logically I thought, and continued to do so through July 2005, that Woodward surely had paid Deep Throat for his cooperation and the attendant risk caused by these revelations. Woodward would have benefitted hugely because of this permission, and Felt, retired by the time of publication, would have received a financial reward for his heroism and the risk he took. Still, such commercial motivations were not attractive and in fact undercut my view of Mark Felt as a foxy but idealistic Hooverite. Indeed, I thought he refused to admit his role for fear of tarnishing his beloved FBI. But if he were paid, and thereby permitted these clues, he risked what he perceived to be a smudge on the FBI's reputation. If so, I had not correctly judged his motives. The circumstantial evidence, again, appeared to clash.

So, I had questions that lingered about this, questions that presented a fundamental conflict between my view of Mark Felt's character and the evidence presented by Woodward's book and movie. I simply could not reconcile the two.

By 1977, my young bride was trying to become pregnant and did not plan on returning to work when she did. I was therefore by necessity preparing myself to interview with civil litigation law firms. I had managed to trade all my criminal cases for civil cases with my friend, young DOJ Civil Division lawyer Robert Mueller III, who happily accepted, eager for a career as a criminal prosecutor.[11] In my view, the Watergate story was complete and was both a vindication of and an improvement upon our system

11 Mueller eventually became at various times the United States attorney in three different districts and later retired after twelve years as FBI director. In 2017, he was appointed as special counsel investigating alleged Russian interference in the 2016 presidential elections.

of justice. It was a vindication because the system showed that it worked, precisely because it relied on honest career civil servants like Mark Felt, who would not easily tumble to pulling investigative punches. The FBI as an institution had shown itself to be essentially incorruptible, save and except for the political robot Gray, appointed by President Nixon. Eventually, forty Nixon administration officials were convicted of crimes. The system worked. It proved self-curative.

Watergate also improved the system. Some of its institutional reforms, such as whistleblower protection and the independent counsel statute, would ensure impartial investigation of politically charged matters. Probably more important even than legal reform were cultural changes. Newspapers and the electronic media embraced the notion of aggressive investigative reporting, especially since the *Washington Post* showed that it could be done to great profit and praise alike. Journalism schools soon were flooded with applications from would-be investigative reporters. The Watergate narrative would embolden ordinary citizens, employed by the government or not, to step forward and speak the truth about crimes.

As I finished my stint with the United States Attorney's Office in late 1979 to pursue a more commercially oriented career, I was proud of the prosecutors and investigators in the Justice Department. And I was gratified by these changes in our society, especially for what they promised for the field of journalism. I looked forward to an era where political corruption and governmental abuse would not be tolerated by honest journalists. Our government and the field of journalism had thus benefited from our country's Watergate pain. Even though I had numerous lingering questions about their collaboration, I could not help but believe that the felicitous friendship of source and journalist–Deep Throat and Woodward–had greatly improved the quality of our civic conversation.

I had great fun pursuing my hobbyist hunt for Deep Throat's identity, but I never thought about publishing what would have been simply one obscure lawyer's opinion summarizing the evidence pointing to Mark Felt. I was gratified by what I perceived to be an increased level of effective whistleblowing but not thrilled by our post-Watergate politically oriented investigative journalism, which seemed harshly partisan and far inferior to the superb work of Woodward and Mark Felt, aka Deep Throat.

For the next twenty-five years, I raised a family and practiced law, thinking of Mark Felt and Woodward occasionally, mainly as a yardstick to measure the failings of modern journalism. Why had it become so partisan, so agenda-driven? Watergate, after all, had instructed the journalism world in the opposite direction, hadn't it? Yes, the *Post* had "nailed" Nixon, but it had done so on the basis of objective fact, albeit perhaps sensationally portrayed.

The journalism following it, clearly seeking the same happy combination of profit, acclaim, and political effect as the *Post* had achieved, nonetheless seemed long on bias and short on presentation of inconvenient facts.

So I clung to the *Post*'s Watergate journalism as the bright, shining exception to the increasingly sleazy rule of modern journalism.

Chapter Four:

MEETING DEEP THROAT

It was a beautiful, sunny April evening in 2002 when my wife, Jan, and I enjoyed a lively, festive night with our daughter and her Stanford University friends at our home in the Marin County hills. Christy and her best buddies had all taken semesters abroad their junior year, so Jan and I had not seen the group together since their sophomore year. Some, having just returned, had barely socialized with their close friends, so the gathering took on the sense of a reunion.

After we sat down to one of Jan's typical feasts of chicken, pasta, and grilled vegetables, I engaged with this group in what they saw as Christy's goofy father's "Big John" badinage, but in fact our conversation soon became meaningful. Because several students had been to South America, I had taken the opportunity to regale the group with stories of my late father's undercover FBI service in Brazil during World War II. According to German records found after the war, the Germans had identified my father just about the exact moment he disembarked in Rio. I claimed to the table that he was the most easily recognized spy in the history of covert operations.

Nick Jones, a great young guy I had known for a couple of years and liked immensely, interjected. "Big John, your dad might have known my grandfather, an FBI agent who also spied on the Germans."

I told Nick that my father often talked about his old FBI friends. "What's your grandfather's name?" I asked.

"He ended up being a pretty high-level official in the FBI. His name is Mark Felt," Nick responded.

I was stunned, of course. Jan and I had gotten to know Nick well, often making a point to bring too much beer and fried chicken to our Stanford tailgates, then giving the excess to Nick, who we knew to have modest resources, to help him scrape by for the week. I had taken Nick under my wing, knowing that he did not have a father who lived with him. But I had never heard that he lived with a grandfather. The fact that Nick's grandfather was the one and only Mark Felt, of course, blew me away. "Do you realize that your grandfather is Deep Throat?" I asked Nick.

"No," Nick replied, "he's always denied it. But," he added, "there have been some hints lately that maybe he was Deep Throat." Nick was referring to a visit by Bob Woodward to Mark in 2000 and a recent article written by a childhood campmate of Carl Bernstein's son, Josh, who had claimed that years earlier Josh told him that his father had named Mark Felt as Deep Throat.

This dialogue did not particularly interest the other diners, who likely thought it was more of my nonsense. As they moved on to more interesting conversations, Nick and I continued at some length. I told Nick I'd like to visit his granddad and convince him to come out. I thought I knew why his grandfather kept mum–he thought respectable "law and order" types would look down on him, I said, but I thought otherwise. After all, I told Nick, his grandfather kept our system free of corruption, so I thought that conservative folks would applaud him. I went on to explain why I thought his grandfather was not revealing himself, and why I thought I had the key to get him to come around. I ended by asking Nick to please talk to his mother about permitting me to come up and visit his grandfather. Nick agreed to discuss it with her, and the conversation that night ended.

Later that week, Nick called to tell me his mother was excited. Could I come up this coming Sunday? I eagerly accepted the invitation.

Joan, thin, lively, and pretty, a former actress and Fulbright scholar, was an energetic college Spanish instructor, perhaps fifty-nine years of age, who held down three teaching jobs to pay for her children's education and care for Mark. She showed me the garage she'd converted into an apartment for Mark, introducing me to her dad as a friend of hers and Nick's, a lawyer whom they could all trust.

Mark was a sweet elderly man who sat in his armchair next to his bed in the modest studio watching TV, a beautiful oil painting of his late wife, Audrey, featured above him. He was a friendly man with a firm handshake, bright blue eyes, big smile, and, despite some senility, a leader's way of making me feel comfortable. He seemed pleased when I rattled off, by design, my federal law enforcement credentials: my father was an FBI agent who spied on the Germans; as an assistant US attorney, I worked with FBI agents for six years; I had worked with Bob Mueller, the current director of the FBI; and my father's partner was Bill Ruckelshaus, former interim director of the FBI, Mark's boss, and deputy attorney general during Watergate. I could tell I had his confidence.

He liked my credentials, and clearly we were bonding as law enforcement guys, which was per my strategy. Then I laid it on him directly. I had long admired this fellow, Deep Throat, I told him, who kept our justice system free of corruption. Other prosecutors and agents had felt the same way. We all thought as young law enforcement personnel that Deep Throat was a hero.

Joan and Nick, sitting near us on the bed while Mark and I sat facing each other, were stunned by Mark's reaction. His hands, which before I brought up Deep Throat had been resting lightly on the arms of his chair, now gripped them tightly, white-knuckled, at the mention of Deep Throat. But as I praised Deep Throat, his blue eyes seemed to melt, as if I were giving him absolution. Joan and Nick both then knew that Mark was Deep Throat, but I wanted to show them even more proof.

I pulled a trick. I switched the third person "he" to the second person "you" in reference to Deep Throat. So, after praising Deep Throat, I told Mark, "you" should reveal "your" identity so "you" can be honored as a hero. And "you" are a true law enforcement hero, I told him, and the rest of the country in today's day and age would think so too. He did not flinch at or argue with the second-person reference. I could see that the eyes of both Joan and Nick were getting wider in amazement. Their patriarch was the legendary Deep Throat!

While Mark had lost his ability to recall the past in any detail, he was "with it" in the moment. He had no touch of Alzheimer's or other forms of dementia that lessen intelligence and was only deficient in his ability to summon detailed memory, a normal consequence of aging. As I was to learn time and again, Mark would not accede to statements with which he disagreed. Yet that day, he offered me not a pip of protest at my suggestions.

I went on to describe all the benefits to him and his family if he were to reveal himself: the honor, the glory, the good for our justice system. As I concluded, he said in a surprisingly firm, booming voice, "I will think over what you have said and give you my decision."

Years later, when we would reveal Mark as Deep Throat, several web commentators thought that this statement was one I simply fabricated, on the theory, I suppose, that Mark was a blithering idiot. In fact, he was a composed, intelligent man who had his wits about him but just could not store or retrieve detailed memories.

To me, the conversation, viewed as a whole, was far more of a confirmation of his identity than if he had quickly agreed, which could have been ascribed to confusion. In this case, he was not overtly agreeing with me but carefully weighing what I said, while not denying. He had heard from Joan that I would keep his confidence as he directed, so he had felt safe. We concluded our meeting cordially.

In the following days, I kept in touch with Joan about her father's attitude. Joan herself had seen her father's reaction and knew intuitively he was, as he had always been to her, a true hero, this time the hero of Watergate.

She soon reported to me that I had apparently stirred up a psychological hornet's nest in Mark. The following day her father had taken his daily drive with his Fijian caretaker Atama, or "Adam," and showed himself to be disturbed by the thought of revealing himself. Referring to Deep Throat in the third person, he told Adam, "An FBI agent doesn't act like that." Obviously, he was forgetting the glowing picture I had painted of his future heroic welcome and was reverting to the hardwired emotions ingrained in him during his Watergate days, surrounded by fellow agents who would not have tolerated one of theirs meeting in secret with a reporter about a pending investigation.

Just days later, with a Watergate anniversary (thirty years) upcoming, Joan and Mark caught a snippet on TV about Watergate. Joan had known it was showing and made sure they watched it so she could gauge his reaction. When the show referred to Deep Throat, Joan asked her father why he thought Woodward's mysterious source acted as he did. "I wasn't out to get Nixon," he responded matter-of-factly, "I was just doing my job." Parenthetically, this comment was consistent with my theory that Mark only wanted to keep the investigation open. In any case, Joan excitedly relayed the conversation to me. We then continued to talk about how to persuade Mark he would be received well by respectable folks.

Serendipitously, soon after that, probably two weeks following my visit, Joan answered a call from Mark's old girlfriend, Yvette LaGarde, a French woman ten years Mark's junior whom Mark had squired around DC after Audrey's death.

Yvette, a little ditzy at the time, had read an article (published around April 26) in the tabloid *Globe* headlined, "Deep Throat Revealed!" The article merely warmed up and served the Chase Culeman-Beckman story (a past campmate of a ten-year-old Josh Bernstein, to whom Josh identified Mark as Deep Throat), along with the story of Woodward's visit in 2000. Yvette misread the article to suggest that Mark himself had revealed his identity.

"Why is Mark revealing himself now?" she asked Joan. "I thought he wasn't going to reveal it while he was alive."

Joan responded, "Reveal what, Yvette?" Yvette, now realizing Joan was not in on the secret, tried to withdraw her admission, only to be confronted with Joan's insistence that she spill the beans.

Yvette finally fessed up. Mark had revealed he was Deep Throat one romantic night on a trip they had taken, just before he was to move to California to care for Joan and her children. Mark made Yvette promise never to tell anyone this romantic secret. She was thrilled and made the promise to Mark.

Joan immediately confronted her father with Yvette's confession. "Well, if that's the case, then yes I am," Mark conceded. Joan, of course, quickly followed with a call to me.

After this, Joan and her brother Mark Jr., a retired US Air Force and American Airlines pilot now living in Florida, conferred. They talked at length with their dad about the possibility of coming out. Mark Sr. was resistant at first but finally agreed to do it for the sake of the family. Joan had played the card that the revelation would help Nick get into law school and help raise some tuition money for her three sons.

I made another Sunday visit. Joan had told me that Mark was still vacillating and had gone back and forth with his admission. She wouldn't let him back out, however. On this second visit, he was still shaky in his admission, not easily moved to state his identity as Deep Throat. I had known from Joan that because Mark couldn't remember details, he would likely feel confident only if he did a public revelation in conjunction with Woodward.

Sure enough, that afternoon Mark was reluctant to admit freely that he was Deep Throat. Finally, with Joan nicely prodding, Mark did admit that "I was the guy they called Deep Throat." This was a trope to which he would tumble over the next two years, even while denying that he *was* in fact Deep Throat. This reaction, we realized, involved a clever defense Mark had hard-wired into his brain over the years. He never considered himself Deep Throat and never called himself that nor answered to it, the essence of taking a name. Therefore, he could honestly deny he was Deep Throat, even though he knew he "was the guy they called Deep Throat."

After some discussion during my next visit, Mark told us that he would agree to release his identity, but only if Bob Woodward did it with him. We understood that Mark's memory was shot, and Woodward's cooperation would solve that problem, so I agreed that I would call Woodward during the coming week. I expressed confidence that Bob would want to do a victory tour with Mark and that the public would applaud Mark for his service.

Before I left that Sunday of his admission, I wanted to get Mark on videotape admitting he was Deep Throat. I knew he was prone to retract his admission, and showing him the tape in the future might bring him back, the same way a witness who revokes an uncomfortable admission could be brought back to the fact by referring to his deposition.

Unhappily, neither Mark nor I were in our best form. He hesitated and stammered, obviously reluctant in the face of the camera to admit his dark secret. It took coaxing to get an admission, and not a particularly impressive one. Clearly, I knew, my "leading" the witness detracted from the force of the historic admission. To make matters worse, I dropped my home video camera during the filming, sure to give nausea to some viewers. But it was something, and it might come in handy someday. And I thought it historic, coming on the first day this reluctant hero had come out for good.

But that was a minor matter. Woodward knew he was Deep Throat, after all, and we were certain he would jump at the chance to help his old friend. So, I was highly excited to call Mark's world-renowned protector.

Chapter Five

FELT'S FRIEND

That Tuesday morning I called Woodward, using a number he had left with Joan. "Hello, I'm John O'Connor, a lawyer for Mark Felt," I told him. "Mark has admitted he was your source, Deep Throat." I explained how Mark wanted Woodward to announce his identity with him by maybe writing a book, giving a series of talks, and engaging in other projects together. I emphasized that it would be fun for Mark and exciting for the public to honor this historic collaboration.

I must give Woodward credit. He was completely calm and spoke as if I were the five hundredth caller representing putative Deep Throat candidates. "Just because I'm talking to you doesn't mean I'm either admitting or denying your client is who he says he is," Woodward began. I expected something like this and quickly agreed to the no-admission concept. This was standard stuff. When discussing settlement or a plea deal, lawyers often agree that nothing should be deemed to be an admission of anything.

"How would I even know he's competent to make the request?" Woodward asked. I assured him that Mark wanted to do this. He had dementia, but that didn't affect his ability to decide important matters, only his ability to remember details.

Joan had a power of attorney, and besides, I volunteered, we could probably see a judge in confidence who could rule on Mark's competence, with the aid of a physician. However, I said, he didn't seem at all interested in whether a court would find him perfectly competent. "If you don't want to do it with us, we'll understand," I told him politely. "We'll do it through another writer. But we think it would be better if you and Mark did it together, since clearly Mark and you were a team."

Woodward did not seem enthusiastic, but, oddly, neither did he sound concerned about Mark's competence. He just plain didn't want to do it. He said he wanted to talk to the family, even though he really didn't say that he would agree to cooperate if the family agreed or if Mark were found competent. Woodward didn't seem like he was truly seeking authority to reveal Mark's identity but, rather, sounded as if he was looking for an excuse not to reveal it. We ended by agreeing to talk again. I had talked vaguely of splitting profits, which may have further dampened his ardor.

The next time we talked, a couple of days later, Woodward now spoke more of his concerns about Mark's competence, but did so in a way that, again, sounded more like an excuse. He clearly didn't want to do this, and it was obvious. He simply didn't engage when I again brought up filing a case under seal and conferring with a judge.

I expected this reluctance, based on his negative reaction earlier, and knew instinctively that he was looking for any reason not to go forward. So I threw a desperation pass, one that would take the competence issue off the table. I said, "Bob, given your concerns about competence, what if we agreed not to reveal Mark's identity during his life? Then, in exchange, you and the family would split the profits from your post-death book?" We could add some family background pictures and FBI insights to the book, I offered. "If we have a deal," I continued, "we won't go public and reveal Mark's identity while he's alive. This should take care of your concerns about competence."

What he said in reaction, and how he said it, told me, unfortunately, everything I needed to know about his intentions. "Let me warn you, John," he stated in a very ominous tone, "*there will be some surprises.*" This statement stunned me.

I responded by asking him to explain what he meant.

"*There will be some surprises*," he reiterated, almost angrily, warning me not to go there. He repeated this a third time, without my having responded.

What did he mean by that, I wondered? The first reaction I had was that he was telling me that Mark was not really Deep Throat, that Deep Throat was a composite, as many had posited, an amalgam of several sources that Woodward used. According to this theory, there was no one Deep Throat but many sources all rolled, so to speak, into one character. In any case, time and again, I could get no response other than this standard warning. My initial reaction, then, was that Woodward was telling me Mark was not Deep Throat. Interestingly, in spite of this angry warning, Woodward said he wanted to talk to the family. I agreed, while continuing to ponder his odd recalcitrance.

The problem with the implied composite theory was that Woodward himself had previously said it wasn't so. And the theory had been originally floated by Mark Felt himself to deflect attention away from him! The composite theory was absurd, especially because it would expose Woodward as a liar in his book and movie when he described the single person that was Deep Throat. But maybe Woodward thought I was dumb enough to fall for it. I relayed the comment to Joan and we, of course, puzzled over its meaning. Although I originally sensed that Woodward was telling us that Mark Felt wasn't Deep Throat, I eventually concluded that it couldn't be so. I *knew* Mark Felt was Deep Throat and *knew* that there was no possibility that there was a composite Deep Throat.

It seemed at first blush that Woodward was simply lying to us, throwing us off the scent, convincing us that Mark didn't really know his own identity but was simply a confused old man. But I couldn't accept that the supremely ethical Woodward would so blatantly lie to the representative of the man who had made his career. No, there had to be something else going on. To believe otherwise would have been to believe Woodward was a deeply dishonorable individual. My client had made millions for Woodward, and now the old guy's family was begging in vain for scraps.

Whether Woodward was sleazy or noble, his rejection of our after-death offer confirmed my instinct that Mark's competence was not a sincere concern but, rather, an excuse. After all, if Woodward in fact could release Deep Throat's name after death, as he often said he would, then Mark's competence wouldn't be an issue in his present refusal to deal with us even after death. Indeed, I had made the offer precisely to push the competence issue off the table.

But if Woodward was refusing to cooperate, competence or no, why would he wish to talk further with the family, as he was continuing to request? A cynical view would hold that he was trying to plant the seed, falsely, with me that Mark was not Deep Throat, while continuing to monitor the family's intentions. He wanted, perhaps, to assure himself that they wouldn't reveal Mark's identity before he did. Simply put, Woodward didn't want to split any money or glory with the family of his source. And if the family were to say they would try it without him, he could beat them to the punch with his own book. He also knew that Mark was unable to prove his own identity, having met with him not long before I did. Therefore, he may have been thinking that it was unlikely a publisher would write the story without Woodward's assent, but he would continue to monitor the situation to ensure that didn't happen. So according to this thinking, he could refuse to confirm Mark's identity until he died and then write a bestseller. And keep all the money.

That was one obvious inference, to be sure. But I just couldn't accept that Woodward would be that cynical. After all, he wouldn't be deceiving mere strangers. If he were being deceptive, it would be to the man who made his career, with whom he claimed to the world to have had a special relationship. No lawyer, fiduciary, or financial advisor should be anything but aboveboard with his client and client representatives; any failure to do so was fraud, plain and simple. Surely Woodward wouldn't defraud Deep Throat and his family! What would the public say if, after Mark's death, it was disclosed that Woodward had defrauded his iconic source? I couldn't believe that Woodward would risk being exposed for such shameful behavior.[1]

Faced with this monstrous inference, I preferred a "saving" hypothesis, which assumed that Woodward would not risk his world-class reputation by acting unethically. Clearly, Woodward at least partially "outed" his source in *All the President's Men* and presumably had his source's permission to out him at his death, as Woodward was planning to do. And the clues and quotes Woodward offered helped an observer such as me to deduce identity. Thus, they certainly had cut a deal. There would be no reason for

1 The fraud would at least be a type known as "constructive fraud." A fiduciary, broadly speaking, is anyone in whom you justifiably repose trust and confidence. Partners, lawyers, corporate officers, and investment advisors are almost always considered fiduciaries. When a person acts as a fiduciary, the law requires full disclosure by the fiduciary regarding all pertinent matters. Failure to do so, even if innocent, is "constructive" fraud. If Woodward was actively deceiving, that would constitute actual fraud as well.

Mark to have agreed to even partial revelation, with the attendant risk he would be found out and disgraced (in his view) while alive, unless he got something out of it.

Mark faced heavy expenses after he left the government, including overwhelming legal bills. Woodward did not mention Deep Throat during the first seventy pages of *All the President's Men*. It made sense that his editor, Alice Mayhew, would have urged him to get his source's permission to partially reveal him after she saw that the book's first sixty-nine pages lacked spice. And it makes sense that Woodward would have struck some financial deal with Mark to gain that permission. Certainly, it would have been a nasty blow to his source to partially out him without permission, an official who clearly did not wish to be unveiled, and do so while Nixon was still in office and capable of revenge. I did not believe that Woodward would do this to his "friend." We knew they at least had a deal that Woodward could reveal Mark's identity at his death, because Woodward had long promised that to the public.

If in fact Woodward had made a deal with Mark, it would be understandable that he would not wish to reveal that to us, which would be tantamount to admitting that Mark was Deep Throat! So perhaps Woodward was in an ethical box: Mark had dementia and wouldn't remember the deal they struck, and thus wouldn't have told us, while Woodward for obvious reasons didn't want to tell us either. When he ominously warned *there will be some surprises*, I now reasoned he was hinting at an arrangement about which he couldn't speak, and perhaps some unethical act of Mark's that he didn't wish to reveal while Mark was alive, indeed, perhaps a crime. He was telling me, in ominous tones: believe me if you do not wish to be embarrassed.

I explained my theory on this to Joan, while assuring her that Mark was Deep Throat and that I could prove it circumstantially six times over. At the same time, I firmly advised her to *never, ever tell Woodward that her father would only be revealed in cooperation with him*. The only reason Woodward would keep talking to her and Mark, I told Joan, would be because he was unsure if we would reveal Mark without him. The only way we could force Woodward's hand was to keep alive that threat. But I hastened to add that I remained pessimistic about his ever coming around.

Over the next few months, both Joan and Mark Jr. asked me on several occasions if I was still sure that their father was Deep Throat. Yes, I assured them, reminding them of key pieces of evidence that nailed it. I also reminded them that Deep Throat, by Woodward's own admission, was not a composite, that the composite seed was cleverly planted by Mark himself.

What was significant to me was that Woodward's talks with them had introduced doubts. I did not press with either at the time as to what exactly Woodward was saying, and neither of them volunteered much to me. I knew that each had his or her own reasons for being tight-lipped. Mark Jr. was a man of duty and military discipline, and likely Woodward told him he was speaking to the family in confidence, inferring that they shouldn't talk to me. Loose lips sink ships. I respected that. Mark Jr. was also, like his mother, a worrier, and Woodward had clearly induced worry in him. I learned later from his widow Wanda's arbitration testimony under oath that Mark Jr. believed Woodward to be warning him that his father was not Deep Throat, telling him time and again of the pain and shame that would befall elderly, befuddled Mark Sr. when his claimed identity was proven false. Woodward, I had concluded, was likely telling Joan the same thing.

Joan, an entirely different personality from Mark Jr., enjoyed what she thought was an increasingly close relationship with her father's friend "Bob," and I didn't wish to intrude on that. Unlike Mark Jr., Joan was inherently optimistic, much attributable to her new-age spirituality. She was strong psychologically, like her father, able to brush off anxiety that would cripple others. While Mark Jr. wanted me to alleviate his anxiety, Joan wanted me to assure her the dream was still alive and that her father was the great Deep Throat. And she didn't want to dampen my enthusiasm. In short, Joan was hopeful and Mark Jr. was anxious.

So, for reasons unique to each, I did not closely probe Woodward's statements to either of them. It was simply not necessary at the time, because I knew Felt to be Deep Throat. I knew Woodward did not want to cooperate and therefore did not care that he was trying to dissuade any revelation.

I felt bad about continually throwing cold water on Joan's hope that Woodward would come around. I felt it necessary, because sooner or later, I would be asking her father, with Joan's help, for permission to pursue the matter without Woodward. Joan was enjoying her talks with Woodward and harbored hope, so I let it alone for a while, continuing to remind her not to disclose Mark's requirement of Woodward's cooperation, which would queer any hopes of Woodward's agreement.

Twice Woodward scheduled California meetings with Mark Sr. and Joan, in conjunction with planned West Coast trips (he had a daughter in California). Each time, though, he cancelled at the last minute, on one occasion saying he had to hurry back to the East Coast. The first planned trip was around August 2002 and the second in November of that year. I interpreted these cancelations in line with my cynical view of Woodward's game. Joan held on to her hope, finding comfort in my continued affirmation of Mark's identity.

Then the expected call came, sadly for Joan, happily for me. In January 2003, Joan was uncharacteristically down on her relationship with Woodward. "I can't understand it, John," she told me, dismayed, almost to the point of tears. "Bob's always been so responsive. We've had this great relationship, but he hasn't answered my calls or emails since right after he cancelled the November trip. What do you think is up?" she asked.

I think she knew, but she wanted me to tell her. I first reminded her that I never thought Woodward was sincere about examining Mark's competence. He was playing us and had no desire for a relationship with Joan, except to monitor our plans. But then I asked the question: "You didn't by chance let Bob know that your dad would only come out with Woodward's cooperation, did you?"

"John," she responded, somewhat guiltily, "I was developing such a great relationship with Bob that I thought by telling him how much Dad needed him, we could push him to accept our offer."

I reminded her of my firm warning and explained that this now gave Woodward assurance that we wouldn't spill the beans independently. Now he knew that he didn't need us. He was going to wait for Mark to die. "Sorry, Joan," I lectured her, "but this is probably good for you to realize so that we can make practical plans to bring your dad into the limelight. Woodward was playing us all along." I did not add that Woodward was waiting for her dad to die so that he could keep 100 percent of the book's proceeds.

I sensed that this conversation had finally hit home with Joan. Several days later she asked me to come up to Santa Rosa to discuss the matter with Mark. I was happy about this and consoled myself that the delay in going elsewhere was probably helpful both to Joan, enamored with the courtly Woodward, and Mark Sr., who needed time to come to terms with the gravity of his intended public disclosure. In any case, on this visit Mark readily assented to my seeking a publisher without Woodward's cooperation. I also used this occasion to elicit Joan's firm promise not to tell Woodward *anything* about our new plans. "It will only hurt you, Joan," I cautioned, "and ruin any chances for you to get some tuition money, and your dad a little glory."

So Joan kept quiet, and Woodward remained incommunicado. Interestingly, after a hiatus of over a year, sometime in 2004, Woodward again got in touch with Joan via email. A pleasant exchange between the two of them ensued through mid-2005, shortly before our *Vanity Fair* article revealing Mark's identity. Woodward's father was elderly, suffering from a form of dementia, and Woodward used this hook to ask repeatedly about Mark's health. I interpreted these communications to be a deathwatch by Woodward, who wished such intelligence so he could prepare for the post-death release of his book naming Mark as Deep Throat and detailing their relationship. Joan heard me, but I could tell she didn't believe me, wondering aloud from time to time if her friend Bob would perhaps come around and cooperate with the family. I continued to remind her of the reality, at least as I saw it, and, after we made a *Vanity Fair* deal, of the need for confidentiality. She would ruin everything, I assured her, if she told Woodward.

My opportunity to convince Joan of Woodward's commercial mind-set finally came in May 2005, after our article was written and while the magazine was being prepared for printing. Woodward wrote another email to Joan, inquiring into Mark's health. The ever-optimistic Joan continued to express the thought that we were missing the chance for good old Bob to collaborate. I was in awe of Joan's positive attitude toward Woodward but saw this as an opportunity to put the matter to rest. I suggested she simply come out and ask Woodward again to collaborate, saying how her dad was so firmly and positively embracing his identity as Deep Throat. "I will bet you a million dollars," I wagered Joan, "that Woodward will go radio silent.

If he does," I asked her to promise, "will you remove all thoughts that this guy would ever, ever have helped us, or would have looked out for anyone other than himself?"

She then replied to Woodward with the email I suggested she write. It read:

> *Dear Bob,*
>
> *Thanks for checking in with me and Dad. Like your father, my Dad has ongoing memory loss, but moments (or periods) of lucidity that can astonish you–as if some channel that had been turned off got turned back on for awhile [sic]. It's mysterious. Another thing I notice is that the aging process reduces or eliminate [sic] inhibitions, so the person is just much more present with the whole of themselves, no longer guarded or self protective. Quite a refreshing development. Anyway, overall Dad is doing very well, stable, healthy and tells me he plans to be a centenarian. He's very well cared for by Bola, so who knows what could happen? He may live up to his plan.*
>
> *It will interest you to know that Dad now says quite openly that he is "the person Bob Woodward referred to as Deep Throat," and he doesn't demonstrate the reserve he had about this topic in previous years. Therefore, I'd like to propose again that you do a book in collaboration with Dad about this now. If you wait until he dies, then he loses out on the acknowledgement and the fun of it, the piece of the action, so to speak. So why not do it now.? [sic] I think it would have much more impact and potential. You fill in all the details that your good memory can afford, and he contributes the living personality, which gets better with each week that passes by. He's such a character, always with a twinkle in his eye, and his heart on his sleeve. He's a person who should be known and enjoyed by the world. Our elders are a much neglected treasure. Once he dies, the story really won't even be about him any more [sic]. And the world will lose a most important part of the puzzle, and a chance to appreciate a one of a kind*

personality who has in some mysterious way, reached his peak performance right about now. I'm sure that if you ask Dad, he will be all for the idea. He likes you; he trusts you. And he wants to be known and appreciated for who he is, all of him. He's not afraid anymore. With regard to the "competency" issue: I think there's an even greater principle that needs to be taken into account now. The man himself needs to speak. And with your help, he will shine.

Best regards,
Joan[2]

Sure enough, Woodward indeed went radio silent immediately. Even Joan, on the eve of the story in *Vanity Fair*, became convinced that he never had any intention of cooperating.

But, still and yet, I did not think Woodward a sleazy reprobate. I knew he was being deceptive but, for the reasons stated, thought he had been forced to deceive to preserve his deal with Mark. Moreover, as lawful as I thought the inferred deal was in fact, I knew it would dampen the glow of Mark's halo. Money drives even heroes, we would be forced to admit. I was unsure of the substance of the deal, how smarmy it would look, and unsure about Mark's guilt in other areas, such as his seeming cooperation with journalist John Crewdson.[3] Perhaps he did commit a technical crime by giving original FBI documents to Crewdson. So, I had better tread lightly, I thought.

In any case, for three years I had sought without Woodward's help to find a publisher for Mark's story, while keeping the matter otherwise absolutely confidential, conflicting ends though they were.

---

2 Joan Felt, "Re: Bob," email to Bob Woodward, May 20, 2005.

3 Felt had leaked to John Crewdson of the *New York Times* that Daniel Ellsberg had been overheard on the notorious Kissinger wiretaps via his conversations with the NSC's Morton Halperin, a Kissinger aide who had been monitored. The ensuing hubbub caused the court to dismiss the Ellsberg criminal charges because the prosecution had not previously disclosed the taps. Later Crewdson interviewed Donald Segretti while possessing FBI reports, some original. The suspicion was that Felt had rewarded Crewdson for his scoop by giving him these reports. An FBI secretary had witnessed Crewdson emerging from the executive suites with a bulging briefcase. A criminal investigation of Felt ensued and was eventually closed. What really happened is itself a fascinating story, which I will tell below.

Chapter Six

MARK TO KILL

I thought that Woodward's failure to cooperate with us robbed Deep Throat's story of much of its richness and prevented public enjoyment of the man's victory lap. But it never occurred to me that Woodward's refusal to accede to his source's request would cause publishers to pass on our story for want of verification of Felt's secret identity. But that's what happened.

Several media companies turned me down cold on the story. But I soon signed a contract with a huge media conglomerate (which had both a weekly news magazine and a book publishing arm), contingent on its satisfaction, after due diligence, that I had the goods. After six months of its investigation, I was told it would write the family a check for the story. In New York at the time, I went to the fifty-first floor to pick it up. After cooling my heels in the lobby, my contact finally emerged to inform me curtly that the managers had reconsidered, unceremoniously handed me my research materials, and departed. After I called the magazine's editor in chief to question this decision, she excoriated me for asking that she and her colleagues risk their jobs over my story.

An almost identical situation transpired with the next publisher, which withdrew for fear of being wrong after assigning a writer and issuing a check that never made it to me. I did receive a Form 1099 erroneously showing that the publisher had paid me! The publisher got cold feet after a two-year University of Illinois study concluded Deep Throat was Fred Fielding, an associate of John Dean!

We had tried for two years to convince a book publisher that we had the goods–that Mark was Deep Throat–but to no avail. Time was passing, and my client was old and frail, so a book was becoming impractical.

Finally, I got *Vanity Fair* magazine to bite, bravely in comparison to other outlets. David Friend was my *Vanity Fair* contact, a close associate of *VF* editor Graydon Carter and an accomplished, multifaceted talent. David, like the others, thought I was only *probably* right but, unlike the others, thought the risk that I wasn't right was worth it. The magazine was part of a closely held empire, and Carter and owner Si Newhouse liked the gamble. Free enterprise fosters the marketplace of ideas, but mainstream journalism for the most part was not truly free enterprise. David regaled me with the story of Carter and Newhouse deciding, over luncheon martinis, that the gamble was worth it.

When I arrived in his office on the publication date of May 31, 2005, David relayed to me, with a look of bemusement, his call to Woodward that morning. Woodward was cool as a cucumber, according to David. He described the call, with Woodward barely registering an emotion to David's communication about the article. "Oh, that's interesting," Woodward had reacted calmly, then repeating the mantra that he would never confirm or deny Deep Throat's identity while he was alive. David's reaction, as expressed to me in turn, was one of wry gallows humor, to the effect that he'd had a wonderful career in journalism and was looking forward to a second one as a house painter.

We proceeded that day with several interviews, most by phone, some via television monitor. Before one interview, as I was waiting for the caller, Andrea Mitchell came on the line, holding the fort until her colleague joined us. We had a delightful chat as we waited. In amused tones, she told me that in the *Washington Post* corridors the staff could hear a great deal of yelling emanating from the conference room where editor Len Downie, Woodward, and Bernstein were conferring–whether this was in person or by phone I did not ask. The obvious drift was that the *Post* editor was displeased that the paper could not exploit the revelation because of Woodstein's stance of non-corroboration.

It was not long before I realized, to my surprise, that the *Post* was not about to praise Mark Felt. I appeared that evening on PBS's *The News-*

Hour with Jim Lehrer alongside former White House press secretary David Gergen, among others. Gergen, very serious, brows knit, immediately began lecturing about the dark side of Mark Felt and the FBI, about Felt's conviction for illegal break-ins of the Weather Underground. He had his thuggish side, Gergen gravely intoned. I then took serious issue, at some length. Gergen was not happy with my takedown.

The following morning my erstwhile buddy Andrea Mitchell, like Gergen a close ally of the *Post*, appeared on *Imus In the Morning*, a popular radio and television morning show. "Follow the money," she advised host Don Imus, emphasizing the monetary motives of Joan and the family lawyer, yours truly.

If I had any doubt that the *Post* was coming after Mark, it was dispelled that same morning with the publication of the morning edition of the paper. On the front page was a still photo taken from a video shot the afternoon before of Mark, who had opened his front door to the roars of the crowd gathered on his lawn. Flanked by his attractive daughter and handsome grandson, Nick, Mark *in the video* was smiling broadly, waving, and looking ecstatically happy, certainly "with it." A news camera crew had caught this scene, which was viewed widely on television Tuesday night. In other papers throughout the country the next morning, pictures of the beaming Mark appeared, eyes wide open, smiling, a picture of happiness.

However, we all blink, and there's always a still frame in any video in which the subject is caught for that millisecond with his eyes closed. The front-page *Post* picture of the family in its moment of glory showed Mark with his eyelids shut, making him look like a confused old man. It took a lot of effort for a *Post* photo editor to capture this fleeting millisecond where Mark was not bright-eyed. But clearly the paper's intent was to make its source and benefactor look like a doddering fool. It was an old newspaper trick, but an effective one.

By the second evening of the story, the *Post* was desperately searching for some way to justify breaking its reporter's claimed sacred vow not to reveal Deep Throat's name until his death. After all, the paper was losing money each day it temporized. So it searched for ways to claim that Felt had consented to his outing, something that should have been obvious from our *Vanity Fair* piece. What was amusing about this effort was my offer in 2002 to have a qualified physician examine Mark as to his competence, followed by a court certification under seal. And of course, I as his lawyer and his adult children would verify his consent, as Mark himself would confirm. All of that was not about to convince Woodward in 2002 of Mark's consent, but that was then. This was now.

So the *Post* sought, it seemed, the aid of Ted Koppel of *Nightline* to get me to admit Mark's consent during our interview. Koppel quickly got down to business and, rather than ask me substantive questions, probed me if Mark had given me permission to write the story–an odd question, since I was Felt's lawyer, from which authorization could be implied. I quickly sussed that Koppel, of *Post* partner ABC, was doing *Post* dirty work, seeking to justify the *Post*'s publishing its own revelation based on Felt's consent to publicize, as admitted by me, his lawyer.

Instinctively, I gave a lawyer-like answer: that I could not reveal what Mark had told me for reasons of attorney-client privilege, which I had no authority to waive. This got Koppel's blood boiling, and he followed with several hostile-toned questions, not quite knowing how to get what he needed by piercing the privilege, about which he had no clue. Finally, after much back and forth, having had my fun, I told him to the effect that, look Ted, you can infer that what I wrote had client authorization. He clearly expressed relief that he had accomplished his mission.

Just then, a voice from a producer interrupted us. "Ted," the voice said, "the *Post* just confirmed that Mark Felt was Deep Throat." We both broke out laughing, and Koppel quickly said in a jolly tone, "Well, John, I guess we'll need to do another interview!" We did just that, amiably conversing about this and that. The point here is that Koppel was freely admitting that he was doing the *Post*'s dirty work. It was clear he had been trying to get my admission that Mark had authorized the *Vanity Fair* article, thereby constituting consent for the *Post* to publish Mark's identity, freeing them from its solemn promise to guard its source's name.

It turned out, then, that the specious basis for the *Post* decision to confirm our claim was that the family had given its implied consent by speaking publicly about their patriarch's identity, ostensibly through Nick Jones speaking from the lawn of his home about Mark's heroism.

What I found so amusingly hypocritical was that this same family and its lawyer had been begging the *Post* for three years to confirm Mark's role, the last such request having been Joan's email to Woodward just weeks earlier. Now a simple statement by Nick Jones–that he considered his grandfather a hero–sufficed to release the *Post* from its sacred secrecy obligation. So, of course, the lesson, I laughed to myself, was that the *Post* will honor its commitments, unless it can make money from their breach!

I eventually smelled that the *Post* was coming after the family, especially Joan, through its aggressive reporter Lynne Duke, who was now in California. Before I flew to New York, we had agreed that the family shouldn't do any unscripted interviews. We weren't sure before the *Vanity Fair* article was released who would be coming after us, but we knew it was inevitable. Now we sensed the identity of at least one assassin, the *Post*, which we had not, perhaps naively, anticipated.

The *Post* and Duke did not disappoint. According to Duke's June 3 *Post* article, the national hubbub surrounding this nice, small-town family was anything but a cute human-interest story. Rather, it was a tale of a carefully crafted plot: "Call it the Felt family strategy, hatched when they told their story to John O'Connor."[1]

The Felt family's humble reticence, according to the *Post*, was just part of a money-grubbing scheme: "The Felts have been told not to talk, not to share their story with anyone just yet, until the prospective big interview deal, big book deal, or big movie deal is secured."

On June 12, Duke reached full snarkiness, quoting an innocent admission of Joan about wanting tuition money, while ignoring her main motivation of showing the world what a wonderful person her father was. Duke delved into Joan's past as a hippie commune-dweller and current New Age spiritual practitioner with a group Duke did her best to make sound like a cult.

Joan called me after reading the June 12 article, sobbing, asking me what her spiritual life had to do with Watergate. Nothing, I answered. This article was so mean-spirited that it was mocked by Columbia Jour-

1 Lynne Duke, "Deep Silence On Redford Place," *Washington Post*, June 3, 2005, https://www.washingtonpost.com/archive/lifestyle/2005/06/03/deep-silence-on-redford-place/85722123-188a-4361-945f-bdb04efc5c7b/?utm_term=.b2277ad005be

nalism Review in a June 12 post entitled, "Joan Felt (gasp!) Was Once Young and Restless!"

In addition to depicting Joan as a money-grubber, the *Post* accused her of taking advantage of her elderly father who lacked mental competence. One pseudo-psychology piece told of the horrors of unlocking family secrets, comparing Joan to Cordelia in *King Lear.* The *Post* consistently suggested, in opinion pieces disguised as news reports, that her father would have preferred to die with his secret (a highly dubious proposition, as it turned out, given his subsequent glowing happiness). All I could do was comfort Joan and tell her to quit giving interviews (she had given one to the local paper, distorted by the *Post* to show her as a financial schemer). As long as the *Post* was in print, anything you say and do, I advised her, will be used, falsely or otherwise, against you.

But this was a small wound compared to the aim of Lynne Duke's mission. Joan called me Wednesday, apoplectic at the feedback she had been receiving. Duke was investigating Joan's spiritual practices in Adidam, a group some call a cult, led by one Franklin Jones, known as Bubba Free John. In the mid-1980s the group had been involved in a sex scandal involving this leader and some young women followers.

By late that first week, she finally learned where Duke was going with all of this. A good friend and longtime member of the group was asked by Duke if Joan's sons, Nick and Rob, were illegitimate sons of...Franklin Jones! No, that's absurd, the friend said she told the reporter. The friend related to Duke that she had known the boys' father, Rocky Jones, who was married to Joan and who she finally was forced to leave after years of problematic drinking. According to Joan's friend, Duke expressed great disappointment, telling Joan's friend she wrongly thought she had a great story, that Joan had borne two love children from Franklin Jones!

Around the same time, Duke experienced some difficulties with an appliance in her room at the Flamingo Hotel in Santa Rosa, located a stone's throw from the Felt household. Called upon to fix the Wi-Fi problem was the property's jack-of-all-trades, a young man from the area with good IT skills named Will Felt. Will was, yes, Joan's first and oldest son, approximately thirty-three years old at the time, quite a coincidence indeed.

Will's fix-it work that day was close to the desk where the guest was working, who Will quickly concluded was Lynne Duke, the same reporter who a day before had his mother in tears. Out of sheer curiosity, he couldn't help but look at the materials on Lynne's desk, trying to get a hint as to what she was doing. Glancing at the computer screen, Will saw something that jarred him. At the top of her screen in large letters was the title of the work: "MARK TO KILL."

Will did a double-take, staring in amazement at the screen. Lynne, preoccupied at first, didn't notice Will's fixation for a moment, then turned to see the young repairman reading her computer screen. Understandably, Duke was upset. "Are you reading my computer?" she demanded of Will. "That's none of your business."

"Oh, no, sorry ma'am," he mumbled while quickly turning and leaving the room.

Will told me the story the following weekend, after Joan had relayed it earlier by phone. "Are you absolutely sure that's what it said?" I prodded.

"Absolutely," he answered. He had stared at the screen continuously because he was so shocked by what it said. There was absolutely no doubt in his mind.

I explored the matter for some exculpatory interpretation. "Couldn't this be a heading, I asked, for items she was 'marking off' so that she could 'kill' them when completed?" Will laughed at the question. "That's not the way it looked to me," he answered. He saw nothing to suggest that this interpretation was right. No checklist or cross off of items. It looked to him like a reporter who was on a mission to kill, figuratively of course, Mark Felt. That's the only interpretation he could get from looking at the screen. As I questioned the sharp, levelheaded young man that day, I got no sense of hysteria or paranoia. The facts are the facts, and he was witness to them.

I couldn't claim at that point that there was enough "evidence" to say with assurance that Duke's intent in writing the piece was an expression of malevolence toward Mark. All I could conclude that day was that the words were all but certainly there on the screen as related by Will.

My assessment was that the actual intent of these words was beside the point. Perhaps there was an innocent meaning, an everyday usage by an organized reporter. But one thing seemed clear: A nice, struggling, striving family had just been put onto the world's stage alongside their ninety-two-year old patriarch. And at that very moment, a billion-dollar enterprise, which owed its success to that man, was trying to destroy his powerless family.

To me, the phrase "MARK TO KILL" on Lynne Duke's screen was at least a symbolic, if not a literal, statement of what was contained in the corporate heart of the *Washington Post*: sheer vituperation toward the historic facilitator of its reputation and riches. But the question remained: what was behind this palpable malevolence? I couldn't comprehend it. Why did these rich and famous people need to crush the old guy and his struggling family? What were they afraid of? It would take me years to find out.

In any event, the *Post* had now corroborated Mark's identity, and I was looking for a simple way to exit this project while assuring some financial reward for the family.

Joan had maintained a good relationship with her friend Bob Woodward, and I had maintained a polite conversational style with him. With Mark's memory problems, why not again attempt to join forces with Woodward?

I hoped to give the family some financial certainty while giving Woodward the upside of a movie contract he would likely not otherwise get. So, on Wednesday morning, I called Woodward's home. A younger (than I) female answered. I asked for Bob. She replied that he had just left. "Who should I say called?" she asked. When I gave my name, she quickly responded, "Maybe I can catch him." Woodward came on the phone within seconds.

I began very cordially, complimenting Bob on having had the good sense to confirm Mark's identity, telling him that if he or the *Post* had simply asked us, we would have gladly given permission to do so. Then I got down to business, offering him a split of the proceeds from his book and our movie, telling him we didn't even need half of the money, just a decent amount to help the family. He agreed that the market would not be hungry for our book in view of Mark's deteriorating memory. When I stated what I thought was obvious–that we would likely get a movie deal and he would not–he did not readily accede to that point. Strange, I thought, since *All The President's Men* was the journalist's story, and already told. The second movie would logically be Mark's story from his point of view, wouldn't it? Yet Woodward clearly thought he owned this second movie story as well! Woodward had been in all our conversations unfailingly polite and courtly, with his midwestern Protestant propriety, and his attitude was in accord for most of this call. He told me, in his slow nasal drawl, very nicely, that there wasn't enough from his book to share with the family.

We continued with this low-key commercial conversation, politely discussing, perhaps arguing, the possibilities for a movie for Mark when suddenly, uncharacteristically, Woodward exploded into a fit of rage. "Why didn't you tell me in advance about your story?" he yelled from close to the top of his lungs. "You know you should have!" I was shocked by the tone, the volume, the vehemence, the obvious anger coming from this low-key, even-tempered personality. To be sure, this type of splenetic rant I had heard many times before, but usually from someone Irish, usually in the evening, usually after ample refreshment, and usually concerning politics or sports.

Coming from Woodward, of all people, and in the morning at that, for some reason it hit my funny bone. I suppressed laughter, at the risk of sending Woodward over the edge. "Well, Bob," I began softly and with a wry tone, "you know I had obligations to *Vanity Fair...*" I hadn't completed my answer when he composed himself and said in the calm voice of Normal Woodward, "Everything here is off the record, right, John?"

Woodward's plea was especially rich in irony because he had taken great pleasure in writing in *All the President's Men* about Henry Kissinger's explosion in response to Woodward's queries about the so-called "Kissinger wiretaps." After his embarrassing fulmination, Kissinger asked Woodward that it be off the record. Woodward cheekily responded, "You knew the rules, Henry." Woodward then explained to Kissinger the long-accepted practice of honoring an off-the-record request only if made before the comment.

I resisted the urge to throw this incident back into Woodward's face and politely told him that everything we would talk about future tense would be off the record, a promise I honor here.

After Woodward turned down my offer, I set about trying to sell our movie, which seemed to me a more attractive property than our book. The main reason I had chosen David Kuhn to be our agent was his deep contacts in the movie industry. Sure enough, he quickly engaged his friend, superagent Sally Willcox of Hollywood powerhouse Creative Artists Agency (CAA). Sally put us together with Universal Pictures and Tom Hanks's production company Playtone and quickly came to a tentative deal whereby Universal would buy the movie rights, reserved for the use of Playtone and Hanks. Hanks himself wanted to play Mark. We were happy, and Mark beamed at the news that Hanks would play his role.

Satisfied that this was in the bag, I took a night off to semi-celebrate by taking two daughters of California friends to dinner on Bond Street. I was interrupted by a call from David Kuhn, talking with a tone of urgency. He had just learned that the *Los Angeles Times* was publishing an editorial the next morning, arguing that Universal Pictures should not buy movie rights from us but rather should deal with Woodward! David said that the editorial was giving the studio and Playtone pause, that maybe Woodward should be the person who had the goods to sell.

"Is this a bad dream?" I asked David. No one writes an editorial telling a business what kind of commercial deal to make, I stammered. Would the *Detroit Free Press* tell Ford Motor Company what kind of tires to buy for its cars? This was crazy. David told me that in fact this was what was happening, agreeing that it was indeed weird. He noted that Michael Kinsley, former *New Republic* editor and Washington, DC, journalist insider, was now running the *Los Angeles Times* and had been wreaking havoc among staff by controlling the editorial page in a dictatorial, ham-handed way. So, whatever would be written was coming through Kinsley.

Sure enough, the next day, on June 9, the *Times* printed an editorial that deserves to go down in *Ripley's Believe It or Not*:

> *A NEW HOLLYWOOD HERO?*
> *A good agent can work miracles, but even Hollywood knows that some challenges are insurmountable. As Halle Berry said to her agent at February's Razzies awards (where she won the prize for worst actress for "Catwoman"), "Next time, read the script first."*

> *The remark came to mind when we learned that Creative Artists Agency is representing the family of W. Mark Felt and the author and lawyer John O'Connor, whose story in* Vanity Fair *identified Felt as "Deep Throat."*
>
> *O'Connor's article created a sensation by naming the most famous anonymous source ever, and every publication in the nation (including this one) would have jumped at the chance to tell that story. Still, we wonder: Did the guys at CAA actually read the piece?*
>
> *It is basically a one-liner padded out by the anecdotes of daughter Joan Felt, some canned history and stilted "how I got the story" details. As a prose stylist, O'Connor's model appears to be the annual Christmas letter ("Jan served her typical Italian-style feast with large platters of pasta, grilled chicken and vegetables").*
>
> *Of course, bad prose does not by itself disqualify a story for the Hollywood treatment–as any reader of "All the President's Men" can testify. Which story, by the way, Bob Woodward plans to revisit in his own forthcoming book about Felt. Maybe CAA is betting O'Connor will be able to tell Felt's version of events, although the former Deep Throat is now 91 and enfeebled by strokes and other illnesses.*
>
> *We know enough about CAA to know it has some kind of strategy here, and undoubtedly it is designed to be opaque to lesser minds like ours. Deep Throat is a franchise character, as they say in Hollywood. We only hope that Mark Felt's legacy is more than that.*

In essence, this editorial was advising CAA to buy Woodward's story, not the Felts'. Of course, I immediately knew that Woodward was at least one of the callers of this "Hail Mary" pass play. He had implied immediately after our *Vanity Fair* article, by yelling at me, that he thought that he had the right to preempt our revelation, and therefore I had a duty to inform him of our plans, even if he admitted no corresponding duty to us. He had refused to admit that we were the logical parties to a movie deal.

We knew also from newspaper reports that he had visited with Robert Redford shortly after Mark came forward, no doubt to try to talk the actor into doing a second movie.

I continued to consider whether Woodward was refusing to cooperate with us because of a deal I hypothesized he had made with Mark many years earlier, pre-dementia. It would make some sense that such a deal would have included Woodward's right to include Deep Throat in both the book and movie version of *All the President's Men*. So perhaps Woodward thought we should be precluded from doing a movie because he had by inference already paid Mark for these rights.

However these thoughts may have been logical, I now began to doubt my presumption that Woodward was an ethical Episcopalian, which I had up until that point used to construct a defense for what otherwise was the reporter's deceptive, unethical series of conversations with Joan and Mark Jr. His actions post-revelation and those of the newspaper he managed now seemed more churlish than churchish.

Certainly if Woodward had made a deal with Mark, he could tell us about it now that Mark's identity was admitted. Maybe, though, he was saving the deal for his upcoming book, thus still keeping on the lid. But I was now doubtful about the imagined deal, because Woodward's attitude was too adversarial.

All of this is not to say that the aftermath of the *Vanity Fair* piece was a drama of pain for the family. To the contrary, Mark and his family, as they had planned, basked in the warmth of the kind letters he received from grateful citizens throughout the country.

I received a number of intriguing calls from acquaintances and strangers alike, offering interesting fragments of Watergatology. Far and away the most revelatory were two nearly identical stories from two unconnected sources. One was a seemingly knowledgeable unidentified man, probably sixtyish. The other was the highly respected Haynes O'Donnell, a Silicon Valley general counsel and former partner at my firm.

Each told me, based upon their respective sources in two New York law firms, that Nixon did not immediately destroy his White House tapes because they promised a post-presidency lifetime of income without taxes. By the time he was required to produce the tapes, no lawyer was brave enough to advise their destruction. Let me explain.

Normally, if an artist, say Picasso, wished to donate one of his own paintings to charity, he could not deduct the market value but only the cost of the paint and canvas. That would also apply, say, to otherwise valuable papers that a writer might have written. But the Constitution gives the president ownership after office of his presidential papers. Somehow, and I don't pretend to understand, he could therefore, according to the tax lawyers, deduct the *market value* of each White House tape he donated to his presidential foundation. Presumably he could wipe out all of his income every year with but a few donated tapes, which were considered presidential "papers" under the Constitution. Each of my two sources claimed that the firm he knew gave that tax advice, although the two named different New York firms. Of course by November 1973, the tide had turned so strongly against Nixon that destruction of the tapes might itself have been deemed impeachable and, for any lawyer so advising, indictable. In any case, I tended to credit this story.

In any event, in spite of the surprising venom coming from the direction of the *Washington Post*, the Felt family was ecstatic with the honor bestowed on its patriarch. I had signed both book and movie contracts, so family members looked forward to glorifying Grandpa.

But as June ended and Woodward's book was due to be released, I was in the main beset by puzzlement. On the one hand, I pondered what dark revelations of Woodward might besmirch our elderly hero. On the other, I had begun to question just how loyal the reporter truly had been to his supposed friend. The thought that now also lingered was the possibility that there was something about Mark or Mark's story that frightened Woodward and his preeminent newspaper.

So I waited with bated breath for Woodward's book about Deep Throat, due to be released July of 2005.

Chapter Seven

THE SECRET MAN

On July 6, 2005, Woodward released his book about Deep Throat. I could now read *The Secret Man* at my leisure, hoping I could glean from Woodward additional insight into my client's psyche and perhaps discern whether Mark had broken any laws. I had turned down appearing on Tom Brokaw's July special on the book for fear that I would be caught unprepared for a revelation of a crime or unethical behavior.

I first quickly flipped through the book to determine whether my worst fears were borne out, specifically whether Woodward had paid Mark for his help. Woodward's source was called Deep Throat specifically because he would only speak on deep background and not be quoted, insisting on anonymity. Yet throughout *All the President's Men*, Woodward directly quoted his source, which helped me identify him. And he told the public he had a supersecret source in *All the President's Men*, while presumably a supersecret source would not want it revealed that there was such a source. Moreover, Woodward provided tantalizing clues about this man, clues I had used to identify him. Surely these contradictions were strong evidence that the source agreed to be so described, at least while the book was being written, which made no sense without his having been paid for this partial outing.

I was happy to learn in *The Secret Man* that Woodward had not paid Mark for his leaks or for his later outing as Deep Throat. But had Mark leaked grand jury transcripts, a violation of federal law? Had Mark given Woodward FBI "302" reports,[1] arguably government property (also a

1 An FBI "302" report is the interviewing agent's summary of a witness statement to them. While prosecutors customarily provide these reports to an indicted criminal defendant, they otherwise constitute highly confidential information not normally publicly shared.

crime)? If he had done the latter, this would make it more likely that he had also given similar reports to John Crewdson of the *New York Times* and would not only be technically guilty of a crime, but also a liar when he penned his detailed denial of having given documents to Crewdson in his own 1979 book, *The FBI Pyramid.*[2] To my mild surprise, Woodward gave no hint of Mark's providing him or Crewdson any documents. In spite of Mark's law-abiding conduct, though, Woodward did his best in *The Secret Man* to portray him as a shadowy character.

So, what was the original deal made between Deep Throat and Woodward in 1972, and how was it changed to accommodate the 1974 book and 1976 movie featuring him? I found my answers on pages 109 and 110 of *The Secret Man*. There, Woodward recounts unsuccessfully seeking permission from Mark to name him in *All the President's Men*! Woodward clearly was not trying to protect Mark, and just as clearly did not understand Mark's motives, as demonstrated by this absurd request. He describes Mark's reaction to this:

> *He exploded. Absolutely not. Was I mad even to make such a request? He went further, suggesting at one point that he didn't know what I was talking about, as if he might be taping the call to create deniability. It was as emphatic a no as anyone could receive. Angry and unhappy, he told me, don't call here again. As I stayed on the line with some more questions, he calmed down, telling me that he had to count on our agreement, to count on me. He used the word "inviolate."*

In *The Secret Man*, Woodward, attempting to justify his seeming carelessness in protecting his source, repeated the agreement he had with Mark:

> *Our agreement was that there would be no identification of him, his agency, or even a suggestion in print that such a source existed. Nonetheless, during the previous year, Carl*

2 In response to a criminal investigation by the special prosecutor, Felt had denied giving FBI reports to Crewdson, who had published Felt's leak that Ellsberg had been overheard on the Kissinger wiretaps, previously denied by prosecutors, resulting in dismissal of all criminal charges against Ellsberg for the crime of leaking the classified information known as the Pentagon Papers.

> *and I had made numerous references in print to FBI files. On one occasion, I quoted Felt anonymously as a source saying that the funding of Watergate was "a Haldeman operation." Felt had never objected to these references, and I thought he gave me some leeway.*[3]

I gasped at this paragraph. I had stayed off the Brokaw special, certain that, if Woodward was the ethical guy I was sure he was, Mark necessarily gave him permission to reveal the character Deep Throat, and as well to quote him and give hints as to his identity. But none of those assumptions were close to true, according to *The Secret Man,* because Woodward promised never even to hint that a big source existed. By Woodward's own admission, then, he had betrayed the guy who made his career! Woodward had promised never to reveal he had a major source like Mark. And Mark had never, as I inferred, agreed to modify the deal.

Let's reflect a bit on this stunning admission. Woodward had solemnly promised that he would not make "even a suggestion in print that such a source [i.e., Deep Throat] existed." Yet, by 1974, millions, perhaps hundreds of millions, of people knew that such a source existed. By dropping hint after hint in the book and movie, moreover, Woodward had started a decades-long search to identify him. Book upon book, article upon article, show upon show, all tried to suss out his identity. As mentioned, a two-year graduate school project at the University of Illinois mentored by the brilliant William Gaines had meticulously researched this mystery. Presidents, Ronald Reagan being one example, vetted employment candidates, such as Fred Fielding, to ensure that they weren't Woodward's source. Woodward's disclosure of the Deep Throat character, I now saw, was an open-and-shut breach of contract case. But the victim couldn't complain for obvious reasons. The enormity of this treachery was mind-boggling.

The quoted paragraph was stunning for another reason. In it, Woodward admits that he not only violated the agreement by quoting Mark regarding Haldeman[4] but moreover admitted mentioning FBI files, contrary

3 Woodward, *The Secret Man: The Story of Watergate's Deep Throat* (New York: Simon & Schuster, 2005): 109–110.

4 Woodward did this to save his bacon for his clear error in reporting Hugh Sloan's grand jury testimony, which did not, as reported, mention Haldeman as a slush fund director.

to his agreement not to refer to the agency. And he used these violations to justify the more serious violation of revealing that there was a Deep Throat! This is like the landlord saying, "I violated the tenant's lease by not picking up his garbage can so therefore, since the tenant did not object, I can turn off his heat and hot water too." Woodward should have been, but apparently was not, ashamed.

Where and when was it that Woodward initially violated the agreement by naming the FBI and/or its files? How about in the very first article published after the first garage meeting? Recall that Bernstein quite accurately referred to this as the most important of their Watergate articles, appearing on October 10, 1972. What was its headline? "FBI Finds Nixon Aides Sabotaged Democrats." The reference to the FBI seemed a clear breach. In Woodward's defense, the headline was most likely not written by him but by his editors.

But the article itself does mention the FBI and its findings numerous times. Let's ask ourselves how hard our intrepid young reporters tried to honor Woodward's promise. This should have–but for Gray's obstinacy–cost Felt his job, because the article pointed right at Felt and his team. The very first sentence of the article read:

> *FBI agents have established that the Watergate bugging incident stemmed from a massive campaign of spying and sabotage conducted on behalf of President Nixon's re-election and directed by officials of the White House and the Committee for the Re-election of the President.*

This sentence, certainly the work of our famed team, violates the supposedly sacred agreement Woodward had with his source. These were the very first words reported after the first garage meeting, where one would think the agreement would be utmost in Woodward's mind.

Another part of the "inviolate" agreement was that Woodward could not name Mark, the prospect of which caused Mark to "explode" when the reporter suggested abandoning this restriction when writing his 1974 book. Nothing in the agreement, as stated by Woodward, allowed him to name Mark–ever. But this was precisely what Woodward had for years been proposing to do upon Mark's death! In *The Secret Man*, Woodward goes through a tortured recounting of his angst-ridden internal deliberations, as well as long discussions with his wife, about whether to reveal Mark's name at death. But in so doing he does not clarify that such identification would breach his agreement with Felt.

Now, of course, when Woodward's first book was published in 1974, Mark could not sue for Woodward's disclosures of the Deep Throat character on pain of revealing himself, nor would Mark be the kind of person who would file suit. Most lawyers reading this would also recognize the lack of damages recoverable by his estate after his death (when Woodward would name him in breach of agreement), because any such damages would have been personal to Mark. In short, Woodward was planning to violate on Mark's death the only corner of the agreement with which he had thus far complied–not naming Mark. Indeed, it was Woodward's announced intention of naming Mark at death that was one factor we used to convince Mark to agree to come out when he did.[5]

Woodward of course knew that Mark did not want to be outed, even after death, because the harm to him personally was not his concern; the damage to his beloved Bureau, which Mark hoped would thrive long after his death, was. Because Woodward knew this, he spent much of the book supposedly searching his conscience while not telling the reader that he knew his source adamantly opposed postmortem identification.

Now even as to this latter promise–not to reveal Mark's name–*The Secret Man* shows a cavalier disregard even while Mark was alive and sweating his outing. Woodward describes playfully bantering about Deep Throat's

---

5 Although we criticize Woodward for his breaches, they paled in comparison to those of other publishers. Felt was identified as a leaker in October 1972 to Attorney General John Mitchell by *Time* magazine's outside counsel, Roswell Gilpatric. Later, in May 1973, after the *New York Times*' John Crewdson broke the sensational story that Daniel Ellsberg had been overheard on the Kissinger wiretaps (leading to the dismissal of all criminal charges against Ellsberg), a man identifying himself as Crewdson told interim FBI director William Ruckelshaus that Felt had leaked the Kissinger wiretap story, resulting in Felt's resignation. Crewdson received from Ruckelshaus's subordinate FBI interview reports on Donald Segretti. Ironically, Felt was criminally investigated for the supposed crime of giving these reports to Crewdson. That criminal investigation, begun in June 1974, was likely spurred by the suspicion of the Nixon administration that Felt was the Deep Throat character described dramatically by Woodward in April 1974. In short, Felt as a confidential source was not treated well by *Time*, the *New York Times*, or the *Washington Post*. So much for principled source protection!

identity with former assistant attorney general Stanley Pottinger at a large Kennedy family Hyannis Port dinner.

In *The Secret Man*, Woodward recounts discussing in confidence with Pottinger grand jury testimony (which, by the way, is illegal to reveal, which seemed to bother neither Woodward nor Pottinger) in which Mark blushingly denied to Pottinger under oath that he was Deep Throat. Pottinger, to his credit, sensed Mark's unease and deleted his lie from the grand jury transcript as not being relevant, realizing that he and Mark both knew he otherwise would have perjured himself.[6] What struck me about this passage was that our former twenty-nine-year-old struggling reporter was now an elite celebrity playing parlor games at Hyannis Port and risking Mark's outing by joking winkingly with Pottinger while other elites looked on adoringly.

Of course, the book is replete with other examples of reckless indifference toward the promises made to Mark, such as the disclosure by young Josh Bernstein of Deep Throat's identity to a campmate. Bernstein obviously told his son about Mark's identity to get points in his broken relationship, and just as obviously had spilled the beans to Nora Ephron, who in turn told reporter Richard Cohen, who in turn was pushed off the scent only by Woodward's mendacity. So even the portion of the agreement that was partially honored–not naming Mark during his life–was executed with an insouciant sloppiness.

I was intrigued by the attitude of *The Secret Man* to the needs and wants of the reporter's source for protection from identification. Woodward and Bernstein were the same reporters from the same paper who had continually warned the public that anonymous sources couldn't always be trusted while they beat their chests about how ethical they were in protecting these sources. *The Secret Man*, then, revealed these nostrums to be the height of hypocrisy because the reporters did little to protect their sources.

In any case, except for these shocking admissions, *The Secret Man* was underwhelming. The first few pages narrate the chance meeting in a White

6 Pottinger obviously had a very strong sense that Mark was Deep Throat. Later, at the Kennedy compound, he and Woodward reveled in their occult knowledge of Deep Throat's identity.

House anteroom between the young US Navy lieutenant Woodward and the senior FBI official Felt. Felt, of course, had nothing to gain by mentoring Woodward, but the reverse was not true. Woodward knew as an ambitious young man that a friendship with a powerful official in Washington, DC, could not help but pay off down the road. And pay off it did.

In his later employment as a local beat crime reporter, Woodward likely would have gone a lifetime without a big story and, if so, he likely would have gone nowhere: he has never been accused of being a prose stylist, and he would have needed a major scoop to advance in the competitive and shrinking field of print journalism. But Woodward got his big scoop almost immediately, thanks to Mark Felt, when George Wallace was shot by a would-be assassin while speaking in Laurel, Maryland, happily within Woodward's "local" beat.

Woodward's movie revealed how Deep Throat (Felt) leaked him key information about the deranged shooter, Arthur Bremer, showing him to be a loner, unconnected either to Democrats or Republicans. From Felt's point of view, this story kept the FBI investigation from being politicized, likely realizing not only that Democrats had begun pointing at Nixon, the chief beneficiary of Wallace's demise, but also that Howard Hunt and Charles Colson were trying to connect Bremer to George McGovern, the Democratic candidate. Woodward's reporting on the solitary, delusional assassin not only gave him a skin to hang on his wall[7] but, more providentially, showed his editors, when the Watergate scandal broke, that he should remain on the story because of his valuable FBI source.

But at this point in *The Secret Man*, surprisingly, Woodward runs out of fresh revelations. There are no long Felt-Woodward talks that would illuminate Felt's motive, no insights fleshing out his character. Sadly, it becomes clear that Felt was "secret" to Woodward, seemingly because the reporter really didn't care to learn about him during Watergate, concerning himself

7 Although Woodward did not discuss this in *The Secret Man*, one could infer that Felt also leaked to Woodward information about corruption under the watch of DC police chief Jerry Murphy, a favorite of Nixon's (after quashing the "May Day" anti-war demonstration of May 1971, jailing twelve thousand demonstrators in squalid makeshift conditions, while the FBI, through Felt, politely declined) and a possible replacement for Hoover. It is interesting that Woodward did not debunk this possibility, widely bruited about for many years, in *The Secret Man*.

only with the next day's story, never delving into what made his source tick. This is probably not unusual for reporters, I surmised. In his typical on-task mentality, Woodward waited until 2000 to attempt an interview of Felt, because not until then did he feel he needed Mark again, this time to write what became *The Secret Man.*

The 2000 visit to Felt's home was thus to complete the reporter's monetization of his source. Learning that Felt's memory was impaired by senile dementia,[8] Woodward knew he had to scramble to produce the watery soup of *The Secret Man*. Helpfully, though, to Woodward, he also gained the insight so useful to him in our later negotiations, to wit, that Mark was incapable of authenticating his identity as Deep Throat. Woodward's "ownership" of his source, he thus learned in 2000, was complete, even if he had waited too long to suck from Mark all commercially valuable information. So where would Woodward go to get enough filler to justify a (presumed) large advance? To paraphrase a publisher's earlier question to me about the Deep Throat story, "Bob, on page 1, you met Mark at the White House. What do you put on page 2?"

My answer came quickly at pages 33 and 34 of *The Secret Man*, where he began paraphrasing Mark's writing in *The FBI Pyramid*. Let me quote a few paragraphs, which tell us what Woodward had in mind for the next 170 pages:

> *In his own memoir, The FBI Pyramid, which received almost no attention when it was published in 1979, five years after Nixon's resignation, Felt angrily denounced the effort to assert political control of the FBI through what he called a "White House–Justice Department cabal."...*
>
> *Felt later wrote that he considered [White House aide Tom] Huston himself "a kind of White House gauleiter over the intelligence community." The four-inch-thick* Webster's Encyclopedia Unabridged Dictionary *defines a gauleiter as*

8 Senile dementia is a common ailment, affecting every person to some degree starting in middle age. It is nothing more than the age-related hardening of arteries that keeps one from retrieving and encoding memories. Everyone over fifty years of age has some degree of senile dementia, even if not clinically significant.

> *"the leader or chief official of a political district under Nazi control."*
>
> *There is little doubt what Felt thought of the Nixon team. During this period, he also stopped efforts by some in the Bureau to "identify every member of every hippie commune" in the Los Angeles area, for example, or to open a file on every member of the Students for a Democratic Society.*
>
> *"This was an utterly ridiculous proposal," Felt wrote. "In the first place, only a very small number of members had actually advocated or participated in violence and there was no justification for investigating the others." It would involve opening thousands of new cases and the FBI didn't have the manpower, he added.*[9]

Clearly, by page 33 Woodward had completed his introduction and presented only scant new facts about his source. So, at this point, the remainder of his book became essentially a rehash of Mark's little-read book, *The FBI Pyramid,* together with snarky anti-FBI comments, as the above excerpt demonstrates.

Woodward's book continues in the vein of the above passage, citing or quoting *The FBI Pyramid* for Felt's attitudes and thoughts about the FBI, Watergate, Hoover, the Nixon administration, and Gray. He uses *Pyramid* to recount Felt's major career events, such as dealing with the 1965 uprising in Santo Domingo, Dominican Republic. He gives us instances of Felt's disagreements with Gray's policies, again lifted from *The FBI Pyramid.* He describes Felt's control of the investigation of Arthur Bremer, who had attempted the assassination of George Wallace. Woodward uses quotes and observations from *Pyramid* throughout the remainder of the book, as needed for his purposes. All tolled, perhaps 80 percent of the biographical material on Felt in *The Secret Man* comes directly or indirectly from *The FBI Pyramid.* The remainder of the descriptions of Mark comes from Woodward's review of FBI memos and his conversations with Mark's family in recent years. And this remainder, to be sure, is replete with Woodward's betrayals of Mark, however softly detailed.

---

9 Woodward, *The Secret Man,* 33–34.

The first point I make, of course, is that Woodward filled a substantial portion of his book with material from *The FBI Pyramid.* As I explained in *A G-Man's Life*, *The FBI Pyramid* was never promoted, was not edited as well as it could have been, and did not even contain a table of contents or index. It was released in the post-Watergate era when the plummeting FBI stock was approaching zero, in no small part, I might add, because of the *Post*'s negative reporting on the FBI and Felt. So, precious few had bought or read the offering, and now that its insights were marketable and of historical significance, it was Woodward, not Felt, who was reaping the benefit.

Woodward may well have stayed within the "fair use" exception of the copyright law, since he claimed to be commenting on another author's published work. In reality, of course, Woodward was doing nothing more than exploiting the FBI official's unique insights that had not previously been widely known.

The ethical question this use posed, then, was whether it would have been immoral for Woodward not to have shared some minor portion of his book's advance with Mark and his family. Once Woodward used quotes, paraphrases, facts, and insights from Mark's book, he went a step beyond simply using Mark as a journalist's raw source of information, as Mario Puzo and Sydney Schanberg had done with their sources.[10] He was now marketing Mark's intellectual property and winnowing profit from it, to the exclusion of Mark. Nonetheless, if Woodward felt remorse or guilt, he did an excellent job of masking it.

Another troubling aspect of *The Secret Man* is its revelation that the *Post* had editorialized forcefully in favor of the Justice Department's 1978 indictment of Felt for his role in warrantless searches of the homes of relatives and associates of Weather Underground members and lobbied as well for his 1980 conviction. When Mark acerbically needled Woodward, as Woodward candidly recounts in *The Secret Man*, about the *Post*'s editorial

10 Schanberg was the author of *The Killing Fields*, a book about the barbaric slaughter of hundreds of thousands of Cambodian people by Pol Pot in the wake of the Vietnam War. Schanberg was aided by local source, friend, and guide, Dith Pran. Mario Puzo used a Mafia source for his inside writings about the mob. As Jon Tierney wrote in the *New York Times*, both of these authors shared their financial success with their prime sources, while Woodward did not.

urging the Justice Department to indict Felt, Woodward, by 1978 a senior editor, begged off, claiming the editorial page was divorced from his news department.

At that point in *The Secret Man*, Woodward abruptly leaves the subject. But what internal discussions were there, we may ask, about the *Post*'s 1978–1980 campaign to indict and convict its important source, Deep Throat? After all, if not for Felt, the *Post* would have remained a sleepy backwater rag–without the oversized influence it had enjoyed in 1978. Did Woodward or Bradlee reveal Mark's heroism in confidence to the editorial board? Wasn't Bradlee its chairman? If not revealed, why not? We are not told. But it is difficult to approve of the fact that neither Bradlee nor Woodward presented, in some discreet fashion, perhaps under an ironclad written confidentiality agreement, that material information to its editorial board. As *Post* editor in chief, Bradlee knew well that Mark had proven himself a man of principle who would seek to obey the law and act according to his conscience. But now his criminal conviction fit the *Post*'s political agenda, no matter how unfair.

The *Post* would thus have had unique knowledge of the man's character and high-minded motives, something the Department of Justice wouldn't have known as it was considering indictment. Was there a moral responsibility on the part of the *Post* at least to advocate for Felt on its editorial page or rail against indictment, when it knew Mark's benign patriotic motives? Since a criminal conviction depends upon "specific intent" to violate the law, the integrity of the target would have been a very important consideration for both prosecutors and grand jurors. As I mentioned earlier, evidence of motive and intent is the key to any narrative and therefore to any trial.

Perhaps, I mused, that is precisely why the *Post* would not have revealed any favorable aspect of Mark's character: it would have interfered with its political agenda against all things "conservative" in the national security arena. The *Post* wanted the indictment, even if it meant indicting its great and highly ethical journalistic benefactor, a truly honest man. There has been no greater injustice in our country's legal history than the indictment and conviction of Felt for doing what is now recognized as perfectly legal under FISA and the Patriot Act, and clearly constitutional, contrary to the civil rights prosecutors who brought the case with righteous post-Watergate fervor. And nothing more damaging could have been done to the country, since this prosecution, we can conclude in hindsight, was inextricably connected to the security failures underlying 9/11, including the infamous "Gorelick wall."[11] So Woodward's mention in *The Secret Man* of the pro-indictment editorial only whetted my appetite for further exploration of the *Post*'s role in the sorry chapter of Mark Felt's prosecution.

Perhaps more significant than what Woodward wrote about Mark's assistance to him during Watergate was what he didn't write: he did not say that Mark ever gave the reporter any 302 field reports or grand jury transcripts, something many commentators had suspected of Deep Throat and for which Felt was criminally investigated in the Crewdson/Segretti matter. Woodward could have directly removed this cloud hanging over Mark, but that would have conflicted with the book's anti-FBI tone.

A larger failure is Woodward's treatment of Mark's motives for assisting him as Deep Throat. The reporter expresses bafflement and claims in *The Secret Man* that he is left to speculation. Perhaps, he throws out, Mark was getting revenge against the White House for not appointing him Hoover's successor. Maybe, Woodward muses alternatively, Mark was undermining Gray, trying to nab his job. Woodward talks about other possibilities, including general FBI thuggishness. At no point, though, does Woodward suggest that Mark was interested in preserving our system of justice while keeping the FBI's reputation free of smudges. Indeed, deliberately and contrary to all evidence, he suggests otherwise.

What Woodward does accomplish is the quashing of any discussion of FBI nobility in Mark's purposes. Why would anyone admire Hoover, Woodward snorts derisively? Rather than discuss the issue of whether the FBI, including Hoover, has been unfairly maligned by modern media such as

---

11 The "Gorelick wall," named after Clinton assistant attorney general Jamie Gorelick, separated information gained from intelligence services and criminal investigations. It was designed to ensure that criminal prosecutions were not "tainted" by national security incursions such as black bag jobs. This "wall" prevented intelligence agents from talking to FBI agents about individuals who became the 9/11 hijackers. Also, recall that a Minnesota judge refused to allow FBI agents to search a terrorist's computer that would have likely led to stopping the 9/11 attacks, conflating standard Fourth Amendment criminal law protections requiring probable cause with national security considerations.

the *Washington Post*, Woodward merely assumed the conclusion that the FBI is and was a disreputable organization, giving the back of his hand to Mark's most heartfelt beliefs, those he expresses in *The FBI Pyramid* but which Woodward conceals. Woodward concludes his discussion of Mark's motives by professing ignorance of a man who for years he had touted as a close friend and mentor. He was, in short, secret.

Interestingly, Woodward was more forthcoming and complimentary about Felt in *All the President's Men*, when he was supposedly shielding him. Yet what is so disappointing about this, again, is not what Woodward says in this bit of speculation but what he omits. In *All the President's Men*, we are left with an impression of Deep Throat as a deeply principled man, one who is coming forward, warily and with great precaution, despite the dangers he faces to himself and his career. Now that Woodward has the opportunity, with Felt's identity known, to specify the heroism of his source, that honorable man seems to have disappeared from Woodward's writing, leaving only the image of a shadowy, unknowable, perhaps ethically challenged FBI official.

He did that, of course, to play to his audience. Liberals, Woodward calculated, were ready to believe in Deep Throat as a man of conscience when they thought that man was not a law enforcement official. But now that the world knew Deep Throat to have been a member of the FBI, Woodward did not wish to offend the reflexive Bureau haters among his audience. So rather than standing up for Mark's integrity, he ran away from it, doing a disservice to the many fair-minded people in the liberal audience.

How, though, one may ask, can we criticize Woodward merely because he has a different view from that which Felt fans might wish? We can't. But we can criticize him for intentionally omitting favorable key facts or presenting politicized facts about the person whose legacy was entrusted to him, his "friend."

For example, a fact to which Woodward alludes mysteriously in *All the President's Men* is central to his description of Deep Throat: "He knew too much literature, too well." Woodward is telling us obliquely in this passage that Mark Felt was motivated by preserving Hoover's version of an independent FBI,[12] freed of political influence, which Felt reads perhaps

12 The 1924 founding proclamations ushering into existence the modern FBI (the for-

too firmly into the FBI's platitudinous founding documents.[13] Why does Woodward choose in *The Secret Man* to ignore this admirable motivation? After all, the last thing we want in law enforcement officials are agents who bend with the political wind. Mark's staunch refusal to do so during Watergate saved the investigation and saved our justice system.

And in *All the President's Men*, Woodward notes Deep Throat's anger when discussing Segretti. As cited earlier, this anger wasn't directed at the criminal acts themselves, which were not heinous, but the seemingly corrupt, politically influenced decision not to investigate the Segretti "dirty tricks." Again, Woodward omits a discussion of this in *The Secret Man*. Why, we ask, does he do this to his "friend"?

In short, that Woodward deliberately concealed facts about Mark's motives, facts that would burnish the reputation of Felt's beloved FBI, is a less than honest betrayal of his supposed friend.[14] Woodward claims disingenuously in *The Secret Man* that he could not fathom Felt's motives but in fact shows in *All the President's Men* that he had a pretty good grasp of them.

There are other instances in *The Secret Man* where Woodward uses his claimed "inside" knowledge of Mark to give the reader a deceptively negative impression of his "friend." In *The FBI Pyramid*, Felt explains the background of the famous Hoover/Martin Luther King feud. There Felt contrasts, from his author's remove, Hoover's prudish nature and King's libertine lifestyle, generally with wry humor and compassion toward both interesting historical figures. He also gives a highly detailed and nuanced history of the events and personalities–including the cynical use of Hoover as a scapegoat by the Kennedy brothers. John and Robert Ken-

mer Bureau of Investigation had been a crony-infested, corrupt political hack squad) promised the FBI independence from political influence–something very easy to promise but hard to enforce.

13 While these founding documents promise the FBI political independence, the Bureau was still under the jurisdiction of the attorney general and Main Justice. These prosecutors, in turn, made key investigative and prosecutorial decisions, such as the early decision not to investigate Watergate beyond the burglary team.

14 The best argument that could be mustered against Felt would be that all of his perambulations in February 1973 were motivated by his desire to get the top job himself. The evidence can be argued this way, of course, but Felt's desire for appointment wouldn't be inconsistent with his motivation to preserve Hoover's legacy, once he realized Gray was part of the cover-up. Had Gray faithfully sought and followed Felt's advice, he would have kept his job.

nedy had given King the false impression that it was Hoover's bias against the preacher, not the Kennedys' political jitters, that motivated the purge of King's communist advisors. In other words, the Kennedys made Hoover the fall guy in King's eyes.

If anything, Felt goes very light on King by showing both Hoover's and the Kennedys' motives. Later in his book, Felt expresses revulsion that the colleague he disliked so much–William Sullivan–would use King's sexual peccadillos to harass and intimidate the civil rights leader. And Felt gently suggests that Hoover's sexual prudishness was partially to blame. Clearly, Felt is not justifying, only explaining, Hoover's attitude toward King. It was Sullivan who, to Felt's disgust, had prepared a montage of the most salacious recordings the FBI had overheard and mailed them to King's residence, with an anonymous letter suggesting King should kill himself, whereupon Mrs. King opened the package. All of this was hidden from Hoover. Meanwhile, Felt had great admiration for King, and the Bureau performed admirably in protecting the Southern desegregation championed by King.

So how does Woodward characterize Felt's writings in this regard? He characterizes Felt as cheerleading for King's shaming:

> *Felt writes approvingly of Hoover's campaign to discredit King, because King was, in the Director's eyes, a hypocrite who did not have the morality to head a civil rights movement. The ends justified the means. Using that information was permissible for a larger, worthy purpose and a judgment that could be made outside the law.*[15]

So, Woodward not only lifts material from Felt's book, but he also does so in a deceptive way, reversing completely Felt's opinions about Hoover and King!

Woodward's lack of candor does provide a "teachable" contrast between his unprincipled commercialism and Mark's principled honor. His failings render *The Secret Man*, viewed as history, particularly tragic. Why would a prize-winning author defame the source that so honestly served him and the public in our country's worst scandal?

15 Woodward, *The Secret Man*, 43.

I found something else Woodward took from Mark in *The Secret Man.* He mentioned in the book that Mark had likened himself to the Lone Ranger, the comparison my book publisher, Peter Osnos of PublicAffairs, had found so compelling in Mark's yet unpublished writings. Woodward was implicitly passing off this revelation as having come from Mark during their Watergate collaboration, but I knew this to be highly likely untrue. Mark Jr. had prodded his father to use this metaphor for the Deep Throat character, without Mark Sr.'s admission to his identity. This did not occur until the 1990s, when Woodward and Felt had long since stopped communicating.

Woodward had clearly picked this item from the manuscript that Mark Jr. had revised with his father and had passed around to various publishers after Woodward's 2000 visit to Felt. In any case, the point I make here is that Woodward had no compunction about stealing this tidbit from Mark's later writings.

Woodward's candid admissions of his betrayals I thought would add nicely to our treatment of Mark's life. We could make a true contribution to our society's views of "investigative journalism," perhaps showings its warts along with its beauty. This anticipated future discussion of reporter and source should get the attention of serious journalists and journalism critics.

I knew that Peter Osnos would be overjoyed at our plans. We would give him, I foresaw, far more than he was paying for; the book would contain a valuable addition to the history of journalism. I could not wait to tell him about my proposed Woodward chapter.

Chapter Eight

THE *POST*'S PUBLISHER

As I mentioned, we had concluded a deal with Universal Pictures to do a movie under the control of Tom Hanks' Playtone. There was one catch: the movie folks insisted upon receiving, in addition to all of our "life rights," the rights to a new book about Mark. As the demand was explained to me by the agent, it made eminent good sense: the producers wanted as much intellectual property as possible, hopefully preventing others from doing a film on the same topic. Fair enough, I agreed; we would do a book on which the movie would then be based.

I came close to concluding a deal with ReganBooks, an imprint of HarperCollins, for a "quickie" book, incorporating Mark's old writings with some notes and comments at the end of each chapter, and doing so for a generous sum of money. The family, to its credit, preferred a book that incorporated substantial new material, even though the inclusion of Mark's little-read previous writings was appealing to them. We eventually arrived at a happy resolution.

ReganBooks had turned down the book before the *Vanity Fair* article for lack of confidence that Mark was in fact Deep Throat, thrown off balance by the University of Illinois study concluding that Deep Throat was Fred Fielding, John Dean's assistant White House counsel. But once the *Vanity Fair* article was released, the publisher was hot in pursuit of the deal, knowing the story was rich. Other publishers, though, backed off when Page Six, the influential gossip column in the *New York Post*, published two items suggesting that ReganBooks was *not* interested because it had months earlier fully vetted the story and found it lacking in substance.

Of course, nothing could have been further from the truth. My agent, David Kuhn, casually told me that ReganBooks had likely leaked the Page Six stories to scare away the competition. It worked, and previously enthusiastic publishers melted away.

I had worked closely many months earlier with ReganBooks, its bright editor in chief Cal Morgan, its founder Judith Regan, and the writer they engaged, the talented Jess Walter. The publisher knew there was much to Mark Felt's story, even if he no longer had a memory that could recall detail.

With all the other publishers backing off the book—at least until I could better outline the story for them—in the family's understandable haste to lock down the movie deal, it was leaning to signing a generous offer from ReganBooks. The unfavorable aspect to this deal was that it called for little meaningful depiction of who Mark Felt really was and no new exploration of his career beyond that in his earlier writings. We were left with a choice of taking a bird in the hand or hoping for two in the bush.

So we were much surprised when Peter Osnos, the founder and editor in chief of the Perseus Books Group imprint PublicAffairs, persisted in aggressively courting us. Osnos described his publishing house as proudly independent, something of a novelty in an industry controlled by a few owners, each with numerous imprints under its control.

To the family's credit, it was not concerned that the advance Osnos offered was much lower than that offered by ReganBooks. The major selling point for the family was that the publisher would allow us the freedom to write deeply about Mark and offered us great research assistance. PublicAffair's independence would allow us to write as we wished, Osnos argued. This meant far more (uncompensated) work for me than with ReganBooks, but telling Mark's story was my goal in signing on, as well as a solemn promise I had made to induce him to come out.

Though I understood the interest of ReganBooks, I was baffled by this ardent courtship from Osnos. He never once asked me what I would write, or what I thought was interesting in Mark's story. Very odd, I thought, when compared to all the other publishing executives I spoke with. My only guess was that, as a former reporter with the *Washington Post* who played a bit part in Watergate, Osnos wanted to share in the reflected glory of Watergate.

In fact, one of his selling points to us was that he knew Ben Bradlee and could likely get him to promote the book. To hear Osnos tell it, Bradlee would be willing to help us because of his friendship with Osnos. I discounted this claim as puffery, reasoning that unless Bradlee or the *Post* had a financial interest in the book, the famous publisher would not break a sweat for us. In any event, far more persuasive was his claim that his imprint's power alley was its ability to promote its books with free media. They had published many serious political books by the likes of former president Jimmy Carter and Soviet refusenik Natan Sharansky and knew how to take advantage of its authors' star power.

One oddity, though, was his professed excitement about Mark's claim, made late in his life at the urging of his son, Mark Jr., that Deep Throat professed to be a "Lone Ranger." Osnos would build the promotion of the book around that phrase, he told us. This idea never floated my boat, but if it led PublicAffairs to buy and promote the book, then fine. We had very low expectations about this mundane theme, in any case. His continued excitement over this sobriquet became even more curious after Bob Woodward included a reference to Mark's "Lone Ranger" identity in *The Secret Man*.[1] The reference by Woodward caused no publicity ripples and, moreover, meant that any revelation of it by us would seem stale. I continued to question Osnos's enthusiasm for the Lone Ranger hook. This one made no sense to any reasonable person, I thought, but he continued to push this bit well after *The Secret Man* was on the stands.

We had our first all-hands conference call with the PublicAffairs editors on August 13, 2005, about six weeks after the publication of *The Secret Man*. I opened the conference by suggesting a chapter to spice up our book by exploring the dysfunctional and conflicted nature of the reporter/source relationship between Felt and Woodward, with *The Secret Man* giving us excellent material for counterpoise.

To my surprise, Osnos erupted at this suggestion, yelling loudly that the book was about Mark Felt, not Woodward. I replied, humorously I thought, that it was hard to write about Abbott without writing about Costello, or

1 I do not believe for a second that Mark ever told Woodward during their Watergate collaboration that he was a "Lone Ranger." As I note, Mark Jr. came up with the tag, and Woodward learned of it through a revised manuscript of *The FBI Pyramid* Mark Jr. had circulated.

Stanley without Livingston. Expecting chuckles, I was met instead by moments of stony silence. Then Osnos firmly told me he wanted none of this nonsense about Woodward, to which I demurred. After Osnos's outburst I considered looking for a new publisher, but I had agreed to a contract with him and wanted nothing to hold up the movie. Osnos then assigned me an editor, the highly accomplished Steve Strasser, a former *Newsweek* editor, which gave me optimism about the project.

I suspected that Osnos's association with Bradlee and former work for the *Post* had caused his reflexive negative reaction to any criticism of Woodward and wrote it off as a personal idiosyncrasy. In the weeks following, I then came up with another idea to add interest to the book, if I were to be limited on Woodward. There were a number of highly intriguing facts about Watergate that emerged years after the scandal, from a variety of sources, facts that seemed to have been anticipated by Felt during Watergate. For instance, in *The FBI Pyramid*, Felt wrote about the FBI's determination that burglar James McCord, a recently retired CIA agent, had been picked up at the DC jail after making bail by a man known only as "Pennington."

Felt suspected that Pennington was McCord's CIA handler and sensed that McCord was not really retired from the CIA during the Watergate burglary. However, when the FBI asked the CIA to identify any agent named Pennington, it told the FBI only of *Cecil* Pennington. After a long wild goose chase to locate Cecil Pennington–who had overseas assignments–the FBI only learned that he had nothing to do with McCord or his pickup. The FBI much later found that McCord had been picked up at the jail by a CIA agent named *Lee* Pennington, a name the CIA had withheld from the FBI purposely, a cover-up broken only because of the honesty of a CIA security officer appalled by the Agency's dishonesty. This tableau suggested CIA involvement in and a cover-up of Watergate, as Felt had originally suspected and told Gray immediately after the arrests.[2]

Felt's suspicion was magnified by the time of his dramatic May 1973 garage meeting with Woodward when he told the reporter, "Everyone's life is in danger!" He explained that the CIA wished to keep investigators

2 Felt's shrewd insight of possible CIA involvement not only proved prophetic but also began the causative chain that resulted in President Nixon's forced removal from office.

from finding out its activities to which Watergate might lead. In *All the President's Men*, however, Woodward and Bernstein claimed that their fears were not borne out in subsequent weeks, implying that Deep Throat had been mistaken. But how could the head of the FBI investigation be so clearly off base?

Additionally, it emerged years after Watergate that the conversations being monitored were largely of sexual assignations between men and women, perhaps prostitutes. The combination of CIA involvement and a prostitute-monitoring operation would suggest not only an alternative to the conventional Watergate narrative but also answers to all the nagging little mysteries of Watergate. For instance, the alternative story would explain why anyone would want to wiretap the DNC before it had any campaign information, and why the taps occurred while DNC chairman Lawrence O'Brien was out of town on an extended decampment to Miami. It would also explain why James McCord stayed on the burglary team, even though he would be clearly associated with the CRP if caught, completely antagonistic to the normal "deniability" designed into any covert operation.

Steve Strasser was initially in disbelief of this angle on the burglary because he had never heard of it before. But I referred him to two works as primers on this topic, *Secret Agenda* by Jim Hougan[3] and *Silent Coup* by Len Colodny and Robert Gettlin,[4] to be followed by examination of the authors' sources. Soon Strasser's initial skepticism turned to unbridled enthusiasm. We talked excitedly about how a concise rendition of this information, dovetailing with Mark's investigative hunches, would add much to our book's appeal.

Steve soon returned to me, speaking dejectedly. Osnos considered *Silent Coup* and *Secret Agenda* to be outside the "Watergate canon" and

---

Gray shared this hunch with Dean, who, claiming the imprimatur of the highly trusted John Mitchell, suggested to the president and Oval Office intimates that the group use the CIA to call off the "Mexican money trail" part of the investigation. Nixon, recorded on a June 23, 1972, White House tape, was caught dead in this obstruction. Mitchell denies the authorization, while Dean maintains it. Author Len Colodny impressively supports Mitchell. But this is a historical swearing contest, the outcome of which is of little practical consequence.

3 Jim Hougan, *Secret Agenda* (New York: Random House, 1984).

4 Len Colodny and Robert Gettlin, *Silent Coup: The Removal of a President* (New York: St. Martin's Press, 1991).

off limits, he related. Our chapter was therefore rejected. I kept pushing Steve. Yes, each author was off on his sweeping conclusions (Hougan that Deep Throat was a White House intelligence plant spying on Nixon; Colodny that Deep Throat was likely Alexander Haig, who was part of a quiet right-wing military coup of the White House). But the underlying factual research of each book was solid, even if a few conclusions drawn were flawed. And why shouldn't I be able to write what I wanted, as long as what was said was factually supported?

After Steve acted for weeks as an intermediary in this minor struggle with Osnos, he told me he had a compromise solution, which he would not describe, but he would have to write this particular part of our book himself without my input. Usually quick in turnaround, Steve waited until the deadline, then produced a few pages that were a good summary of the revisionist narrative but a bit weak at key inflection points, which I did not understand. He did not show, for example, the infiltration of the White House by the CIA but only claimed it may have been interested in this same prostitution ring as the White House. And the centrality and meaning of the Maxie Wells desk key was also missing, although Steve mentioned offhand that the burglars had a desk key. I wanted some strengthening so that the story would appear both as credible fact and as far more damning of the CIA. That said, the summary Steve wrote of my take on the revisionist theory was decent and well written, even if more vanilla than it should have been.

Before the "wrap" meeting in New York, as deadlines approached, I finally unburdened myself to my agent, David Kuhn, about the restraints put on us both about Woodward and the alternative narrative. David, somewhat surprised, in turn pushed our case to his friend Susan Weinberg, now Osnos's designated successor. He reported that our book was still Osnos's baby, according to Susan, but that she would present our case to him.

What shocked me about this exchange was news of Osnos's ouster. By whom was he ousted? I asked myself. From speaking with Osnos at the outset, he gave me the impression that he *was* the imprint, as "founder" and editor in chief of this relatively low-advance house. But obviously others were in control. Who were they? I was puzzled. In any case, David advised that he informed Susan of our wishes to quickly supplement our manuscript with these offerings, something we could do while still adhering to our schedule of an early summer release. We thought a couple of weeks would suffice.

At the November wrap meeting, Osnos immediately announced that he was moving up the book's release to an earlier date, on the absurd theory that every publisher looks to distribute summer beach books but that there is a spring hiatus in offerings, just prior to the summer books, where we would have little competition. Clearly, he was looking for a reason to say we had no time to add to our work. Was Osnos the only publisher in New York who had this brilliant insight about the pre-summer, pre-beach books? After asking a younger female associate about the editing schedule, he then calculated, right then and there, as if for the first time, that the final processing had to begin...that night! Of course, no more substantial additions would be possible, he said. Clearly, he was using his contractual powers to edit and distribute to silence our rights to write our own work. This was obvious nonsense.

David and I then pushed our case for supplementing the Woodward and revisionist treatments. Certainly, we urged, there should be time to revise a bit. Osnos was becoming visibly upset, his tanned face becoming red to the point of crimson. Finally, after much back and forth, he shouted loudly, "Do you know who signs my paychecks? Do you? Ben Bradlee, that's who!" He repeated this for good measure. His neck veins seemed to be popping. He was, in short, unglued. Susan immediately called for a break. Needless to say, the revelation that my publisher was controlled by the *Washington Post* stunned me.

At break, I received various answers as to the *Post*'s role in PublicAffairs. Some employees told me that PublicAffairs was an "independent" house but didn't know who owned the stock. A highly reliable source, whom I will not name, told me matter-of-factly that the *Post* owned the publisher. In any case, Ben Bradlee was chairman and controlled the imprint's affairs. I understood now why the publisher would care so much about my laying off of Woodward. But why would the *Post* be so hostile to the revisionist narrative? Yes, it added new matter to the *Post*'s fine reporting during the scandal, but why would that upset *Post* loyalists? In any case, as I write this, the imprint has been sold to a reputable publishing house, Hachette Book Group.

When he returned from the break, Osnos finally allowed me but a day to add some material about Woodward, but from this I knew that essentially the book would be unchanged. He then announced, in fact theatrically loudly, as if being recorded, and then repeated, "Go ahead, John, whatever you want to write you can write!" But as noted, he had given me twenty-four hours, an absurd limitation.

Before the meeting ended, Osnos had bullied me into removing my suggestion, already in the manuscript, that Woodward had acted dishonorably. I had written that even though both Felt and Woodward had acted to advance their own interests, at least Felt had acted honorably. Osnos angrily told me that I was "slapping Woodward in the face." I agreed to remove the reference, further weakening my already tame treatment of the reporter.

I saw very little opportunity to reformat my treatment of Woodward so as to meaningfully treat his perfidy, which I had to complete by the following afternoon. So I settled for a few sentences expressing my surprise that Woodward had provided rich clues about Deep Throat in *All the President's Men*, but without the compensation and agreement between the two I assumed would have occurred.

As I was finishing up, I took a restroom break from the room I shared with Steve. When I returned, I caught Steve defensively assuring someone on the phone, "No, no, no, he's just added a few sentences..." It seemed he was calming down his communicant. When he hung up, I asked with a grin, "Peter?" Steve just smiled.

However, even though I added only a few snippets, given Osnos's reaction, I developed the sense that he was now not keen on promoting our offering. My fears were borne out when days before the book's release, the *Post* published a scathing review of it, which in effect was, through Bradlee, approved by my publisher! The review, by Richard Gid Powers, actually did not describe the book but said in essence, "Don't bother reading it because nothing is new here." The review was immediately posted on our book's Amazon web page, meaning that PublicAffairs had consented to quashing its own book by allowing this review on its site! It stayed on the web page for years, while favorable reviews from the *Post* are nowhere to be seen. Oddly, the review criticized the book's structure, combining my fresh writings with Mark's past work, a design ordered by Osnos, and vicariously by the *Post*, the paper now criticizing it.

If there was any doubt about the motivation behind the review, it was made clear at its conclusion. Bear in mind that our brief treatment of Woodward, even-toned though it was, could not be described as favorable to him, telling the close reader that Woodward's outing of the Deep Throat character in *All the President's Men* was not authorized by his source. In a very mild, unsensational tone, we accused Woodward of betraying his friend. But Powers said just the opposite, claiming, amusingly, that Woodward was proven in this book to be a "stand-up" guy:

> *Still, Woodward emerges in Felt's book, as he did in* The Secret Man, *as a straight shooter whose preservation of Deep Throat's secret helps explain his amazing access to officials at the highest levels; his sources know that when Woodward says he will keep their confidences confidential, he means it. Felt's book and his earnest but unavailing efforts to recall his relationship with Woodward make it clear that Woodward was far more than just a press conduit for Felt. He was a friend. Similarly,* The Secret Man *showed that Felt was far more than just Deep Throat to Woodward, who was boyishly eager to reconnect with the old wizard during Felt's sad years of decline. Felt and Woodward appear in the two books as kind, thoughtful men of honor: In a characterization both men seem to relish, they are "stand-up guys."*[5]

Of course, the review was patently false in its depiction of our book. Obviously, the *Post*'s enmity to us was continuing, perhaps escalating, as it was now actively burying our book and displaying it on our Amazon page!

That Osnos was playing games with us, at least since that fateful August editorial phone conference, was obvious. The difficulty for a nonintuitive person like me was discerning what was a dishonest game and what was sincere but incompetent. An example was the choice of Mark's first interviewer for our promotional campaign.

5 Richard Gid Powers, "Secret Agent Man," *Washington Post*, April 23, 2006.

We had been keeping our powder dry, not yet allowing any interview–a risky undertaking given Mark's condition–until our book came out, and under conditions comfortable for Mark.

From the outset of the project, I let Osnos know that Katie Couric was hot for the interview. She hosted the *Today* show, which had great ratings, and as the book project moved along, she was strongly rumored to be in talks with CBS to be the prime news anchor on the *CBS Evening News*. So to capture a national prime-time audience, Couric would be a great bet, and she had personally told me she wanted the interview.

Oddly, Osnos never seemed excited by this, even while lacking a prime-time interviewer. (Clearly Couric could have garnered prime time.) After I continued to press for Couric, Osnos off-handedly informed us, I believe for the first time at our wrap meeting, that he had Morley Safer (of *60 Minutes* fame) lined up to do a special, and the deal with him was all but done and dusted.

I still preferred Couric, but she was rumored to be in the CBS talks, which would have put her in conflict of interest if she talked to me about a CBS interview when she was still working for another network.

Safer would have been fine because, after all, he was a respected national news figure. But I never felt that Osnos truly had Safer in hand, and if I, with terrible intuition, intuited that, it must have been obvious. But I could never press to lock up Couric because she was not answering my calls, as was safe on her part. I left messages telling her I understood her position and imploring her to call me the moment she was free of conflict.

Unfortunately, that moment did not come soon enough. As we were finishing up the galleys for the book, I recall around February 2006, Osnos calmly announced that Safer was unavailable for the interview because he had a daughter studying abroad in Italy, and he would be traveling there. I questioned Osnos about how this didn't make sense, because at most interviewing Mark would be a three-day project. Surely his daughter's presence in Italy wouldn't really keep him from this, I argued. Osnos verbally shrugged me off.

But in my heart of hearts, I knew there never had been a Morley Safer interview in the works. The lack of content about Osnos's discussions with Safer and/or his producer, the lack of other detail, always made me feel I was being BSed. Now I knew I was. But to what purpose? I assumed simply it was an excuse not to put all our eggs in Couric's basket.

Several days later, I received an excited call from Osnos's PR exec, whom I will call "Meredith." She told me that Larry King of CNN had agreed to a special program for Mark. I had great respect for King's interviewing abilities, which would be needed to get the most out of Mark. Since I hadn't yet heard from Katie Couric, I had no choice but to agree, and I was not unhappy to arrange a session with King's production staff in Mark's Santa Rosa living room. Indeed, I was pleasantly surprised that Osnos had arranged a legit interview.

As the gods would have it, it was no more than a week after firming up the deal that I received a nice call from Katie Couric, who had just signed with CBS. She wanted to do Mark's interview and a special with it. I had given my word to the King people, thought Osnos was acting in good faith, and had, sadly, to turn her down. I regret doing so to this day, but my father taught me that your word should be your bond. Looking back on this decision, I should have recalled my father also saying that every rule has its exception.

That said, I was fatalistically preparing for some subterfuge or undermining by Osnos. The King interview, even though not Couric, was a nice promo for a great hero, if completed without sabotage by Osnos.

In mid-March, Larry King traveled to Santa Rosa to interview Mark in his living room, decorated by the King team to look like we were in King's studio. Larry did a nice job of speaking with Mark, getting right to the heart of his psyche as Deep Throat, his motivations. I, along with the family, was overjoyed. Larry King had been masterful, and Mark came off well for an older guy. Though I was still wary of Osnos, all was looking good for the show.

Given my wariness, I was somewhat surprised when Woodward, Bernstein, and Bradlee had agreed to appear on the one-hour *Larry King Live* Deep Throat "special" along with the family and me, ostensibly to help promote our book. CNN promoted the special with a continuing advertising barrage the weekend before, featuring not only Felt as Deep Throat but the three *Post* stalwarts.

However, the show's capable producer, Eleanor McManus, called me in a panic on the Monday following, in advance of a Tuesday show. "Bradlee, Woodward, and Bernstein will not appear with you, John," she said. "Would you please agree to appear, as they wish, only in the last minutes, after these three have gone off the air?" Eleanor was now worried that without Bradlee, Woodward, and Bernstein, the show would be a bust, after advertising all weekend that promised the *Post* stalwarts. So I conferred with my most trusted advisor, my daughter Christy, who urged me not to abandon my clients Mark and Joan. I agreed with her that I could not leave my clients unrepresented, and I declined their request, assuming that they intended to beat up on Joan. Their bluff called, the three then relented and agreed they would appear after all.

Because I liked both Bradlee and Woodward personally, I was disappointed that the first comments they made in the show about my elderly client were uncharitable, emphasizing his old age decline:

> *KING: What Mark Felt had, by the way–has, is vascular dementia. It's called old age and if we live that long, we're all going get it. Bob Woodward, what's your reaction to seeing him like this?*
>
> *BOB WOODWARD,* WASHINGTON POST: *Well it's clearly a different phase of his life. When I saw him six years ago, I saw the same indicators that he didn't have the kind of specific memory and, you know, that's evident from your discussion with him.*
>
> *I think of him–I was just saying to Ben Bradlee here that he was one tough SOB. He was somebody who really wouldn't answer a lot of questions, gave us some information, some hints, laid out a blueprint, was vital to the coverage.*
>
> *But he was in control and, you know, now in this phase of his life, he's not. I also think of him, you know, he's the guy who told the truth and all of the discussion about whether he*

> *should or whether he shouldn't, he told the truth and that's not a bad starting point for any of us...*[6]

> *KING: Is he a hero to you?*
>
> *BEN BRADLEE, VICE PRESIDENT AT LARGE,* WASHINGTON POST: *Oh, boy, yes, he is. And my reaction at seeing this is one of sadness. I mean, especially with–I believe, Bob, that he was one tough SOB. And that makes me feel good about the FBI and about him. But he isn't now and he's sort of sad and I found myself holding my breath hoping he wouldn't screw up and do something that would change his image.*[7]

After this, the two spent much of their time talking about how the *Post* got just about everything right in Watergate, but for the one mistake about Hugh Sloan's testimony, which did not in fact name Haldeman.

I was puzzled about their motives in defending the *Post*'s reporting. Why did Bradlee feel the need to defend his paper's coverage of Watergate? Wasn't that excellence implied if he simply noted Felt's contribution to his paper's reporting?

I did not appear on this show to fight these fellows but rather to praise my client, so I did not engage. But again, I thought Bradlee's defensive tone somewhat odd. Had he volunteered to appear on the show simply to reaffirm the celebrated *Post* reporting? Everyone in the Western world knew of the paper's plaudits. So why would they need to do this, while stooping so low to insult Mark?

As I thought about this after the show, I realized that these *Post* loyalists, having failed to keep me from appearing, were preempting any negative remarks they thought I was planning on making by filling the air with self-congratulation. I had never intended to ruin Mark's night in the limelight by starting a donnybrook with the *Post*, so if there was anything sad about the show, it was Pulitzer Prize winners sucking the oxygen out of a nice old man's tribute show.

---

6 Woodward, interviewed by Larry King, *Larry King Live*, CNN, April 24, 2006.

7 Ben Bradlee interviewed by Larry King, *Larry King Live*, CNN, April 24, 2006.

So, to sum up, these *Post* journalists had, first, tried to keep Mark's lawyer essentially off the show, and, second, not having accomplished that, damned its key source with faint praise while straining their rotator cuffs to pat themselves on the back. They were very guilty, and very worried, about something they thought I might say if given a chance. What was it they feared? What made them so defensive? I was not sure.

Following this show, given the palpable antipathy of Osnos to our book, I was not surprised that PublicAffairs told me that I need not do any bookstore talks, and, indeed, the PR executives discouraged me from doing any such talks. So the only bookstore appearance I scheduled, on my own initiative, was at Santa Rosa's Copperfield's, part of a large celebration among family, friends, and locals of their hometown hero, with which PublicAffairs had no involvement.

Strangely, shortly after committing to this one event in Santa Rosa, I received an excited call from Meredith telling me they had garnered for me a real plum speaking spot in a *bookstore*! This was no ordinary bookstore, she emphasized, it was Politics and Prose, a very prestigious Washington, DC, venue with broad influence. So, oddly, no other bookstore in the country but this one was worthy of a talk!

I politely turned her down, because the date they had selected was the day before the Santa Rosa event. "Well, we'll keep this on the Politics and Prose schedule just in case," Meredith stated matter-of-factly. Puzzled, I told her that this was not necessary, because I was not going to miss the Santa Rosa event. She said she'd keep my talk on the schedule anyway on the theory that we could never regain a slot with this coveted platform.

However, several days before these two events, Meredith called, beside herself with thrilling news. "*Book TV* is going to cover your DC talk at Politics and Prose," she told me. "You have to go!" Reluctantly I agreed, because I knew *Book TV* would be an extremely important promotional forum for our book. She also told me she had a radio show to be taped in Maryland the following day, *Books on Tape*. I would therefore have to miss Santa Rosa. In short, I felt obligated to go to DC because of my contractual duties to promote the book.

Then she added a caveat: she was telling me about the *Book TV* appearance in confidence. She was almost positive they would be there, but she was not supposed to know. A rookie in the publishing world, this uncertainty did not strike me as odd.

I felt terrible about missing the Santa Rosa celebration because it was the culmination of four years of effort to get the patriarch his warm bath of applause, surrounded by his loving family. But as much as this was a personal disappointment, I took pride in my sacrifice for my client. *Book TV!* What a great show, one that would recycle good talks, especially about famous subjects. So I felt as if I could fulfill my promises to Mark of four years earlier. I would tell his story widely.

When I arrived at the Politics and Prose store on Connecticut Avenue, I encountered an impressive "crunchy," non-chain bookstore, not a megastore by any means. I approached my gray-haired speaker's liaison and enquired of her about *Book TV*. Where was the camera? I asked. She looked at me quizzically, as if I had asked her about a Martian invasion. No, she said, she knew nothing about *Book TV* being there. So I proceeded to speak to thirty mostly middle-aged, intelligent listeners, a very staid event. The next day, I did *Books on Tape* in Silver Springs, Maryland, and flew home.

I spoke with Joan the day after the Santa Rosa event, which she said was a fantastic celebration of her father. Needless to say, I had wasted two days of my life and missed a meaningful event. I continued feeling mixed emotions of personal sadness and professional pride.

I also noticed another feature of the book's Amazon page. It showed the book would not be available until May 25, which was a month after the Larry King special. So anyone watching the show who had the urge to order our book on Amazon would be discouraged by the date listed on the site. I had pointed out to PublicAffairs this erroneous date many weeks before and repeated my concerns. Peter Osnos and Meredith had both told me that once the book is published, they have no control over these things. I asked repeatedly for them to fix this with Amazon. They said they would try but were not hopeful. So, in addition to the Powers hit piece being featured prominently, our Amazon listing discouraged any immediate order of our book.

Having been lacerated by the *Post*'s non-review review of the book, I was gratified that we received generally positive reviews elsewhere, including a very lengthy, thoughtful one in the *San Francisco Chronicle*. This review correctly decried our limitations in summoning Mark's memories but complimented us on our research. Other reviews were similar. I was quite appreciative of the reviewers' recognition of our use of multiple sources to capture Mark, including his past writings and diaries, his FBI files, and interviews with past friends and colleagues. But we still had on the PublicAffairs website with Amazon the absurdly negative review by the *Post*. I had no dreams about our book becoming a bestseller.

I had earlier hoped that the television promotional appearances—so enthusiastically promised by Osnos as part of PublicAffairs' "free media" sweet spot—would bear fruit. But like all other aspects of the book's promotion, the television appearances were ineptly handled.

PublicAffairs scheduled on several days' notice an appearance on the then-popular Keith Olbermann prime-time pundit show. But on the appointed day, we were told that Olbermann had the night off, scheduled days in advance! No attempts were made to reschedule. I was shrugged off when I suggested doing the interview when Olbermann was actually there.

Our only appearance—Nick Jones and I—was on *The Chris Matthews Show*, that night hosted by sub David Gregory. The appearance was an amateur twilight zone episode. Nick and I were situated far away from the camera, the table in front of us removed, and the light kept unusually low. Gregory seemed barely awake, asking us uninspired, mail-it-in questions. My friends and family remarked on its eerie strangeness. I was ashamed that I had led the family to sign with what I concluded was a third-rate publisher.

I harbored no illusions about a career in writing and in fact had grown weary of a long process, without pay, for which I had not originally signed up. So I left this chapter of my life with a sense of pride at having helped Mark and his family, but with much relief as well. And I put in perspective the conflicts and tensions I experienced in my dealing with PublicAffairs and Woodward, much as I had done hundreds of times at the end of a litigated case.

I liked Woodward and found myself defending him from time to time over the years against what I thought were ill-informed attacks on various aspects of his reporting. It appeared to me that what he had reported in

Watergate reflected the best information available to him. Personally, he was unfailingly gentlemanly and cordial in our talks. If he was fiercely commercial, that was his right, even if not highly principled.

So, yes, Osnos had, likely for fear of displeasing Bradlee, put the clamps on us, and the *Post* had not been kind to Mark, his family, or our modest but insightful book. Woodward had not been square with the family when they tried to publish their patriarch's identity and had competed with the family in selling movie rights. The family members were unsophisticated, and I was an amateur author, so that cynical people tooled us around should have come as no surprise.

I think of myself as a fighter, but not much of a hater. So I left this chapter of my life with a sense that the family had accomplished what it set out to do. I saw no reason to harbor grudges against other people who were simply protecting their own interests, however opaque they were to me. Gratitude, not loathing, was my default setting as I ended, I thought, this chapter of life. If the *Post* had screwed us, let the shame be on it. I was not about to let my frustrations linger.

Chapter Nine

WOODWARD AND BERNSTEIN VISIT DEEP THROAT

In late 2008, Joan called me, overjoyed that Bob Woodward had contacted her. He and Carl Bernstein were coming to visit Dad, she told me excitedly. Carl and Bob were speaking in the area, and Bob thought it would be a great occasion to have a visit and bring along Carl. Carl hadn't met Mark before, likely the reason for Woodward's initiative. Mark's health was failing, so this was perhaps the last opportunity for them to meet.

Joan's son Rob and Joan's friends and neighbors were there to witness the visit, which Joan audio-recorded, in part, for posterity.[1] Mark was dressed in his best red jacket and was very much aglow in anticipation of the visit, even though he was but days away from the end of his life.

The four of us–Mark, Woodward, Bernstein, and yours truly–were seated in a tight conversational circle, with Joan and friends forming an outer circle of observers. Bob acted as the moderator and did a good job of keeping things moving. Of course, Mark couldn't talk coherently for very long, didn't remember Watergate details, and was not particularly having a good mental day, as much fun as he was having. In essence, we were just filling the air with nice conversation, as one might do during periodic visits with an aging grandparent.

Bob brought up for discussion the broad subject of the "unanswered" questions of Watergate, its "mysteries." I'm not sure he really meant to have a serious conversation, but it seemed like an appropriate topic to throw around with Mark and Carl in attendance. Again, attempting to

1 Unfortunately, during key parts of our talk, her recording device was not activated.

fill the air and give everyone the impression of a real conversation, I responded to Bob's polite conversation starter by talking about questions concerning the CIA's possible infiltration of the White House, and how the burglars were not really directed to Larry O'Brien's telephone but rather to that of Spencer Oliver Jr. Moreover, I noted, the burglars seemed to be more interested in Maxie Wells's desk key than in wiretapping any phone, and I explained the importance of the key. And I brought up the "sixth burglar" issue. I went on for about forty-five seconds on these topics, hoping that Bob or Carl would jump in to respond because I had for some time wondered what their take was on the "revisionist" version of the scandal.

Although I thought I would get them excited by a semi-intelligent conversation, both reporters looked at me quizzically. Carl had a blank expression on his face, as if he didn't know anything I was talking about, but Bob took on a look of alarm.

Finally, Woodward interrupted, as I hoped he would, but not, as I had hoped, to prolong this conversation. "How is it you know all this?" he asked, quite aggressively. It was almost an accusation, a demand that I justify myself. I immediately felt on the defensive because of Bob's tone and answered, almost apologetically, that I came across these facts during research to corroborate proof of Mark's identity. Bob reacted to this with obvious relief and a seeming grant of dispensation. "Oh, okay. I understand," he said. His nod seemed to indicate that he was satisfied with the explanation that I had given a valid excuse for looking at heretical texts. Strangely, I in fact felt absolved, like I had just passed the Spanish Inquisition.

Soon after this exchange, Bob somewhat abruptly said he needed to go to his car to get something for Joan. He suggested I could get books for Carl and him, which I had earlier told him I had in my car. I happily agreed. The conversation, after all, was just air-filler. So we took a break.

As soon as the two of us got outside the door and off Joan's porch, he stopped me to talk and looked at me with concern on his face. "Do you think you are going to do something more?" he asked. We both knew what he was asking: Was I going to write another book? I didn't respond immediately, searching for a response, when he asked me again in different words. He was looking at me with his sad, sincere eyes, intently, perhaps plaintively. I told him, truthfully at the time, that I wasn't planning on writing anything. He seemed relieved. We soon returned to the living room and exchanged thoughts on more conventional Watergate themes. All attendees felt they had witnessed a meaningful Watergate reunion.

As the days passed, I began reflecting that I had done nothing to cause Bob alarm that I would be writing about him, but I did, of course, give him reason to think I would be writing about the CIA/prostitutes revisionist version of Watergate. Over the following months, as I thought about this, I concluded that was likely what caused his concerns. But why did he care? I asked myself. What is the skin off his nose if I were to write about the CIA and naughty boys and girls?

The visit cemented my friendly attitude toward Woodward, for his reaching out as he had to the family. Yes, it may have been to his benefit, too, to put the reporters, especially Bernstein, perhaps closer to Mark in the public eye than they were in reality. But still, their visit was a real jolt of excitement for this family in Santa Rosa. This type of interaction, after all, was exactly why they wanted Mark to come out with his identity when he did. Joan and the family were greatly appreciative of the two reporters' effort to see Mark, sensing that the visit validated their patriarch as a hero. Mark, thanks to his dementia, no longer remembered his serious grudges against Woodward over thirty years earlier. And so what if Woodward refused to cooperate with the family on a coming-out book? It all worked out, after all, didn't it?

Weeks after the visit, on December 18, 2008, Mark passed away. Joan asked both Bob and Carl to speak at the service, which was to be held in mid-January 2009. To my surprise, but not to Joan's, they both agreed to attend. Each of them gave a stirring oration and thrilled the hometown crowd of about four hundred. The town was abuzz with these two journalistic celebrities eulogizing the hometown hero. It was an exciting event for little Santa Rosa.

That night, I hosted everyone who came in town for the funeral at a very nice upscale Chinese restaurant in town. It had a full bar, important for our crowd, and a big secluded table for our large group. Mark Cummings, the young lawyer who had represented Felt in his "black bag" trial along with Brian Gettings, was there, as was Willy Regan, former heavy-duty

Weather Underground undercover FBI man, who had worked closely with Mark. Talented writer–and later director–Peter Landesman and successful director Jay Roach from the movie team also were in attendance.

At dinner, we went through all sorts of interesting reminiscences about Mark, Watergate, and his criminal trial. Mark Cummings was fascinating, Peter and Jay had wonderful tidbits to add, as of course did Bob and Carl. As usual, I didn't keep my mouth shut either. Woodward was ecstatic at the wonderful conversation. "This dinner should be shown on C-SPAN!" he exulted several times.

While each at the table took turns regaling the group with wonderful stories about Mark, I tried out a pet theory on Bernstein. In late September 1972, when the Watergate reporting was dying down, Carl had received an anonymous call from a "government lawyer" naming one Alex Shipley, an assistant attorney general for Tennessee, as a source to contact. Shipley in turn led the reporters to the sensational Segretti "dirty tricks" story. I always thought that the anonymous "government lawyer" was Mark Felt, calling Bernstein because Carl would not recognize Mark's voice and therefore could never testify that the reporters had been given confidential information from an FBI file. This source has never since been named by the reporters.

"No," Carl emphatically told me, "I was called by an assistant attorney general, a state official, not by a government lawyer, and certainly not Mark Felt." We argued until finally Carl got very hot under the collar, yelling at me that I didn't know my keister. All were quiet, eyes trained on the two gladiators, when I yelled laughingly, "But Carl, I have solid proof!"

"What is that?" he demanded, almost snarling.

"Your book!" I shouted.[2] The crowd loved it, laughing uproariously. Carl turned red as a beet.

"He hates you," my perceptive wife whispered to me.

As I observed Woodward that night having fun, exulting in the reunion-type stories, I thought again about his earlier question as to whether I would "do" anything more. I had no desire to write about Woodward's

---

2 Actually, in Bernstein's defense, the text is ambiguous since the caller made sure to throw in the confounding detail that he had seen Shipley at a picnic. For a host of reasons, I conclude this was Felt being clever.

odd treatment of Deep Throat. If he had not protected Mark Felt as well as he should have, any harm was all in the past, unremembered by Mark. And I would leave it to someone else to write a definitive Rashomon-effect book about the revisionist version of the scandal.

The earlier reunion at the Felt house in December 2008 and the bigger gathering at his January funeral service put a fitting cap on my serendipitous involvement in this fascinating story. It ended a nice chapter in my life and did the same for the Felt family.

Chapter Ten

THE EPIPHANY

Late one weekend evening in 2010 I found myself on our family room couch, channel surfing. After Jan and I had returned from a social event, she immediately had gone to bed, and, with a second wind, I was alone to pass the time. As I hopped from bad movie to dull interview to recycled sitcom, I eventually found myself on *Book TV*. Normally on *Book TV* I would encounter an articulate middle-aged author, alone at a podium, calmly discoursing at a relatively high intellectual level on the subject matter of the author's book.

The scene I encountered that night, however, was like nothing I had ever seen on *Book TV.* There were several enthusiastic people surrounding a stand-up microphone, themselves surrounded by a number of friendly onlookers. The scene had more the feel of a postgame celebration than a book disquisition. I checked the channel again. Was I really tuned in to *Book TV*? Yes, I was, indeed.

As I listened to discern the subject matter, I got the feeling that I knew the casually dressed, handsome thirty-something man talking about what a great guy this fellow was–always positive, fun, one who complimented everyone with whom he came in contact, a man who had a kind word for all. This sounded more like a celebration of a deceased man's life than a book report. Then I heard the young man mention how patriotic his grandfather was, what a great FBI career he had. It came to me then: he was talking about Mark Felt! This was Will Felt, his grandson! I thought I knew him and I did. Focusing now on those surrounding him, I now saw Joan Felt, and then recognized Nick and Rob Jones, her other sons.

This was the *Book TV* program, I quickly realized, about *A G-Man's Life*! It was taking place at the Copperfield's bookstore in Santa Rosa, the venue to which I had originally committed to speak, only to shift my talk suddenly, at the insistence of Meredith and PublicAffairs, to the Politics and Prose bookstore in DC. I immediately felt like I had been punched in the gut. In an instant, I realized what had happened years earlier when I had been sent to Washington, only to encounter there a few gray-haired bookworms but no *Book TV*. I had been sent there, it was now obvious, to avoid *Book TV* coverage, not to garner it. That's why, I now understood, I had been scheduled for a date in DC the day before the Santa Rosa date, even though I had announced my intention to attend the large Santa Rosa event right from the get-go.

Of course, as I now understood through this epiphany, *Book TV* couldn't just pop into a bookstore unannounced to film an author's talk without having made prior arrangements with the store. The podium, with proper background for video, had to be set up. Recording equipment needed to be put in place. Above all, *Book TV* would need the assurance that the author was speaking, and I had been on the Santa Rosa bookstore list as a speaker for weeks. I would have been certain to come to this big Felt-centric celebration at this well-known local bookstore, just a few miles from where Felt lived. I was scheduled to attend and, just as clearly, *Book TV* had counted on my attendance. *Book TV* had been defrauded every bit as much as I had been.

It was now easy to conclude that *Book TV* had scheduled its taping well in advance of the Santa Rosa event and had certainly let the publisher know in order to assure my attendance. So, to avoid my saying something negative about Woodward or the *Post*, or, moreover, promoting sales of a book they did not like, PublicAffairs and the *Post* had contrived to prevent my speech in Santa Rosa. And if they had informed *Book TV* well in advance that I would not be attending the Santa Rosa event, then *Book TV* could have found me somewhere else. It made perfect sense for PublicAffairs and the *Post* to keep me scheduled for Santa Rosa. This would entice *Book TV* to cover the event, all while PublicAffairs was making sure that I would be three thousand miles away!

After I initially had resisted their entreaties to go to Washington simply for the prestige of the venue, they felt compelled to resort to an out-and-out fraud to get me there: they told me that *Book TV* was likely showing up in DC, while concealing its scheduled attendance in Santa Rosa. Obviously, I now realized, they had no indication of a DC *Book TV* taping, which is why the nice gray-hair at Politics and Prose was so surprised when I asked her about *Book TV*. Now I knew why PublicAffairs told me that the speaking slot they had arranged for me in DC was the only possible time I could get into the bookstore's schedule.

Obviously, I felt very stupid. I thought more about the effort that PublicAffairs had expended in order to get me to DC. First, they had to exaggerate what a prestigious venue this was. It was a nice bookstore with a well-known speakers' program, but in reality, it was only a cute shop in a prosperous residential neighborhood. (To be sure, the store featured impressive speakers, but my later research revealed that the speakers usually were scheduled at the store's larger, more centrally located branches.) So, the second deceit was that this was the only day the bookstore could squeeze me in. Clearly this store was open for speakers on 250 other nights that year, at least, and the store often had several speakers in a day. And by booking me in advance, and then telling me they were going to keep the DC talk on the schedule (for reasons which were never clearly explained), Meredith and Osnos made it seem credible that *Book TV* had planned to show up in DC.

I was also clear now that this deception had been planned so very carefully and well in advance. It would have looked fishy if PublicAffairs had set me up for a talk on the exact same date as the Santa Rosa event, which was already in place when Meredith got the DC date. Scheduling me for DC on the day before the Copperfield's event, three thousand miles from Santa Rosa, would make it difficult for me to get back on time. But to make sure I didn't return to the Bay Area immediately, they scheduled me for a *Books on Tape* interview the next day.

What should have tipped me off, had I thought it through, was Meredith's professed uncertainty about whether *Book TV* would really show, and her hints to me that she was operating on secret inside information she wasn't supposed to have. On reflection, I realized this made no sense.

After all, why would *Book TV* hide its light under a bushel? Obviously, it would be in *Book TV*'s interest to let the publisher know when and where it was taping an author precisely so that the author would show. A *Book TV* filming is not equivalent to a visit from a restaurant food critic, which rests on the element of surprise for a fair evaluation. Now I fully understood that there would be no reason for Meredith to guess about *Book TV*'s appearance, nor to have gained this information only from secret, back-channel whispers, as she implied.

What also *should* have tipped me off was that this was the only bookstore appearance PublicAffairs scheduled for me. And it just happened to prevent me from attending the only one I had personally scheduled, the Santa Rosa event!

Throughout all my prior tribulations with Osnos and the *Post* gang, I had concluded that their major worry was my spouting off about their hero Woodward. But as I reflected now, I realized that I had never been strongly outspoken about Woodward's breaches of trust. I peeped up a bit in the wrap meeting but had meekly submitted to adding only a few sentences and had removed a direct reference to Woodward's lack of honor after Osnos harangued me. I had been widely interviewed and had never harshly criticized Woodward. There had to be something more.

In piecing this together, I thought back to my pontification in Santa Rosa in December 2008 on the facts of the revisionist narrative. It was my little disquisition that truly troubled Woodward, and his alarm about whether I would write a future book was directly related to the alternative version I was spinning in the Felt living room that day. Putting a finer point on it, he first interrupted me when I spoke about the key found on Watergate burglar Eugenio Martinez, with the sixth burglar lurking nearby. The topics I was discussing were precisely those facts and their interpretation, which I was first required to leave out of *A G-Man's Life* entirely and later to accept a bowdlerized version. It made sense that Woodward would think I could have been intending to write more about this topic, weaving together all the meaningful underlying facts such as the key and the sixth burglar.

What had concerned Woodward had likely been Osnos's big concern as well, since Osnos was likely carrying Woodward's water, and certainly

Bradlee's. The *Larry King* show antics told me that Bradlee shared the same concerns as Woodward and Osnos. The primary motive for all of this seemed to be a quashing of the discussion of, as Woodward would have it, the truly unsolved mysteries of Watergate. But why would they care to such an extent that they would stoop to such childish games? Osnos was the editor in chief of a respected, albeit small, publisher, and Bradlee and Woodward were world-renowned figures. They would not be doing this unless it was both significant and deeply troubling to them.

I reflected now on the curious goings-on at the Richard Nixon Presidential Library. Mark Felt had passed away on December 18, 2008. It was not long after that, in June 2009, when I happened upon a little blurb in *Newsweek* magazine. Nixon loyalists were reportedly upset because the Nixon Library had invited as a speaker at an anniversary event (thirty-seven years since the Watergate break-in) one John Wesley Dean III. It seemed that the Richard Nixon Foundation had recently lost control of the library to a board appointed by the National Archives, and one of the first acts of the new trustee was the invitation to Dean. The selection of Dean at this key event, together with the endorsement it implied, enraged these loyalists. It bothered me greatly as well, for reasons I subsequently shared in part with these loyalists.

The selection of Dean was not an isolated act by the new trustee. It came on the heels of the trustee's initiative to remove a number of stands and stations at the library depicting aspects of the revisionist narrative. To be sure, some of the offerings followed themes put forth in *Silent Coup*, suggesting that certain ultraconservative military forces may have intentionally pushed Nixon out of office, using Watergate as a convenient excuse. As much as I thought the factual research behind *Silent Coup* to be solid, perhaps brilliant, I disagreed with the "coup" theme. But there can be little doubt that Dean's perfidious role in Watergate, so perceptively chronicled in *Silent Coup*, mitigated the guilt of the president.

It seemed to me that the new curators of the Nixon Library were engaged in an ongoing battle against the revisionist narrative of Watergate, in which Dean's actions figured significantly.

It was with little surprise, then, that I learned of the content of Dean's speech at the Nixon Library. Dean, it was reported by the *Post*'s partner *Newsweek* in favorable terms, blasted the "revisionists" who were constantly trying to change the true and tested mainstream Watergate history. The translation was, of course, that a revisionist was anyone who argued with the *Post*'s rendition of events. The motive of these revisionists, Dean in essence told the audience, was that they were... conservative! Since it was assumed that most conservatives are venal, that was all he needed to say.

Newsweek of course was a wholly owned organ of the *Post*. Its editorial slant seemed to be hostile toward the Nixon Foundation's previous efforts to fill in gaps in the Watergate story. Why did *Newsweek/Post* care about how the dispute between the Nixon Foundation and the Nixon Library turned out? What did they have to win or lose in this game? This Nixon Library contretemps and the opposition of the *Post* and *Newsweek* to the revisionist account doubled the curiosity I felt when learning of the fraud that took me on a Washington, DC, wild goose chase.

I began trolling the internet about the revisionist facts to see if I could gain clues about their attitudes. Of course, this led me to *Silent Coup* and *Secret Agenda*, the two works to which Osnos had so vehemently objected as not in the "Watergate canon." I happened upon a couple of reviews of these two books, and to my surprise, they were ravingly positive,[1] even though there were a few negative reviews. So my question now was *whose* "Watergate canon" was Osnos talking about? That of the *Washington Post*?

---

1 **Sample reviews of *Secret Agenda:***
"If even half of this is true, *Secret Agenda* will add an important new dimension to our understanding of Watergate."–J. Anthony Lukas, *New York Times*

"Hougan is an imaginative scenarist with a computer memory for shady characters and suspicious details–but whatever his 1001 leads ultimately lead to, Watergate will never look quite the same."–*Kirkus Reviews*

Sample reviews of *Silent Coup*:
"A very solid piece of sleuthing."–Robert Sherrill, *New York Times*

"Modulated in tone and dense in fact, it clearly deserves a respectful hearing, and is pregnant with a wealth of material for both journalism and historians to follow-up."–Doug Ireland, *Village Voice*

"An impressive revisionist history."–Prof. James D. Fairbanks, *Houston Chronicle*

"Densely packed, tightly woven...*Silent Coup* is a reminder that this chapter of history is by no means closed."–Peter Copeland, Scripps-Howard News Service

One clue was the reference to critics who had discarded *Silent Coup* and *Secret Agenda*. A typical example was the one I found in a review of *Silent Coup* by Robert Scheer of the *Los Angeles Times*:

> *A very readable yet detailed book...Before you turn the page away from what must seem preposterous charges, consider that this book is more carefully researched and solidly documented than some more well-received books on Watergate... There is just too much troubling documentation for this book to be dismissed out of hand as some critics have done.*[2]

Then I ran across a fascinating editorial in the *Washington Post* from February 4, 2001, which verified my suspicions about the *Post*'s stance. It seemed that Gordon Liddy had read the same factual research that I had and believed it explained his nagging questions about the scandal. So on his radio show, he repeated the prostitution theme and was promptly sued by Wells and Oliver,[3] represented by, among others, a lawyer who had represented John Dean in his libel suit against Colodny. The jury returned a strong seven-to-two verdict against the plaintiffs, meaning the evidence showed that the plaintiffs had not proven the prostitution theme of the revisionist narrative to be false.

It is odd indeed that such a defamation defense verdict would cause a major newspaper to publish an angry anti-verdict[4] editorial, but the *Post* did just that:

> *Courts are a capricious venue for arguments about history. Sometimes, as when a British court last year resoundingly rejected the Holocaust denial of "historian" David Irving, litigation can help protect established history from those who would maliciously rewrite it. But conspiracy theorizing generally is better addressed in the public arena by rigorous*

2 "The Deepest Throat: *Silent Coup: The Removal of a President*, by Len Colodny and Robert Gettlin," *Los Angeles Times*, June 23, 1991.

3 Spencer Oliver Jr.'s phone had been tapped by the burglars. Oliver, a minor official networking with Democrats throughout the country, was often out of town, and his secretary, Maxie Wells, set up visitors in one of the suite's offices.

4 Media outlets generally favor defense verdicts in defamation actions.

confrontation with facts. That's true both out of respect for freedom of speech–even wrong-headed speech–and because historical truth does not always fare so well in court. A jury in Tennessee in 1999 embraced the looniest of conspiracy theories concerning the assassination of Martin Luther King Jr. And this week, in a federal court in Baltimore, the commonly understood and well-founded history of the Watergate scandal took a hit as well.

The forum was the defamation case of G. Gordon Liddy, the Watergate felon and radio talk-show host, who has promoted in speeches a "revisionist"–false would be a better description–account of the scandal. Mr. Liddy has argued that the burglary was not an attempt to collect political intelligence on President Nixon's enemies but an effort masterminded by then-White House counsel John Dean to steal pictures of prostitutes–including Mr. Dean's then-girlfriend and current wife–from the desk of a secretary at the Democratic headquarters. The secretary, Ida Wells, is now a community college teacher in Louisiana and was understandably offended by the implication that she was somehow involved in a call girl ring. She sued Mr. Liddy, and the battle has dragged on for four years.

The jury failed to reach a unanimous verdict, but it split overwhelmingly in favor of Mr. Liddy; the majority of jurors felt that Ms. Wells's lawyers had failed to prove his theory wrong. They found this in spite of the fact that Mr. Liddy relies, for his theory, on a disbarred attorney with a history of mental illness. The call girl theory "is possible," one juror told Post *staff writer Manuel Roig-Franzia. "It sure makes me more curious." "We'll never know" what happened, said another.*

The danger of such outcomes as this one is that this sort of thinking spreads. For whether or not Mr. Liddy's comments legally defamed Ms. Wells, we do know what happened at Watergate–and it had nothing to do with prostitutes.[5]

5 "The Courts and History," *Washington Post*, February 4, 2001, B06.

Why, I asked myself, was the *Post* so invested in denying that any prostitution was involved? And why go so far as compare this to Holocaust denial and the Martin Luther King conspiracy? There was a "wounded" tone to the *Post* complaints. They weren't defending Wells so much as defending the story they told their readers during Watergate.

But now, putting it all together, I saw that the *Post* would have had this strident, defensive reaction to the Liddy verdict, and later go to great lengths to keep me off the airwaves, only if they were covering up their own journalistic misreporting about Watergate.

Surprising myself, I was not angry so much as bemused. I began thinking obsessively about a possible *Post* cover-up, much in the same way I was so deeply curious about Deep Throat's identity thirty-some years earlier. Did the paper cover up facts, I wondered, as opposed to simply hyping White House guilt? After all, there was plenty of Nixon White House guilt to report.

As my new hobby, I decided to collect all of the *Post*'s Watergate articles, then compare them to facts known or easily knowable at the time. If the *Post* reported all known facts, even with an anti-Nixon take, there would be no basis for criticism. But if the *Post* hid inconvenient material facts from the public, then it was guilty of a cover-up every bit as reprehensible as that of the White House. Indeed, perhaps more so because Nixon was not publishing reports every day vouching for their truth like the *Post* was.

I was acutely aware of what I had observed as the tendency of "investigative" journalists to bend the facts to fit their preconceived narrative. I did have some solid proof of a *Post* cover-up already but acknowledged to myself that its sins may have been mere peccadilloes. I thought I would find that the *Post* had beveled some edges on Watergate, based upon its extreme reaction to the *Wells v. Liddy* verdict. If I focused on something interesting, I may, I thought, make a magazine article out of it, perhaps my most comfortable métier.

I looked forward to my new pastime. I began with the suspicion I would find something, but the extent of my eventual discoveries was stunning. I will share what I found out about the *Post*'s reporting on the key players and evidence: Mullen and Howard Hunt, the CIA, James McCord, the sixth burglar, the key, and the other intriguing characters and facts in the most significant political drama in American history. But first let me summarize the factual research I had reviewed that solidly establishes evidence[6] that appears not to have been part of the conventional Watergate narrative. After this review, I will analyze whether these facts were unknowable or unknown by the *Post* during its Watergate reporting.

---

6 Evidence can be direct or circumstantial, and the law does not provide that one is necessarily better than the other. Circumstantial evidence in a particular case (e.g., a fingerprint) may be stronger than direct evidence (e.g., defendant's denial he ever possessed the weapon with the fingerprint). In Anglo-American jurisprudence, the parties may each have presented conflicting evidence, as to which the fact finder must decide whose is more compelling. As I summarize "evidence" of the revisionist or "unexplored" story, I rely on evidence of pertinent facts, evidence that others may find unconvincing or not as persuasive as other facts considered to be evidence. Evidence to a writer or historian is not necessarily evidence which that person could adduce on a witness stand but is often evidence that some individual could competently get in evidence if alive and sworn in. The point is that saying there is "evidence" of a fact is not the same as saying there is either conclusive or winning proof of it.

Chapter Eleven

THE UNEXPLORED STORY

In the three years before our *Vanity Fair* article was published, I had engaged in wide-ranging research aimed at defending my conclusion that Mark Felt was Deep Throat. In the course of this study, I was surprised to learn evidence of many seemingly newly discovered facts[1] that, in my opinion, substantially revised the commonly received Watergate story, especially concerning the involvement of the CIA and the actual meretricious targets of the eavesdropping. It was this evidence that led me to propose writing about a revisionist narrative in *A G-Man's Life*.

"Evidence," of course, is different from conclusively proven fact but instead is information that should be presented to the jury–in this case, that of public opinion. The evidence I will outline in this chapter is information I would have wanted to consider during the Watergate scandal. Much could be subject to good faith debate, which is precisely my point in presenting it.

Now that my curiosity was piqued by the strange actions of the *Post*, I wondered how much of the these "recent" discoveries weren't recent at

1 Far and away the two best collections of research revealing previously unexplored facts were the seminal works *Secret Agenda* and *Silent Coup*, the two works that upset Osnos so greatly. But, in addition to their original investigations and cited research sources, see also, without pretensions to completeness, Anthony Lukas's *Nightmare* (J. Anthony Lukas, *Nightmare: The Underside of the Nixon Years*, New York: Viking, 1976); *White House Call Girl* (Phil Stanford, *White House Call Girl: The Real Watergate Story*, Port Townsend, WA: Feral House, 2013); *Will* (G. Gordon Liddy, *Will: The Autobiography of G. Gordon Liddy*, New York: St. Martin's Press, 1991); the Senate Minority Report on Watergate (Baker Report); the transcripts and opinions in *Wells v. Liddy*; FBI Watergate 302 Interview Reports; the Earl Silbert hearings on his confirmation as US Attorney; and the Nedzi Committee hearings into the CIA's involvement in Watergate.

all and had been known or knowable by the *Post* during the scandal. In other words, when Woodward looked alarmed, almost terrified, at my disquisition on these facts during our 2008 meeting at the Felt home, was it because the *Post* had hidden these facts?

In the conventional version as reported by the *Post*, there were many lingering mysteries, as Bob Woodward often said. For instance, why did the burglars choose as a target the Democratic National Committee, which in June 1972 had no meaningful campaign information? What interested them, if anything, in Larry O'Brien, who, in any event, was not and would not be in his DC office for months? These new revisionist revelations from a variety of sources answered many of these questions while putting a far different slant on the scandal. What had been intriguing about this research was that it was quite consistent with the investigative hunches of Mark Felt, hypotheses he could not follow through on because he did not stay in his job long enough.

As we discussed in *A G-Man's Life*, Felt had been pushed into retirement by interim FBI director William Ruckelshaus, based on Felt's admission that he had confirmed the Kissinger wiretaps story to John Crewdson of the *New York Times*, thereby freeing Daniel Ellsberg. After Crewdson gave up Felt to Ruckelshaus,[2] Felt's premature departure from the Bureau kept him from taking to ground all his investigative hypotheses.

One tentative conclusion Felt immediately reached upon surveying the first blush of burglary evidence was that the caper was a White House operation, a CIA operation, or both.

2 In *The FBI Pyramid*, Mark had written that he had been investigated in an intentionally humiliating fashion by the FBI and special prosecutor for the suspected unauthorized transmission of original FBI 302 reports to John Crewdson of the *New York Times*. An FBI secretary had witnessed Crewdson emerging from the FBI's executive suite, where Felt had an office, with a briefcase bulging with documents. The hypothesis was that Felt had given these documents to Crewdson as a reward for reporting, per Felt's leak, the government's overhearing of Ellsberg on the Kissinger wiretaps. The investigation began in June 1974, immediately after the release of *All the President's Men* featuring Deep Throat. As I learned in 2007, from John "Jack" Ruckelshaus, William's brother, a man identifying himself as Crewdson called Ruckelshaus to implicate Felt as Crewdson's leaker. Crewdson, wishing to catch up with the *Post* on Watergate reporting, received the Segretti "302" reports from Ruckelshaus's underling, not from Felt, seemingly as a reward for giving up Felt. In *Leak*, Holland speculates that the caller may have been William Sullivan, Felt's enemy, posing as Crewdson, speculation that seems absurd to this author. Whatever the case, Crewdson received the FBI's Segretti interview reports from Ruckelshaus's team, not from Felt.

Two of my sources supporting CIA involvement in my earlier book were, intriguingly, Felt's own book, *The FBI Pyramid*, and the transcript of his criminal trial in *U.S. v. Felt*, where he discussed the relationship of both the White House and the CIA to the FBI's program of warrantless entries, often for the purpose of wiretapping. It was a traditionally accepted legal doctrine that the Bill of Rights did not apply to presidentially authorized national security orders, based upon the president's status as commander in chief of the armed forces, endowed with supreme authority over national security. Abraham Lincoln, for example, could free the slaves in belligerent states on the basis of national security, even if otherwise forbidden by the Bill of Rights.

Felt had written in *Pyramid*, following up on his similar comments to Woodward as Deep Throat, that the White House got into the break-in business through the "Plumbers" because the FBI had quit performing them for the White House. Though legal if done for legitimate national security purposes, according to Deep Throat it was inevitable that the White House would slide toward performing these operations for political ends, which of course would be illegal.

Felt had amplified this theme by expanding upon the background of the so-called "Huston Plan," the controversial 1970 initiative, named after White House aide Tom Huston, that authorized wide-ranging, aggressive actions by all intelligence agencies (under the FBI's supposed supervision), including warrantless entries, wiretapping, mail openings, and related activities. If performed for legitimate national security purposes, these acts would be constitutional. The plan was likely authored by Felt's noirish rival, William Sullivan,[3] using Huston as a front man while covertly currying the support of the CIA, which presumably would have freer domestic rein.

Originally approved by Nixon, Hoover (likely on urging by Felt) and Attorney General Mitchell soon withdrew any support for the Huston Plan, and Nixon rescinded it after but a few days in operation in July 1970. A

3 It was Sullivan who likely responded to Henry Kissinger's reported purple-face rage when the Cambodian bombings were leaked to the press in May 1969, sparking widespread campus riots. In response, Sullivan wiretapped both Kissinger's National Security Council staff and several prominent newsmen. Hoover was forced by Sullivan's initiative to go along, but, after also tapping columnist Joseph Kraft in Paris, Hoover let it be known the Bureau was through doing black ops for the White House.

disgruntled Huston left the White House, leaving some of his duties for Dean. There remained some in the White House who were frustrated at the loss of this continuing black bag capability by the White House. Added to this milieu, as Felt described it in his criminal trial, the CIA was not pleased with Hoover's previous 1966 halt to performing warrantless entries for the Agency. Felt testified that because the CIA's charter forbade its performance of domestic operations, the FBI had to perform black bag jobs for the CIA, if performed at all. This national security power had been delegated to the FBI, Felt testified, since 1938, when President Franklin D. Roosevelt authorized the capabilities in order to hunt for communists and Nazis. The CIA's interest, it appeared from Felt's trial, involved in part breaking into foreign embassies in the United States, presumably to insert wiretaps and room bugs.

However, Hoover grew increasingly concerned about the CIA's underlying cowboyish basis for these operations, and by 1966, with the winds of civil rights blowing fiercely, the legendary director decided enough was enough. He banned these black bag jobs for the Bureau as a whole, careful not to single out the CIA. But restraint of the CIA was Hoover's primary motive, Felt testified (not calling the CIA by name but referring to it as "Program C"). So, the Huston Plan was something that not only some FBI intelligence officials such as Sullivan wanted but also was ardently desired by the CIA.

Felt's initial opinion that Watergate may have been a CIA operation may well have been an astute assessment. But, if so, what was its target? Would CIA Watergate involvement explain why Larry O'Brien was not likely the target of the burglaries? I thought so. But, if not O'Brien, who or what was the true target?

The answer comes from *New York Times* reporter Anthony Lukas's definitive and well-regarded 1976 overview of Watergate, *Nightmare*. In this book, Lukas summarizes evidence that the true target of Watergate wiretapping may well have been meretricious calls between men and women.

To be sure, as Hougan notes in his 1984 book, *Secret Agenda*, some observers wrongly assumed that the aroused women on these calls were DNC employees and that the men were outside the DNC. Several researchers have since asserted that the women were call girls at the nearby Columbia

Plaza apartments, a known haven for high-class prostitutes.[4] The men were likely out-of-town visitors to the DNC.

But how would these motifs–the CIA and the call girls–be reconciled into a consistent narrative whole? Occam's Razor tells us that one unifying explanation is to be preferred to several unrelated ones, each partially explanatory. Why, in short, would the CIA be interested in call girl talk?

The career backgrounds of both Howard Hunt and James McCord suggest that each was at the time of Watergate falsely retired from the CIA[5] and was operating undercover for the CIA. Both Hunt and McCord had worked with the Office of Security (and within the Office of Security, or OS, the highly secretive Security Research Service, or SRS) within the CIA. The OS was a special compartmentalized counterintelligence unit within the CIA, reporting directly to CIA director Richard Helms, the only section to do so. At the time of Watergate, it appeared that Hunt and his part-time boss at Mullen and Company, Robert Bennett, both reported to CIA case agents.

The intensive interest of the OS in sexual activity over the years was geared to understanding, and perhaps manipulating, a political subject of interest. The CIA's taping of a drugs-and-hooker operation through a program set up in San Francisco by Colonel George White in the 1950s had been revealed in the post-Watergate congressional investigations, as had the CIA's horrid "Operation Bluebird" covert drug experiments, on which McCord worked, resulting in the death of one unwitting victim. As Hougan brilliantly details, in the 1960s the CIA had become interested in Duke University's research suggesting that with sufficient personal information, a psychological "machine" could be constructed predicting the behavior of the individual in certain situations.[6] The combination of the CIA, electronic eavesdropping, and hookers made for a consistent, unifying explanation of CIA involvement in Watergate. It was, in short, looking for claimable presidential "authorization" for its prostitute-taping program, even if White House lieutenants did not realize that they

4 Hougan, *Secret Agenda*; and Phil Stanford, *White House Call Girl*.

5 Hougan, *Secret Agenda*, 9.

6 Hougan, *Secret Agenda*, 52-53.

were so authorizing the Agency and thought they themselves were the only beneficiary.

Several seemingly reliable witnesses had stated that shadowy alcoholic private eye Lou Russell had bragged prior to Watergate about taping prostitutes and their johns. Russell was unknown to Liddy and not on his payroll but was instead paid by sterile check from McCord and Associates, McCord's private-investigation firm. If Russell was involved in Watergate, or in the taping of prostitutes, it was as a CIA contractor through McCord, not a CRP or White House agent.

This hypothesis of a CIA operation, though, still was missing a key ingredient in any complete narrative. While I have just described the motive and related intent of the CIA, I have not yet ascribed the motive and intent of the White House and its campaign organ, the Committee to Re-elect the President. If in fact this was an operation to tape call girls and their patrons, why would the White House and its election campaign (which supplied the funding) have an interest in listening to this naughty talk? Wouldn't the White House be focused on information related to the campaign?

This question was answered by Len Colodny and Robert Gettlin in their brilliant 1991 book, *Silent Coup*, which followed on up on Lukas's *Nightmare*, Hougan's *Secret Agenda*, and Liddy's *Will*[7] (again, accounts denied by Dean). Colodny showed how Dean, as he recounts candidly in *Blind Ambition*, saw opposition intelligence (read "dirt on opponents") as a promising strategy of advancement in the Nixon White House. Under this narrative (which Dean denies), Dean likely knew of an arrangement set up in the fall of 1971, in which a DNC secretary, at the request of prostitution lawyer Phillip Mackin Bailley, would refer out-of-town DNC visitors to the Columbia Plaza call girl operation.

Dean knew that the campaign would soon have plentiful funds for security operations and that he could use its money–and the unguided missile Liddy–to feather his own intelligence nest. Dean had persuaded Liddy in late 1971 to leave the White House for the CRP, where, Dean promised the credulous Liddy, he could ramp up a sophisticated intelligence operation with a half-million-dollar budget "for openers," according to Liddy.

7 Liddy, *Will*.

Hunt as well may have sold Dean on the juicy dirt available at the DNC, although this is simply inference. If the CIA had been monitoring these same conversations and wanted to legitimize the entirety of the CIA call girl taping operation in the process,[8] it would have been easy, one may infer from Dean's book, to inveigle Dean's authorization, ostensibly for his own ambitious purposes.[9]

The origin of the wiretapping was thus seemingly a combination of the CIA's desire to give its domestic operations the tincture of legitimacy and, combining Dean, Colodny, and Liddy, Dean's desire to gain career advancement. While this is only inference, we do know from Liddy that Dean was the driving force behind what became Liddy's Gemstone Plan. Indeed, long before Liddy hatched the Gemstone Plan of campaign intelligence black ops, Dean had White House detective Tony Ulasewicz, through former Nixon administration security operative Jack Caulfield, "case" the DNC offices in October or November 1971, according to Caulfield and Ulasewicz,[10] (and weakly denied by Dean), when the Bailley referral operation was just beginning. And Dean had at the same time also commissioned Ulasewicz to look into New York's "Happy Hooker" ring, looking for prominent Democrats (which he may have found, but also reportedly found Republicans).

On June 9, 1972, two weeks after the Watergate bugging began pursuant to the first break-in, an article in the *Washington Star-News* about Bailley's unrelated arrest and indictment[11] for corruption of one particular girl, described a "call girl ring" with a client list that included "one lawyer at the White House":

---

8 This prostitution operation, it now appears, was cooperating with the CIA, which in turn could protect it from the police. Its madam asked Bailley to set up a DNC referral operation, according to Bailley. It is entirely possible that the madam had in turn been put up to this request by her CIA protectors.

9 Dean again denies, and again, we have a swearing contest. Colodny quotes both Hunt and Magruder as to Dean's approving the burglary, and Liddy writes of Dean's encouragement of his Gemstone Plan.

10 Ulasewicz has the date wrong, suggesting April 1972, which is unlikely because Caulfield was already gone from the White House.

11 Bailley was indicted for a Mann Act violation involving a single University of Maryland coed who he had persuaded to perform sexual tricks for his friends. No prostitution "ring" was involved.

> *The FBI here has uncovered a high-priced call girl ring allegedly headed by a Washington attorney and staffed by secretaries and office workers from Capitol Hill and involving at least one White House secretary, sources said today.*
>
> *A 22-count indictment returned today by a special federal grand jury names Phillip M. Bailley, 30, as head of the operation.*
>
> *Sources close to the investigation said that among the clients of the call girl operation were a number of local attorneys holding high positions in the Washington legal community and one lawyer at the White House...*[12]

That same day, Dean summoned Bailley's prosecutor, John Rudy, from the US Attorney's Office to the White House, where Dean examined the evidence Rudy brought with him, seized in a search of Bailley's office.[13] Bailley's address books, examined by Dean (though Dean claims he only glanced at them), contained at least five listings of Dean's girlfriend (later wife), Maureen Biner, by one name or another, including "Mo," "M. Biner," "M.B.," and "Clout." The reference to "Clout" was her seeming influence as the girlfriend of White House counsel John Dean. Rudy had no knowledge of Dean's connection to Biner. These references most likely would have been due to Bailley's innocent social friendship with Biner, since many of the listings were of personal friends.

Also, that same day, Friday, June 9, according to *Will*, an astonished Liddy was told by his supervisor Magruder that he may have to again enter the Watergate, which as in the first burglary seemed to Liddy to be of no campaign value. The following Monday, June 12, 1972, Magruder ordered Liddy's team to reenter the DNC offices. Slamming his hand on his lower left desk drawer for emphasis, Magruder told Liddy that what he should be seeking was what was in this drawer (meaning dirt on opponents, which the Republicans normally kept in that drawer). So, Liddy wrote in *Will* in 1980 that the burglars were seeking, in this second burglary, primarily documents showing the dirt that the Democrats had on the Republicans.

12 "Capitol Hill Call-Girl Ring," *Washington Star-News*, June 9, 1972.

13 Dean admits to meeting with Rudy but claims prosecutor Earl Silbert suggested it because he was concerned about the article.

Liddy years later came to believe that the dirt included information connected to prostitutes.

When the burglars were arrested, as Colodny describes, Eugenio Martinez tried to get rid of a metal object in his suit pocket, putting his life in great danger in the process. After almost shooting Martinez, the arresting officer, Carl Shoffler, retrieved a small desk key, which days later the FBI tied to the desk of Maxie Wells, secretary to Spencer Oliver Jr., the minor official whose phone had been successfully tapped for the prior two weeks.

Liddy has subsequently disclaimed any knowledge of the key. Even though he knew that the operation was targeted to retrieve opposition dirt that the Democrats had on the Republicans, he was not aware that the incriminating material would be in the drawer of Maxie Wells, and in fact it appears he had believed the target was Larry O'Brien's desk. Of course, Hunt, who supervised Martinez, knew about the key, as likely did Baldwin and McCord, but not, apparently, Liddy. Following the June 12 order, Baldwin, posing as a nephew of former Democratic National Chairman John M. Bailey, wanting to see "Uncle John's" old office,[14] made contact with Maxie Wells on the pretext of looking for his friend and her boss Spencer Oliver Jr., thereafter touring that area of the office. Clearly Baldwin and his boss, McCord, were seeking the exact location of Wells's desk. The presence of the key on Martinez revealed both the target of the burglary and the secret agenda of McCord, Hunt, and Dean.

So, this new evidence, in my opinion, made a very coherent narrative out of what had been a puzzling, seemingly senseless and bungled burglary. The motive of the CIA to legitimize an otherwise illegal domestic prostitution monitoring operation merged with the motive of an ambitious White House lieutenant to develop an intelligence network harvesting personal dirt on Democrats. Its only connection with the election was campaign funding, which set aside plentiful cash for campaign security.

Dean pushed Liddy from the White House to the temporarily wealthy CRP precisely because Liddy would do anything asked of him, especially if the much-admired Hunt was involved. Magruder was an easy-to-manipulate weakling formally reporting to Mitchell but in fact was under the

14 Tom Condon. "From Hartford 25 Years Later, A Watergate Player Reflects," *The Hartford Courant*. June 15, 1997. Web.

control of Dean as a seeming loyalist of Haldeman, Magruder's lifeline to the White House. Magruder was never a Mitchell man and had been foisted on Mitchell so that Haldeman would have eyes and ears at the CRP while ridding himself of an inept weakling. Dean, who was close to Gordon Strachan, Haldeman's assistant, we infer could control Magruder, claiming sanction by Haldeman for his directions to Magruder.

With this framework in mind, minor mysteries become explicable. McCord left tape on the Watergate's doors (he lied to the other burglars about having removed it), even though all the regular team had entered and a taped lock was not needed to exit. Why? To allow his own agent Lou Russell, the mysterious "sixth" burglar, to enter and lurk, unbeknownst to the other burglars, for CIA purposes–likely to curate the "take" before given to Liddy.

What for thirty years had been a highly opaque scenario now became with this background crystal clear. This revisionist narrative–showing intent and motive both on the part of the CIA and Liddy to burglarize, Dean and McCord to lie, and the CIA and Dean to obstruct–made sense. The desk key was the pivotal piece of evidence that defeated the opposition claims of campaign spying. This revisionist narrative, I firmly believed, made sense of an otherwise senseless burglary.

So this unexplored story, sensed in part early on by Mark Felt and stymied by CIA obstruction, seemed, in my opinion, to be the true narrative of Watergate.

But it is one thing to show the CIA was behind Watergate and that it had instigated it through eager young White House dupes and quite another to say that the *Washington Post* should have uncovered what was a cleverly covert scheme, perpetrated by professional secret-keepers. After all, the CIA lies professionally, and the White House was hardly candid.

So what categories of evidence should we examine to determine whether the *Post* knew, hid, or intentionally ignored probative facts implicating the CIA?

The first area for exploration, I thought, was the status of Howard Hunt and his part-time employer, Mullen and Company. Hunt, Mullen, and its president, Robert Bennett, we now know, were engaged with the CIA through Mullen as a "front," or CIA cover company. But such a cover status by nature is confidential, presumably classified, information. Did the *Post* learn of this cover status? If it did, then its Watergate reporting failed to shine any light on the CIA as it should have, or to examine whether the Agency bore some responsibility for the burglary. And if the burglary was indeed an Agency caper involving prostitute taping, it is highly unlikely that Richard Nixon, John Mitchell, or other White House higher-ups had anything to do with it.

If the *Post* had such evidence, even if inconclusive, to consider, reporting it would have been important information for the American public. Along the same lines, if the *Post* knew Hunt was planning a "CIA defense"–that is, that he was not guilty because he was working on a valid CIA mission–the paper would have been remiss for not reporting a likelihood or possibility, again, that the burglaries were in fact in part CIA operations. And if the *Post* knew of the sexual context, seemingly the target of the wiretappings, then it can be faulted for covering up the real aim of Watergate.

So, generally, we should determine whether there were any factual tidbits, clues, inconsistent statements, or other evidence suggesting a DNC cover-up, CIA guilt, or simply overheard girly talk, any of which was known to the *Post* but not reported or reported deceptively.

My planned methodology in this new venture was to examine the key articles of the three thousand or so *Washington Post* Watergate reports. Then I would compare what was reported against what was known. What was known, in turn, would be determined by FBI reports, congressional and Senate transcripts and records, witness statements, and any relevant litigation records. Finally, I would examine published reports of other newspapers and magazines, as well as memoirs of various Watergate participants.

My mind-set going into this project was that one or two instances of palpable, material deceit, either by concealment or affirmative misstatement, would be sufficient to indict the *Post* for a Watergate cover-up, a fraud on its trusting readership. After all, Richard Nixon was pushed out of office after having been held to that same standard. If, on the other hand, as I thought reasonably possible, the *Post* simply slanted the news here and there, without materially misstating the true narrative, it should be chided but not condemned.

When a man is charged with a crime, the most execrable wrongdoing of a prosecutor is to withhold potentially exculpatory evidence. I wanted to find out if the *Post* did so in its prosecution of Richard Nixon.

Chapter Twelve

MULLEN AND HUNT

As I have described above, in early July 1970 William Sullivan's and Tom Huston's carefully laid plans fell apart when Nixon, at the urging of Attorney General Mitchell and J. Edgar Hoover, withdrew his approval of the Huston Plan. The CIA as a result would not have domestic break-in or wiretapping capability through the FBI. With Hoover's 1966 edict banning black bag jobs once again in effect, the CIA hungered for "dark" domestic operational capabilities. So did the White House.

Their problems–the CIA's and the White House's–were completely different but mutually solvable. The White House had inherent authority to conduct black ops if done for legitimate national security purposes, but it had no operational capabilities. The CIA, on the other hand, had operational capability in abundance but no authority to conduct same domestically. Their mutual need, while theoretically synergistic if optimally and legally pursued, by the very same token also threatened mutual destruction if not. The true history of Watergate should be viewed as awkward efforts of each of these two groups to fill the vacuum left by the FBI, efforts which should have doomed both but destroyed only one.

The White House had previously sought to develop its own in-house investigative muscle by the hiring of detective Jack Caulfield, who kept under wraps his pulp fiction sleuth, former NYPD detective Tony Ulasewicz. After the demise of the Huston Plan, Caulfield optimistically cobbled together Operation Sandwedge, an outline of clandestine programs likely to be carried out by an outside contractor such as, for example, Jack Caulfield, who planned on soon leaving the White House. Sandwedge would have cost around $250,000 per year, a goodly amount in 1971 dollars. Caulfield's plans, which included break-ins, were less imaginative than those later proposed by Liddy in the Gemstone Plan but still were of doubtful legality if pursued for political, as opposed to national security, ends.

Eventually, after the Pentagon Papers were released, the White House commissioned Kissinger aide David Young and Ehrlichman protégé Egil Krogh to plug national security "leaks," thus giving rise to the humorous sobriquet of "the Plumbers." Deep Throat told Woodward that there was nothing wrong with the White House performing its own security operations but it was inevitable that, without professional discipline, they would eventually stumble over the boundary of legitimate national security and into illegal political operations.

What about the CIA? In the summer of 1970, it was about to lose its staunchest ally in the FBI, Felt's shady rival, William Sullivan. After its loss of the Huston Plan's imprimatur on domestic CIA black ops, Howard Hunt ostensibly retired from the Agency and joined DC public relations firm Mullen and Company as a "copywriter." The job was not as absurdly inapt for a former CIA agent as it might appear, since Hunt had authored numerous potboiler spy novels. Still, the idea of a Bay of Pigs veteran penning the praises of United Fruit bananas was a bit much to swallow. It was obvious to anyone with common sense and knowledge of the CIA that Hunt was hired to do the CIA's bidding undercover. No sooner had Mullen hired Hunt in mid-1970, with CIA director Richard Helms' endorsement, than Mullen's president Robert Bennett and Hunt approached the White House's unprincipled hatchet man, Charles Colson, for a part-time White House gig for Hunt, ostensibly to help Colson carry out his dark special projects. Colson, like Hunt a Brown University alum, demurred, whereupon both Bennett and Hunt hinted that Hunt would work without pay. It goes without saying that this unusual offer suggested that Hunt and Bennett had a hidden agenda, and the offer only made sense if Hunt represented attempted infiltration of the White House by the CIA.

Hunt got his break a year later when the Pentagon Papers scandal erupted in early June 1971, with Daniel Ellsberg soon prosecuted for leaking classified material. Colson then hired Hunt, with Oval Office blessing per John Ehrlichman, to help with discrediting Ellsberg and other secretive chores or "sensitive projects." At the Ervin Committee hearings, the CIA's deputy director Robert Cushman testified that, upon hiring Hunt, Ehrlichman called him to ask for the CIA's "carte blanche" in assisting Hunt. Ehrlichman has stoutly denied that request, and with great credibility.[1] After all, Ehrlichman was not directly involved in Colson's dirty work regarding Ellsberg and would have little reason to know of any specific way Hunt would need CIA help. And if Hunt did need the help, wouldn't he be the one to make that call, or ask Ehrlichman to make it? The fabricated call was alleged after the Watergate arrests to explain the Agency-wide support that had been provided to the supposedly retired and detached Hunt.

One of Hunt's first jobs was suggested by the CIA's Medical Services staff, via Bennett and Hunt, to the Plumbers: if you can get Ellsberg's psychiatric records, we can do a fine job of profiling him,[2] the Medical Services staff related, but without them, we can do no better than the weak, superficial effort we have attempted. At Bennett's suggestion, relayed by Hunt, David Young and Egil Krogh of the Plumbers requested Ehrlichman's approval to obtain these records covertly, to which Ehrlichman assented by written authorization, later denying that he was authorizing a burglary or other illegal means to get them. The CIA now had its hooks into the White House.

According to Hunt, as he reported to a disappointed Gordon Liddy, the break-in of Dr. Lewis Fielding's office in Beverly Hills was unsuccessful in finding and photocopying Ellsberg's records. Oddly, in Liddy's view, the burglars and Hunt celebrated with champagne that night. Fielding later said that Ellsberg's records had obviously been located and thumbed

---

1 This supposed request, it appears, was claimed by the CIA later in order to justify the extraordinary and widespread support it provided Hunt and colleagues over the next year, culminating in Watergate. If Ehrlichman was telling the truth, as it seems he was, then the CIA is indicted by that fact alone, since its support for Hunt was deep and wide, involving almost every division of the Agency.

2 After a year of trying to persuade White House hatchet man Charles Colson to hire him part-time for cloak-and-dagger jobs, Colson had hired Hunt for "sensitive" assignments in the wake of Ellsberg's release to the *New York Times* and the Washington D.C. of the top-secret Pentagon Papers. Nixon, egged on by National Security Advisor Henry Kissinger, sought to discredit Ellsberg, the main rationale for hiring Hunt. Hunt then relayed the CIA's suggestion that the CIA psychiatrists could produce a negative psychological profile of Ellsberg.

through, therefore likely copied by the crew's document-copying cameras. Indeed, burglar Felipe de Diego has stated that he helped copy the files. Intriguingly, the CIA was sure to keep a "casing" photo of Hunt and Liddy in Fielding's parking lot. This picture was later incriminating of both Ehrlichman and Liddy but was likely kept by the CIA because it would have been exculpatory evidence (showing White House authorization) should someone later claim this to have been an illegal CIA domestic operation. This break-in–with White House support, a seeming CIA initiative, begun with a suggestion by Hunt and/or Bennett, and sequestering of the fruits by the CIA–set a pattern for virtually all of Hunt's "help" for the White House.[3] It would not be irrational to see this operation as a template for Watergate.

If in fact the Fielding burglary was a CIA operation, then it is quite a reasonable inference that Watergate was also. Is this as obvious as we here claim? Certainly Charles O. Morgan Jr., a Democratic American Civil Liberties Union (ACLU) lawyer retained by the DNC to suppress Watergate burglary trial testimony about the meretricious phone conversations, thought so. And Morgan was anything but a pro-Nixon advocate.

Because of Morgan's legally "unprecedented longshot" intervention into the burglary trial, Judge Sirica allowed him, along with other counsel, to listen to the tape of Baldwin's interview with the *LA Times*. To Morgan, it was amusingly but outrageously obvious that the Fielding burglary was a CIA operation, and he said so to anyone who would listen. Baldwin related

3 The following are examples of operations suggested by Hunt/Bennett, seemingly for White House benefit and so approved, but which were in fact covert CIA operations in which any "take" was seemingly grabbed by the CIA to the exclusion of the White House. Howard Hunt interviewed former CIA operative Lucien Conein regarding the Kennedys participation in the plot to assassinate President Diem of South Vietnam. While seemingly for White House political purposes, the Agency was also likely an interested consumer. But Hunt claimed the recording device implanted under Ehrlichman's office couch cushions failed to activate. Hunt interviewed Clifford de Motte about his knowledge of Ted Kennedy's Chappaquiddick imbroglio, claiming that de Motte had no information. Hunt's Mullen boss Robert Bennett had urged Hunt and Liddy to break into the safe of *Las Vegas Sun* publisher Hank Greenspun, promising information for the White House that "would blow [Senator Edmund] Muskie out of the water." Watergate itself, as I will show, fit this same pattern: a venture likely proposed by the CIA through Hunt, wherein the CIA, through McCord and Baldwin, would edit the take. Note that McCord had sidestepped Liddy's request that the conversations be taped. See Hougan at notes 62-63.

on the tape that his lawyer, John Cassidento, held a similar opinion. They also believed the CIA was involved in Watergate.

Another oddity of the Hunt activities was the timing of his burglary team's formation. He recruited a number of Cuban Bay of Pigs veterans in April 1971, when he had the Mullen job in hand but not yet the White House consultancy, and not any hint by the White House of the Watergate or Gemstone plans. The Cubans clearly understood that they were back in business with the CIA, hopefully leading to a deposition of Fidel Castro. One of the Cubans, Eugenio Martinez, was an active CIA agent, which the *Post* knew at least by January 1973. Obviously, Hunt knew he would be carrying out black ops, whether with White House authority or otherwise, even if the White House yet had no clue. After all, the Ellsberg debacle did not hit publicly until early June 1971, the occasion for Hunt's part-time retention by the White House.[4]

In the summer of 1971, as Hunt was being hired, Hoover confided to a friendly newsman that the White House was going to get in trouble with the CIA men it was hiring. To whom beyond Hunt Hoover was referring was unclear, although others besides Hunt, such as White House aide Alexander Butterfield, were suspected intelligence operatives. Perhaps Hoover was referring to the Cubans.

All of this is but necessary prelude to the situation Woodward, Bernstein, and the FBI observed post-arrest on June 17, 1972.

It was June 17, 1972, when young *Washington Post* crime-beat reporter Bob Woodward received a call alerting him to the arraignment of five men for the burglary of the Democratic National Committee headquarters in Washington, DC. Woodward soon learned from DC police sources of the odd nature of this burglary. All the men, it seemed, wore business suits and rubber gloves, while some were carrying hundred-dollar bills numbered in sequence. At the arraignment, Woodward gasped when one of the defendants, James McCord, told the court in a whispering voice that he was recently retired from the CIA. This was indeed a curious affair. It

4 The Pentagon Papers were given to the *Times* by Ellsberg in March, perhaps one motive for Hunt to form his team. The CIA was deeply interested in Ellsberg because of his close relationship with liberal firebrand writer Frances FitzGerald, daughter of legendary CIA black ops stalwart, the late Desmond FitzGerald. See Hougan at notes 48-49.

would become even more curious when Woodward learned of the connections of all the burglars to the 1961 Bay of Pigs invasion of Cuba.

Woodward was alert enough to notice that one man stood out in the seedy surroundings of the petty criminal court venue. Whereas the "Fifth Street Lawyers" normally populating the courthouse were sloppily dressed in bad suits and sport coats, one man in this weekend court session did not seemingly belong, expensively dressed and tastefully coiffed. Who was this fish out of water? Woodward described this memorably curious scene:

> *Woodward went inside the courtroom. One person stood out. In a middle row sat a young man with fashionably long hair and an expensive suit with slightly flared lapels, his chin high, his eyes searching the room as if he were in unfamiliar surroundings...*[5]

The man was one Douglas Caddy, a lawyer associated with Mullen and Company, the same DC public relations firm that was Hunt's part-time employer. He had hired Joseph Rafferty, a criminal defense lawyer, to represent the defendants. But Woodward already knew from jailhouse sources that the burglars had made no telephone calls that night. How did Caddy know about the arrests? Woodward asked him. Caddy, clearly uncomfortable, refused to comment.

> *Caddy didn't want to talk. "Please don't take it personally," he told Woodward. "It would be a mistake to do that. I just don't have anything to say."*
>
> *Woodward asked Caddy about his clients.*
>
> *"They are not my clients," he said.*
>
> *But you are a lawyer? Woodward asked.*
>
> *"I'm not going to talk to you."*
>
> *Caddy walked back into the courtroom. Woodward followed.*
>
> *"Please, I have nothing to say."*[6]

---

5 Bernstein and Woodward, *All the President's Men*, 17.

6 Bernstein and Woodward, *All the President's Men*, 17.

Caddy soon claimed to Woodward in explanation that he had received a worried call from the wife of burglar Bernard Barker, concerned that her husband had not come home. Caddy claimed to have had a "sympathetic" conversation with Barker a year earlier, which apparently led to his wife's outreach to him.

The *Post* stuck for days with this absurd story that Caddy had been hired by Barker's wife, ostensibly without a payment. However, at the very same time, Woodward, on a tip from Deep Throat, had both identified and reached Howard Hunt at his Mullen office. Thereafter, the *Post* blared headlines of Hunt's employment as a White House consultant, an employment directly confirmed by the White House switchboard, clearly familiar with Hunt.

However, with Hunt's emergence, and the knowledge that he worked part-time for Mullen, where Caddy also worked, the Barker story made little sense. Hunt, after all, was a copywriter with the PR firm while Caddy was a lawyer who had an office at Mullen headquarters and represented one of its big clients, General Foods. In late June and early July, the *Post* reported:

> *Douglas Caddy, a lawyer originally retained by five suspects arrested in the incident Saturday, worked in one of Bennett's offices while he was liaison between Bennett's firm and General Foods, a major client of the firm.*[7]

> *"Caddy and Hunt were good friends and the relationship continued after Caddy left here," Robert F. Bennett, president of the Mullen firm, told a reporter last week.*[8]

On two consecutive days, June 21 and 22, 1972, the *Post*, having repeated the story that Caddy told about the "sympathetic" conversation with Barker, now added Robert Bennett's comment that Hunt and Caddy were personal friends and had once shared an office at Mullen. This per-

7 Bernstein, "Employer of 2 Tied to Bugging Raised Money for Nixon," *Washington Post*, June 22, 1972, A9.

8 Woodward and Jim Mann, "Jury Probes Lawyer in 'Bug' Case," *Washington Post*, July 1, 1972, A1.

sonal friendship, of course, was put forth to counter the obvious inference that if a Mullen lawyer showed up at arraignment regarding a burglary in which a Mullen employee was involved, then perhaps this was a Mullen operation. Stressing the personal friendship, as ludicrous as that was, was meant to explain the involvement of two known Mullen agents. Clearly, the PR firm's role would need to be explained.

Bennett once again provided the lifesaver for Woodward to float. Bennett was closely tied to the White House as an organizer of "dummy" fund-raising committees,[9] he volunteered to Woodward, raising money for Nixon while keeping secret the donors' names. This was reported in the body of the June 21 story, but to make sure the readers would not miss the connection of Mullen to Nixon, a June 22, 1972, *Post* headline—"Employer of 2 Tied to Burglary Raised Money for Nixon"—blared above a Bernstein article:

> *Robert F. Bennett, president of the Washington public relations firm in whose office two figures mentioned in the Democratic National Committee bugging case have worked, acknowledged yesterday that he was the principal organizer of dummy campaign committees to raise money for the re-election of President Nixon.*[10]

In the same June 22, 1972, issue, Woodward, in a separate front-page piece, had written the same with more embellishment:

> *Robert F. Bennett, President of the Washington public relations firm where two figures mentioned in the bugging incident have worked, acknowledged that he was the prime organizer of the dummy Campaign Committee designed to collect money for Mr. Nixon's reelection without listing the donors' names.*[11]

9 In fact, Bennett, laundered client and CIA asset Howard Hughes' contributions to Nixon.

10 Bernstein, "Employer of 2 Tied to Bugging."

11 Woodward, "Democrats, GOP Tighten Security After Watergate 'Bugging' Case," *Washington Post*, June 22, 1972, A1.

Given the CIA connections of all six known burglary participants, the question of Mullen's and Hunt's CIA connections lingered. The question was explicitly raised and answered by the *Post* on July 8, 1972. The paper reported that Caddy had told a grand jury that he had "intimations" that Mullen had done work for the CIA, apparently noted by prosecutors in open court proceedings. What those "intimations" were should have been the subject of deep digging by the *Post*.

The *Post* told its readers what those intimations supposedly were in its July 8 article, citing the ubiquitous quote machine, Bennett, to say Caddy must have been referring to Mullen's work for Radio Free Cuba "in the 1960s," which everyone knew was CIA-sponsored:

> *During Caddy's appearance in court, it was revealed that he told the grand jury of "intimations" that Robert R. Mullen Co.–the Washington Public Relations firm where he and Hunt once shared an office–did work for the CIA.*
>
> ***Robert F. Bennett, President of the Mullen firm said this week that Caddy was probably referring to work the firm did in the 1960s for Radio Free Cuba, widely reported to be funded by the CIA.***[12]

Certainly Woodward and the *Post* can be criticized as being both gullible and incurious for their seeming acceptance of Bennett's assertion, without energetically testing it. But in assessing whether the *Post* engaged in a deliberate cover-up, let's first focus on Woodward's close relationship with Mark Felt, who had just given his reporter friend the Hunt scoop.

Immediately after the burglary, on June 21, 1972, the FBI requested, and the CIA gave, a description of Mullen's cover arrangement with the CIA. Later CIA documents reflect that *Time* magazine's Sandy Smith, one of Felt's close journalist outlets, called Bennett in February 1973 to inquire whether Mullen was a CIA front:

> ***Mr. Robert R. Mullen, President of Mullen & Company, telephoned CCS on the morning of February 28 to advise us that***

12 Bernstein and Woodward, "Nationwide Search Ends–Bug Case Figure Faces Quiz," *Washington Post*, July 8, 1972, A4.

Sandy Smith, reporter from Time Magazine was in the Mullen office late on February 27. Smith started off by saying that a "source in the Justice Department" had informed him that the Company "is a front for CIA." Mullen denied the allegation stoutly...Smith had many questions concerning Howard Hunt, such as how he secured Mullen employment and his salary. Mullen told him the Company paid him a salary initially and later on a consultant basis when Hunt began to work for The Committee to Re-elect The President....

Bob Mullen again telephones CCS at 1650 hours on February 28, 1973 as a follow-up to his morning call, as reported above.

Sandy Smith, the Time reporter was again in the late afternoon and told Mr. Mullen that he had just seen, through an FBI contact, a paper allegedly personally delivered by a high official of CIA to Mr. Patrick Gray, acting director of the FBI during the height of the Watergate flap and investigation of Howard Hunt last summer.

It was evident that Smith at least knew of the existence of such a document, but Mr. Mullen could only guess that Smith had not seen it long enough to digest it or said so little that Smith has not developed more information....

Mullen would like to know what exactly we gave the FBI so that he can tell Smith what he already seemingly knows from our memorandum to the FBI...

...Mr. Colby would recommend...that Messrs. Mullen and Bennett be allowed to read the June 21, 1972 memorandum to the FBI and that they be asked to continue to deny any allegation of association with the Agency...

It developed that Mr. Bennett had been present during the second meeting with Mr. Smith. Messrs. Bennett and Mullen were of the opinion that Smith had not seen the memorandum. They suggested that he had only heard of its existence or had seen the FBI report which summarized the memorandum and said only that the company had provided cover for

> *the Agency. They felt that if he had seen the memorandum he would not have re-visited them or would have accused them on the rather specific information contained in the memorandum.*[13]

According to CIA documents, Smith had clearly been tipped off (read: likely by Felt) but did not have all the information contained in the CIA report to the FBI. Bennett, of course, denied all to Smith, and Smith did not go public. But the point is that Smith's source was in the FBI (likely his friend Mark Felt), and the FBI had the evidence in hand in June of 1972. All of this shows a strong likelihood that Woodward had the goods on Mullen from the FBI if he wanted them.

Unfortunately for the *Post*, any missing certainty is supplied by another internal CIA document, a report by a CIA officer recounting what Bennett's case officer in turn reported about Bennett's doings. First off, the document we have verifies that Bennett was a CIA asset reporting to a case officer, incontrovertible proof of his own CIA agency and of a *domestic* cover arrangement. But moreover, in this report Bennett brags about his supposed deal with Woodward, in which Woodward promised to "protect" Mullen, presumably meaning not spilling the beans on the company's status:

> *Bennett said also that he has been feeding stories to Bob Woodward of the* Washington Post *with the understanding that there be no attribution to Bennett. Woodward is suitably grateful for the fine stories and by-lines which he gets and protects Bennett (and the Mullen Company).*[14]

Although this document is dated March 1, 1973, the statements of Bennett to the CIA reflected in the report go as far back as July 10, 1972. It is of course absurd to believe that Woodward needed stories from Bennett and therefore covered up Mullen's status. Indeed, the stories cited were the definition of bland.[15] So if Woodward was "protecting" Mullen, it was

13 Eric Eisenstadt, "Memorandum for the Deputy Director for Plans," Central Intelligence Agency, March 1, 1973.

14 Eisenstadt, "Memorandum."

15 Bennett was likely puffing up his role in keeping Mullen out of the news as a CIA cover company. The stories Bennett claimed to have planted were not exactly teacup-rattlers. See

for the *Post*'s purposes, not Bennett's. And Woodward's knowledge about Mullen was gained before Bennett's July 10, 1972, report to his case officer, whereas Bennett had not given him any "story" before that date.

We do know, certainly in hindsight, that whatever interest the *Post* had in keeping Mullen and its CIA sponsor out of the news, it would be one that the *Post*'s philosophical twin, the DNC, shared, just as the two shared Joseph Califano, a prominent Democratic politician and general counsel to both the DNC and the *Post*. We should keep in mind that exposing the CIA's participation would inexorably have led to questions about the mission's target, which the Democrats would not want to occur.

In fact we know, thanks again to a helpful CIA memo, that the DNC, as did the *Post*, apparently shared the same interest as Mullen and the CIA in keeping Mullen/CIA out of the news. We know this because Bennett noted to his case officer on July 10, 1972, that he, through lawyer Hobart Taylor, had made a "back door entry" to the DNC law firm Williams, Connolly & Califano (WCC), which was representing the DNC in its litigation against the CRP. The entry was designed, again, to keep Mullen's CIA connection from being exposed:

> *Mr. Bennett related that he has now established a "back door entry" to the Edward Bennett Williams law firm which is representing the Democratic Party in its suit for damages resulting from the Watergate incident. Mr. Bennett is prepared to go this route to kill off any revelation by Ed Williams of Agency association with the Mullen firm if such a development seems likely. He said that he would, of course, check with CIA before contacting Mr. Williams for this purpose.*
> *Mr. Bennett presently believes there is little likelihood of exposure of our current cover arrangements. He did not even mention [deleted] and said only that [deleted] was shocked by Hunt's alleged participation in the Watergate plot.*[16]

This clear evidence–seemingly conspiratorial confessions by Mullen to the DNC and the *Post*–was, we can safely conclude, that Mullen had been

N. Horrock, "Whispers about Colson," *Newsweek*, March 5, 1973, 21.

16 Martin Lukoskie, *Memorandum for the Record*, January 17, 1974, reflecting the July 10, 1972, memorandum.

acting as a CIA front. And of course the *Post* appeared to have helped Mullen and the CIA hide this crucial connection. But in January 1974, independent confirmatory evidence emerged not only tying Hunt and Mullen to the CIA, but also supporting the hypothesis that a main goal of the OS's Security Research Service was acquiring sexual dirt on key political players, thus explaining Watergate.

It was then that Rob Roy Ratliff, an aide working for the CIA as a White House attaché, emerged to tell the CIA's inspector general of the packages which Hunt had been regularly couriering from the White House to Dr. Bernard Malloy of the CIA's Psychological Services Branch, a practice which he learned had predated him.

In short, the packages contained explicit sexual gossip about various key White House figures. To Ratliff, it was certain that Hunt would only do this with the highest Agency authorization. The sexual nature of this information is consistent with both the Ellsberg/Fielding burglary, directed to Ellsberg's sexuality and the DNC wiretapping of lurid calls.

The Ratliff statement of January 17, 1974, now partially redacted but still informative, soon became available not only to the Select Committee, but also the House Judiciary Committee.

On June 21, 1972, Mark Felt told Patrick Gray that the break-in was a White House job, a CIA operation, or both. He likely told the same to Woodward, which in any case should have been obvious. But even if Felt did not tell Woodward, at some point he would have shared Mullen's cover arrangement with his close friend, just as he later did with Sandy Smith, the latter perhaps because the *Post* had remained silent on the issue.

While Woodward and the *Post* can try to wiggle out of these inferences, they cannot escape the implications of Bennett's claim of a deal with him to cover up Mullen's role. Nor can we doubt at this remove that the DNC, through WCC, was actively involved in keeping the lid closed. The DNC, in turn, should be viewed as a close *Post* partner. If the DNC was covering up the Mullen cover arrangement with the CIA, so was the *Post*.

We must find the *Post* and Woodward guilty as charged, by a preponderance of the evidence, of covering Hunt's and Mullen's cover status, a key fact that the public should have learned from the paper.

Chapter Thirteen

THE HERMÈS NOTEBOOKS, THE CIA DEFENSE, AND DEAN

As I described in the last chapter, Mullen's president Robert Bennett energetically strove to keep the PR firm from being identified as a CIA front, thus blowing his cover, displeasing his Agency sponsor, and endangering a lucrative contract.

But Bennett was not facing prison like Howard Hunt was. If Hunt was really on a CIA mission, his belief in the president's national security authority would make the mission legal, and prison would be off the table. But if he proved he was on a CIA mission, he would have to describe it. And by doing so, subsequent investigation might uncover years of illegal domestic CIA black operations that did not get prior White House approval. The top brass might go to prison or lose their pensions, but likely not Hunt, who previous to Watergate had been for the most part a foreign operative.

It would therefore be best for the CIA and Mullen for Hunt to be a good soldier and take one for the team, spending several years in a nearby white-collar, low-security prison. But this would not necessarily be a good outcome for Hunt personally. He was a deeply devoted family man and was revulsed by the prospect of prison.

In Hunt's short White House tenure, there had been a number of operations approved by someone in the White House that were really the initiatives of Hunt and Mullen. The Lewis Fielding burglary was clearly a CIA brainchild, as Hunt relayed the need of the CIA Medical Services staff for Ellsberg's psychiatric records (supposedly to do a better profile for the

White House), copies of which the CIA ultimately kept for itself to the exclusion of the White House. Bennett had convinced Liddy to explore with Hunt breaking into the safe of Hank Greenspun, *Las Vegas Sun* publisher, on the pretext that they would find information that would "blow Muskie out of the water." Oh, yes, and Greenspun also allegedly had dirt on Howard Hughes (a CIA asset), which the Hughes organization should want. Although Hunt and Liddy explored this caper, the Hughes representative wisely vetoed it.

It appeared also that Hunt had tricked Liddy into helping a clear CIA mission, Operation Mud Hen, which was in essence an intimidation of columnist Jack Anderson. Anderson had notice of the plan to break into the DNC[1] long before it was a glint in Liddy's eye,[2] and long before the falsely claimed (by Magruder) March 30, 1972, approval by Mitchell. Liddy was brought by Hunt into a meeting with a retired CIA poison specialist, Dr. Edward Gunn, to explore ways of incapacitating Anderson. Liddy erroneously thought Hunt had a White House principal behind the discussion and eagerly joined in. In fact, Hunt had brought Liddy into the meeting to again gain tincture of White House authority should bad things later be uncovered. The White House was not interested in silencing Anderson, in short, but the CIA was.

Hunt had scrupulously noted these various White House/CIA operations, and their White House approvals, in his operational Hermès notebooks,[3] one of the purposes being to document a national security/presidential authorization defense should the need ever arise. Because the

---

1 *Manhattan Tribune* editor William Haddad, a small-time muckraker with intelligence sources, alerted Anderson to the rumors in February 1972.

2 Liddy had always considered Watergate to be only an optional target, and at that, only after the campaign was underway in fall 1972. Prior to March 30, 1972, even according to Magruder, no Watergate entry had been suggested by Mitchell, and no budget for Gemstone had been approved. Around November 1971, Dean had White House detective Jack Caulfield send his operative Tony Ulasewicz on a "casing" walk-through visit of DNC headquarters. This was long before Liddy began planning Gemstone and months before he took a job with the CRP. So the break-in may have been contemplated by Dean, likely at the suggestion of Hunt. Intelligence community members began hearing of such plans around December 1972, again before Liddy drew up his plans.

3 A "Hermès" notebook was a stylish notebook sold by the fashion designer Hermès and Company.

national security action would be on behalf of the CIA, this defense has been called the "CIA defense" by defense lawyers and later by journalists. In sum, after his arrest, Hunt knew he had a possible CIA defense available to him, based upon his documentation of CIA and White House approvals of ostensible national security operations, the latest being Watergate.

Hunt proved to have been less of a true-blue CIA diehard than James McCord. His aspirations of assuming control of the lucrative Mullen CIA contract, already subject to internal dispute prior to Watergate, now appeared doomed as the Agency considered yanking its Mullen cover contract altogether. Hunt's wife, Dorothy, presumably a CIA agent undercover with the Spanish embassy, had been fired in the wake of the arrests. With nothing to lose from his now-destroyed CIA relationship, Hunt was entertaining a CIA defense with his attorney, William Bittman, his close family life being his controlling motivation.

To pursue this defense, Hunt needed his two clothbound Hermès notebooks, which he kept in his White House safe, showing notations of these various White House/CIA operations up through the burglary and memorializing both White House approvals and CIA direction of them. Hunt and Bittman were also convinced that the prosecution had used information from the notebooks to indict Hunt so that if they were seized in violation of the Fourth Amendment search warrant requirement, Hunt must go free on that basis.

However, when the prosecution turned over to Hunt's lawyers the contents taken from his safe–by Dean, at the request of the FBI–the two Hermès notebooks, one operational, were missing. Without these books, Hunt would have difficulty establishing his CIA defense. The operational notebook would have, according to Hunt, shown Dean's authorization of the Watergate burglary and Ehrlichman's authorization of the Fielding burglary, the latter at the request of "Plumbers" David Young and Egil Krogh, after the CIA advised the two naïfs that it needed the psychiatric records for a meaningful Ellsberg profile. Hunt had made his motion for his operational notebook on October 11, 1972, and went to the courthouse in November 1972 to examine the evidence, here described in his book, *Undercover*, with emphasis in the original:

> *I searched the seized material for my operational notebook, files and telephone list, but did not find them. Bittman [Hunt's attorney] asked Silbert if he was holding them in another area, but Silbert declared that what I had reviewed was all there was. It was sufficient to convict me,* but any material that could have been used to construct a defense for me was missing; *my operational notebooks, telephone lists and documents in which I had recorded the progress of Gemstone from its inception, mentioning Liddy's three principals by name: Mitchell, Magruder and Dean.*[4]

Although Hunt's desire for this notebook would later be characterized by the *Post* as aimed at showing an illegal search, this passage shows that Hunt wanted the operational notebook mainly to establish his CIA defense.

Dean had withheld the books from the FBI and never showed them to his White House conspirators. He discussed with Ehrlichman having withheld them, likely a relief to a guilty Ehrlichman, but there is no evidence Dean ever showed them to him. There is also no evidence that Ehrlichman or any other White House official thought, rightly or wrongly, that they would most likely have implicated Dean in the Watergate burglary. In short, the withholding of the notebooks, while a dirty secret of both Ehrlichman[5] and Dean, was likely, we infer, far dirtier for Dean, although only he and Hunt knew what the notebooks said.

Interestingly, had Hunt grabbed his notebooks when he opened the safe the morning of June 17, 1972, following the arrests, history would have been radically different. His eventual use of these notebooks would have had two spectacular effects. First, the public would have known of the CIA's secret sponsorship of the Watergate burglary, taking heat off the White House and destroying the campaign-spying theme, thus making the White House a type of victim. Secondly, it would have likely shown that White House authorization for the DNC break-in went no higher than Dean, again absolving higher-ups, causing Dean's firing and ending any

---

4 E. Howard Hunt, *Undercover: Memoirs of an American Secret Agent* (New York: Berkley Publishing, 1974), 277.

5 Ironically, while the notebooks would have harmed Dean, they would have helped Ehrlichman, who was denied a legitimate national security defense for the Fielding burglary.

cover-up. Martinez and Gonzalez, who always thought they were on a CIA mission, and whom history has written off as Hunt's dupes, would convincingly corroborate Hunt's defense if they became emboldened to speak out in trial, as they eventually did post-trial.

Hunt has since admitted that the logs in the notebooks would have shown authorization of the burglaries by Dean, Magruder, and, mistakenly, Mitchell. Just before Dean suffered his first amnesia attack in December about having seized the notebooks, Hunt's recently retired CIA agent wife, Dorothy, died in a United Airlines crash as the plane was to land in Chicago. The "bag man" for some of the hush money payoffs, she had been traveling to Chicago with $10,000 in hundred-dollar bills to pay off bug manufacturer Michael Stevens, who was unknown to the White House conspirators but one who could identify McCord as having been on a CIA mission. (Stevens will be discussed at length below in connection with his customer James McCord.) Thus the inference was strong that any payment of hush money from Dorothy Hunt, intended for Stevens, was for the purposes only of the CIA and not of the White House. After all, Stevens could not implicate this White House beyond facts already well known. Hunt's wife's death simultaneously destroyed one of Hunt's witnesses for a CIA defense[6] and his desperate desire not to go to jail to preserve his domestic life. So if the CIA did not cause the plane crash, it was a very lucky organization, serendipitously benefiting from it.

Shortly after a despondent Hunt pleaded guilty on Dean's urging, lacking both his Hermès notebooks and his wife, Dean supposedly "found" the notebooks among Nixon's personal estate files Dean kept in his own office. It was then that Dean went through what he described as the "sweaty"—and difficult—act of shredding the thick clothbound books, he later admitted in his book. It would be difficult, one would think, to forget such an important and gut-wrenching act, which, based on the timing of Hunt's plea, occurred in late January or February 1973. However, when questioned

6 Investigator and conspiracy theorist Sherman Skolnick claimed there was evidence that the plane had been sabotaged. I have no opinion other than to say that if the CIA didn't cause the crash, it benefited greatly from it. Hunt likely saw this as a shot across his own bow. At this point, the cause of the crash remains in the world of speculation. It is of interest that the crash was investigated by the FAA soon to be headed by Colonel Alexander Butterfield, long rumored to have been an undercover defense intelligence plant.

exhaustively just months later both by the regular prosecutors, beginning in March 1973, and then by the special prosecutor and the Ervin Committee, Dean neglected to tell them about the books and their destruction.

He "remembered" them again in early November 1973, just before his sentencing, when he told Judge Sirica about their destruction. His sudden regaining of memory may have been triggered by the imminent release of presidential tapes on which Dean was overheard telling Ehrlichman about the withheld notebooks.

We do not know with absolute certainty what Woodstein knew about Hunt's plan of a CIA defense in the fall of 1972, but we do know that such a defense would have completely altered the promising anti-Nixon narrative so carefully developed through the joint efforts of the DNC and the *Post* (and "back door" by the CIA). What did Woodstein know about this defense, and when did they know it?

We know from the later confirmation hearings of nominated US attorney Earl Silbert that he and his assistant Seymour Glanzer were actively preparing for a CIA defense in the fall of 1972, making sure always to call the defense "spurious" or "phony":

> *Senator HART. Later, and this would be in November or December of 1972, you indicated that you became concerned that a spurious defense based on CIA sponsorship might be raised, and again you contacted the CIA.*
>
> *What was your inquiry of them at that time?*
>
> *MR. SILBERT. Well, Senator, as I indicated in the report, we were trying to anticipate at the trial which way the defendants might go. It was Mr. Glanzer's thought, one of my colleague's thought, that one of the defenses they might raise would be, as you indicated, a spurious CIA defense...*[7]

At the Silbert hearings, Senator Sam Ervin referred to press reports of the possible CIA defense:

---

7 Silbert Testimony of April 23, 1974. Nomination of Earl J. Silbert to be United States Attorney: Hearing Before the S. Comm. on the Judiciary, 93rd Cong, 129.

> *Senator ERVIN. Well, now, you felt at that time that since there was a feeling, or at least it had been stated in the press, had it not, by some from the time the Watergate burglars were discovered, it was suggested, about that time, in view of the fact that Hunt and certain, one or more, of the residents of Miami had connections with the CIA in times past, there was some discussion in the press to the effect that the defendants might, that anybody arrested might, defend the case on the grounds of a CIA operation?*
>
> *Mr. PETERSEN. Well, I don't recall precisely when that theory was developed. I think that it developed much later in the proceedings, and I think it was suggested by Mr. Glanzer of the prosecution team. My recollection of it would fix it sometime as a possible defense some time around December, but not at the time of the first delivery of documents.*[8]

But as we will have seen in so many aspects of the *Post*'s cover-up, an item in any newspaper other than the *Post* is not part of the narrative unless and until it is adopted by the *Post*, and if another paper did reveal this defense, then the *Post* ignored it.

We now know that in fact Hunt and Bittman had been exploring the CIA defense up through late December 1972, when they urged McCord lawyer Gerald Alch to explore the same defense with his fiercely resistant Agency diehard client. Would Bittman have been willing then or later to reveal these plans to inquiring reporters? It seems as though he would have had no reason not to. We also know from the later Silbert hearings that the prosecutors were girding in November and December 1972 for a CIA defense.

We know that when the subject of the missing Hermès notebooks was publicly raised around the time of the Gray hearings, after Hunt had pleaded guilty, Bittman willingly gave an interview to Woodstein about his earlier motion to retrieve them and at least one purpose in so doing. Woodward and Bernstein quoted Bittman in a March 3, 1973, article as confirming

8 Henry Peterson Testimony of June 20, 1974. Nomination of Earl J. Silbert to be United States Attorney: Hearing Before the S. Comm. on the Judiciary, 93rd Cong, 444.

his desire for the notebooks as part of his efforts to show an illegal search of Hunt's office:[9]

> *"At that time we thought the FBI had them and had used them in their investigation," Bittman said. "I was going to argue that the government's whole case was tainted because their information had come from material (the notebooks) obtained in an illegal search. I was going to call Dean and other people at the White House to show that Hunt was still using his office in June and that he had not abandoned his property in the White House."...*[10]

Interestingly, the article also made reference to Dean's desire to thwart investigators who wanted to use the notebooks to show that higher officials were involved, with the implication that this was not Hunt's or Bittman's concern:

> *In its Feb. 12 issue,* Newsweek *magazine quoted "a source close to the Watergate defense" as saying that Dean "actually removed documents" from Hunt's office that "might have led the G-men to Administration top siders." The same report said Dean received orders "to try to prevent federal investigators from tarnishing any figures in the President's inner circle."*

Clearly, the defense source, likely Bittman, is supposedly telling *Newsweek* why the *investigators* wanted the notebooks and why Dean and others may not have wanted that to occur. But nothing in this quote or in the entire article suggests that *Hunt as well wanted to show the approvals of*

---

9 The recent entries in the book would have shown that, contrary to the prosecution's claim, Hunt had not "abandoned" the office, his safe, and the property in it and therefore had a reasonable expectation of privacy, protected by the Fourth Amendment, thus requiring a warrant. Note that the Bittman quote in the March 3 article has ellipses and did not purport to be *all* that Bittman told Woodward. For what other defenses were these notebooks relevant?

10 Bernstein and Woodward, "Watergate Case Notebooks Missing," *Washington Post*, March 3, 1973, A3.

high White House officials in order to bolster his CIA defense. Remember, it was Hunt, not the prosecution, who made the motion for the notebooks.

Did Bittman tell Woodstein of the CIA defense as a reason for wanting the notebooks? If he did, the reporters should have reported that hot item. Hunt had already pleaded guilty, and it was likely that he would have emphasized to the Probation Office, like Martinez and Gonzalez, that he thought the burglary was a legal national security incursion. We also know that McCord later claimed a form of that possible defense[11] as well to the *Post* and to the Ervin Committee (a defense that, as related by McCord, would not implicate the CIA) and thus likely told the same thing to the Probation Office. So it is more likely than not that Bittman told the *Post* of the CIA defense, since its essence was approval by White House "top siders" for purposes of national security.

Bittman had no motive to shy away from the CIA defense in speaking with Woodstein. We know he readily told *Secret Agenda* author Jim Hougan years later about wanting the notebooks for the CIA defense; Hougan wrote about this in his book. So in short, after 1973–although we don't know positively whether Woodstein concealed Bittman's exploration of the CIA defense or of the notebooks' connection to CIA operations–I put in the "more likely than not" category that Woodstein willfully suppressed evidence of Hunt's potential CIA defense in March 1973. Indeed, if Woodward and Bernstein did not get this low-hanging fruit, they were not the thorough reporters they claimed to be.

However, by late May 1973, the Post clearly knew that in fact McCord's lawyer Gerald Alch had raised this defense shortly before trial and that McCord was forced to admit this in his testimony. The Post knew this could be explosive, since the defense would be discussed only if there was factual predicate.

11 McCord did not claim that this had been a CIA operation but did state to the Senate that he thought Watergate was a national security intelligence operation apparently approved by the attorney general. This thought unwittingly reveals the CIA rationale for infiltrating the White House, i.e., any CIA operation approved by the attorney general would be legal (even if violating the CIA charter). Baldwin had described the same national security defense to Jack Nelson of the *Los Angeles Times*, strongly implying that McCord maintained a CIA connection. Baldwin's Democratic lawyer, John Cassidento, a former federal prosecutor, thought that the CIA had involvement in the burglary, as Baldwin related to the *Times*.

To soften the blow, the *Post* suggested that McCord was exaggerating and that no lawyer had actually suggested the defense: "One contended that the defense lawyers simply asked their clients if the CIA was involved, and the other said he could not recall...."[12]

What the *Post* article missed, seemingly purposefully, was that Alch's approach was likely suggested by Bittman, in turn based on Hunt's urging. Certainly, reporting that the burglary team's supervisor was willing to testify to an undercover CIA operation would have been earthshaking. So the Post minimized what McCord had already minimized. At least the New York Times printed on May 24 colloquy not only of McCord but also of Alch:

> *Q. Now as to Mr. McCord's first complaint that you suggested he use C.I.A. involvement as a defense, it is true, is it not, that the question, at least of C.I.A. involvement, was the subject of discussion between you and Mr. McCord on two occasions in December, one at the Monocle Restaurant and another time in your office in Boston?*
>
> *A. I specifically asked him whether or not there was any factual basis to the contention that the C.I.A. was involved....*
>
> *Q. In your statement on Page 10, you say during the meeting with defendants in December, and prior to your Monocle meeting with Mr. McCord, "the question arose as to whether the C.I.A. was involved." Would you tell us how the question arose, who raised it? Do you know how that was raised, this question? Who raised it?*
>
> *A. I am not sure. It may have been Mr. Bittman. I cannot be positive...*

12 Paul G. Edwards, "McCord Disputed on Idea of Linking Burglary to CIA," *Washington Post*, May 23, 1973, A12.

... Q. So it is no fiction, really, that Mr. McCord was deeply concerned over what he believed was a conspiracy to have him implicate the C.I.A. in the Watergate case?

A. I have no knowledge to contradict that statement by Mr. McCord.

Q. Actually according to your own statement, when you first raised the C.I.A. involvement with Mr. McCord in the Monocle Restaurant, you said he did not really respond to it, but launched into a complaint about how the White House was treating the C.I.A. I think that was your statement.

A. That is correct.[13]

McCord also testified, consistent with Alch, that Hunt, via Bittman, had been pushing this defense, including proposing evidence of the CIA practices of false retirements and plausible deniability of blown operations.

Even more damning was a series of alarmed letters to the CIA from McCord as the CIA defense was being pushed, all introduced into evidence in the hearings. McCord especially expressed worry in these letters, sent between December 21, 1972 and January 5, 1973, that supposedly "perjured" testimony from an MPD (Metropolitan Police) intelligence officer, Garey Bittenbender, would be introduced to the effect that McCord had admitted to him in the jailhouse after arrest that this had been a CIA operation. Only when the maverick Hunt finally agreed to plead guilty in early January did McCord express relief to his presumed CIA bosses.

Hunt's proposed "CIA Defense," along with the Cubans' belief they were on a CIA mission, was actually buttressed, not weakened, by the loyal McCord's reporting to what appeared to be his Agency handlers. Indeed, his letters were so incriminating to the Agency that the Agency withheld them for months before reluctantly disclosing them.

Accordingly, by May 24–25, 1973, it was now unmistakable that Bittman and Hunt had been exploring the CIA defense. And if Hunt, a CIA

---

13 "Excerpts from Transcript of Testimony Before Senate's Committee on Watergate," *New York Times*, May 25, 1973.

veteran, was exploring it, one would infer, there must have been a sound basis for it. So merely reporting that this CIA veteran had wanted his notebooks because they supported CIA involvement in Watergate would have been explosive. But our Pulitzer Prizewinners carefully refrained from suggesting any such thing or from printing the full testimony of Alch or McCord on the CIA defense.

However, if the *Post* had written an article about Hunt's defense plans in that summer of 1973, such a planned defense would immediately have bolstered the notion that Gonzalez and Martinez, who claimed they believed they were on a CIA mission, were heady agents who knew of what they spoke and would have erased the picture of them as dupes. But the *Post* did not honestly portray this defense, covering up a key fact.

Woodstein and the *Post* had no motive in March 1973 to whitewash Dean's perfidy, but rather to the contrary, because in March 1973, Dean had not yet turned prosecution witness.

By the time Woodstein was writing their book in late 1973 and early 1974, however, Dean was the critical accuser of the president at a time when the availability and complete content of the presidential tapes was yet unknown. If the *Post* was falsely to slant its reporting to get Nixon, it would want, as of November 1973, to portray Dean as a choirboy caught in bad company. This was the case when Dean, spurred by the tapes' upcoming release right before his sentencing in early November 1973, suddenly remembered getting and destroying the Hermès notebooks. The fabled team did not write about this admission at the time, which they left to an article on November 6, 1973, by the *Post*'s Timothy Robinson, who explained Hunt's motivation for wanting the books:

> *The notebooks were important, according to Hunt, because they could have been used to support a defense that he thought the Watergate operation was legal because it had been approved by high government officials.*[14]

As noted above, when Woodstein reported in March 1973, they noted that the *investigators* would have wanted the notebooks, according to

14 Timothy S. Robinson, "Dean Admits He Destroyed Evidence," *Washington Post*, November 6, 1973.

the defense, to nail top-siders as part of the *prosecution*'s case. But when Robinson reported on Dean's admissions of destroying the evidence on November 6, 1973, he described Hunt as wanting them *to show a defense* of "approval by high government officials," a horse of a different color. This, of course, was only a defense if part of the CIA defense–that is, the approvals had to be of a national security CIA operation. So most likely Bittman had revealed, and Woodstein intentionally omitted, a key fact in March 1973 when they reported on Hunt's motives in wanting the notebooks, specifically that Hunt hoped to prove his CIA defense. But whether or not they hid this fact in March 1973, it appears the *Post* was still hiding the CIA aspect of this defense in November 1973, even if Robinson was more forthcoming in his reporting. Why wouldn't the *Post* explain exactly why approval by "high government officials" was a valid defense? This freely given admission by Hunt/Bittman to Robinson suggests that the exact same thing likely was told to Woodstein for their March 3, 1973, article.

In the same November 6, 1973, article, Robinson described the objections of Gonzalez and Martinez upon learning of Dean's notebook destruction, which was that it destroyed evidence that the operation was, as they believed, an ostensibly legal intelligence operation:

> *Attorney Daniel Schultz, who represents conspirators Bernard Barker, Eugenio Martinez, Vergilio Gonzalez, and Frank Sturgis, argued his clients' position that they should be allowed to withdraw their pleas because they thought the break-in was a legitimate government intelligence operation.*[15]

But Robinson did not connect Hunt's defense of high-level approval with the Gonzalez/Martinez defense of a "legitimate" national security "intelligence" operation.

At the time of publication of *All the President's Men* in April 1974, the *Post* was now protective of Dean, on deck as a key impeachment witness against Nixon. So when Woodstein wrote about Dean's destruction of the notebooks in their book, published when Nixon's impeachment was gaining steam, they did so in a misleading way in order to protect him:

---

15 Robinson, "Dean Admits."

> *In late 1973, John Dean acknowledged that he had destroyed the notebooks, which he had found the previous January in the President's personal financial file. The White House said, "The President did not know the notebooks were in his estate file," and declined further comment.*[16]

The omission of the true location of the "President's personal financial file" (which was in fact in Dean's office in his safe, as opposed to presidential custody) keeps the reader from inferring that it was Dean, not the president or his men, who hid these notebooks, thus concealing Dean's guilt and Nixon's innocence for that obstruction.

Once again, we must give the paper, and especially Woodstein, a failing grade for intentionally ignoring the CIA defense and Dean's role in destroying the missing Hermès notebooks, dishonestly protecting this star anti-Nixon witness. The evidence therefore strongly supports a verdict of deliberate suppression of evidence by the *Post* and its star reporters.

Now it is true that the *New York Times* did publish the Alch and McCord testimony. But it did so, without any accompanying framework of analysis, as part of a much larger publication of testimony, and in the context of seeming agreement by Senate questioners that the CIA involvement was simply a false defense briefly considered by a guilty defendant. The public in any case was not looking to the *Times* for analysis.

So informing the public of a nonfrivolous CIA defense to be presented by Hunt, who was apparently a CIA operative acting undercover through Mullen, would have caught public attention and diverted it away from the question of high-level White House participation. This would now raise a question that had never been a central issue in Watergate journalism: Exactly what were the burglars looking for, if not campaign information? Put another way, what would interest the CIA in Democratic National Committee phone calls?

One gateway into that subject would be the observations of the wiretapping monitor and seeming lookout, Alfred Baldwin III. To him the story now turns.

---

16 Bernstein and Woodward, *All the President's Men*, footnote on 273.

Chapter Fourteen

THE BALDWIN COVER-UP

While a somewhat obscure character in the popular lore of Watergate, Alfred Baldwin III is to serious students a key player in the scandal. That is so because he was for three weeks prior to the arrests the monitor of the wiretapping resulting from the prior burglary, one not initially known to the public. The phone calls to which he listened were not recorded, so he was the lone figure who could testify with personal knowledge as to the nature of the monitored conversations. The nature of these communications–so eagerly sought to be documented by the burglary's directors, on the phone of an unimportant figure, who was not even a direct DNC employee–should have removed the mystery surrounding what otherwise was an inexplicable third-rate fiasco.

But Baldwin's name was not known until relatively late in the reporting, and in his published interview and testimony, as we will see, he was not allowed to repeat conversations he actually heard. Indeed, at the criminal burglary trial he was not permitted to describe even the general nature of the conversations. So the public never got to hear his full account, which would identify the purpose of one of history's most impactful scandals.

Oddly, his failure to testify as to what he heard occurred while the trial court's feisty Judge John J. Sirica was loudly and continually demanding that the government prove the "motive and intent" of the crime, issues which could be elucidated immeasurably by Baldwin's identifying the true target of the burglary by describing its fruits. Ironically, Sirica was named *Time* magazine's Man of the Year for 1973 for his insistent demands in the face of what appeared to be a government cover-up to protect the White

House. Yet as we shall see, both Sirica and the prosecutors were stymied by the Democratic-friendly appellate court from hearing the most important evidence in this historically significant trial. And as we also shall see, the *Washington Post* stayed silent on what remained hidden by this unwarranted restriction of the public's right to know, an unforgivable cover-up of a cover-up.

How Baldwin was chosen to be on the burglary team has never been made clear and raises a number of puzzlements. Originally, Baldwin helped James McCord with personal security for Martha Mitchell, the former attorney general's somewhat erratic, alcohol-challenged wife. One assumes, of course, that McCord hired Baldwin on May 1, 1972, with the likelihood in mind of using him to monitor any wiretapping project.

We start out by describing what Baldwin actually heard. Prosecutor Earl Silbert's office extensively interviewed Baldwin in the fall of 1972 as a prosecution witness, as did the FBI, while the DNC lawyers interrogated Baldwin's lawyers. What did they learn? According to the most widely respected summary of Watergate, written by *New York Times* reporter Anthony Lukas, Baldwin was listening to lurid talk on the phone and extensions belonging to minor Democratic official Spencer Oliver Jr.:

> *Several secretaries used Oliver's phone because they thought it was the most private one in the office. They would say: "we can talk; I'm on Spencer Oliver's phone." Some of the conversations Baldwin recalls were "explicitly intimate"...Ehrlichman, after debriefing Magruder (in the wake of the arrests), reported, "what they were getting was mostly this fellow Oliver phoning his girlfriends all over the country lining up assignations." So spicy were some of the conversations on the phone that they have given rise to unconfirmed reports that the telephone was used for some sort of call girl service catering to congressmen and other prominent Washingtonians.*[1]

From Colodny and Gettlin's *Silent Coup*, we have the following summary of what was overheard:

---

1 Lukas, *Nightmare*, 201.

> *In a recent conversation with us, Howard Hunt said that the bugging target was not Wells or Oliver, "they just happened to be on the same phone, that's all."*
>
> *For corroboration that the phone tapped was in this area, and that the overheard conversations pertained to Cathy/Heidi's call-girl operation, we have to leap ahead in time...The evidence establishes that in the period just after the burglars had been caught and identified, and their criminal trial was imminent, the government's lead prosecutor, Assistant U.S. Attorney Earl J. Silbert, believed that the fruits of the Watergate break-in were embarrassing tapes of a sexual nature... Silbert believed that Hunt had intended to use the telephone conversations that Baldwin had overheard for purposes of blackmail.*
>
> *The evidence includes the fact that Baldwin characterized the conversations overheard as "explicitly intimate." In addition, federal prosecutors have confirmed that the telephone tap conversations were "primarily sexual" and "extremely personal, intimate, and potentially embarrassing."*[2]

The FBI soon got to Baldwin and in early July interviewed him about what he had heard during those two weeks. Bits of what Baldwin had overheard can be pieced together, albeit in fragments collated from several locations. Most assuredly, what he monitored was primarily intimate sexual talk of men arranging trysts with women. In a 1996 libel case deposition, the DNC's Robert Strauss testified to these assignations:

> *Some of the state chairmen (who) would come into (Oliver's) office and use the phone to make dates...in connection with the use of the telephones, some of the calls...could have been embarrassing to some of the people who made them.*[3]

2 Colodny and Gettlin, *Silent Coup*, 138–139.

3 Deposition of Robert Strauss, *Maureen and John Dean v. St. Martin's Press et al.*

James Rosen, then a stalwart reporter for Fox News, had interviewed Strauss. Rosen testified in the *Wells v. Liddy* trial to some astounding admissions by Strauss:

> *Democrats in from out of town for a night would want to be entertained..."It wasn't any organized thing, but I could have made the call, that lady could have made the call"–the reference was to Maxie Wells–"and these people were willing to pay for sex." Those were his exact words.*[4]

Liddy's lawyers had interviewed Maxie Wells's (Oliver's secretary) successor at the DNC, Barbara Kennedy Rhoden. Asked if she said, "It was likely that Spencer Oliver and Maxie Wells were running a call-girl operation," Rhoden replied: "I might have said that..." But, she added, "I have no knowledge that they were."[5]

Indeed, in Baldwin's first FBI interview in early July 1972, he told agents that the first call he listened to after McCord handed him the earphones was between "a man and a woman discussing their marital problem." He later said he had listened to "explicitly intimate conversations," which he repeated on September 28, 1972, to the *Los Angeles Times*, in excerpts published on October 5, 1972, albeit an admission buried deep in its recounting of Baldwin's experience.

As we will describe later, Baldwin was precluded from publicly testifying in the criminal trial by characterizing what types of conversations he overheard. But his deposition testimony years later, summarized below by Jim Hougan, makes it clear that the conversations were not innocent:

> *Baldwin was even more specific in a deposition that he later gave. According to the former FBI agent, many of the telephone conversations involved dinner arrangements with "sex to follow." And while he never heard "prices" being discussed, Baldwin testified, he guessed that "eight out of ten" people would have thought the calls involved prostitution. But he himself did not. As a former FBI agent, Baldwin knew that*

4 Testimony of James Rosen in the first *Wells v. Liddy* trial.

5 Testimony of Barbara Kennedy Rhoden, *Wells v. Liddy*.

> *for prostitution to occur, there has to be a promise of money. But money was never discussed, he said, or at least not in his hearing.*[6]

By mid-September 1972, if the *Post* did not know that intimate calls were a big portion of what Baldwin had overheard, every other interested player seemed to. Spencer Oliver Jr., for instance, was livid that the FBI was so energetically inquisitive about whether and how he had "marital problems," an inquiry clearly flowing from Baldwin's recountings. Oliver was so open with his discontent that the *Baltimore Sun* reported it fulsomely in a front-page story on September 22, 1972:

> *A Democratic party official whose phone was bugged says he finds it "frightening" that an FBI investigation is seemingly more concerned with probing into his life than with getting evidence on the wiretappers...*
>
> *...Oliver said four FBI agents have been spending the past week interviewing 80 staff members at party headquarters and asking such things as whether Oliver has marital problems and whether he works late at night in his office...*
>
> *..."They're asking the staff here what kind of person I am, do I come in here late, if I have marital problems."*[7]

The *New York Post* published an essentially identical piece on September 25, 1972, so the *Washington Post* cannot claim that it had no notice of what would seem to be a newsworthy story.

It would seem obvious that the FBI agents were not asking just about Oliver, since there were a number of callers using Oliver's line. Wouldn't some of these eighty staffers have been willing to share with Woodstein the very personal lines of inquiry the FBI was pursuing? It seems so.

Around the same time, by memo of September 15, 1972, John Dean advised the president's Oval Office team by memo that the Cubans' defense lawyer, Henry Rothblatt, was digging into the sex lives of DNC officials, based upon scuttlebutt relayed by CRP lawyers Paul O'Brien and Kenneth

6 Hougan, "On the New Inquisition," JimHougan.com, http://jimhougan.com/WatergateInquisition.html.

7 *Baltimore Sun*, September 22, 1972.

Parkinson. Rothblatt had taken Oliver's deposition on September 8, 1972, and CRP, DNC, and burglar lawyers knew he was inquiring into the lurid talk overheard by the wiretappers. If these lawyers attended Rothblatt's deposition, and Dean learned of these questions, wouldn't the great reporters from the *Post* have access to similar information?

According to the Silbert confirmation hearings, in the fall of 1972 his office investigated the motive for overhearing intimate conversations:

> *We never were able to determine the precise motivation for the burglary and wiretapping, particularly on the telephone of a comparative unknown–Spencer Oliver. Baldwin had told us that McCord wanted all telephone calls recorded, including personal calls. They were, many of them being extremely personal, intimate, and potentially embarrassing.*[8]

Silbert later testified:

> *Now with respect to the blackmail, possible blackmail. Baldwin had told us that McCord was interested in having him listen in to all of the conversations on the wiretaps, not only those relating to political intelligence but those that related to personal matters, and a number of those conversations were personal. And for that matter, why would he want that kind of information? And the logical inference that we drew, Senator, was that there might be some attempt to compromise, blackmail, compromise either the participants in those conversations, and that is why we suggested that not as the motive but as one of a possible variety of motives that might have impelled the conduct of these defendants, particularly Hunt and Liddy.*[9]

If during the scandal the broad public audience knew of this lewd talk, many would certainly have at least questioned whether the burglary was re-

8 "J. Response to Criticism Concerning Prosecutors' Suggestion of Political Blackmail as a Possible Motive," nomination of Earl J. Silbert to be United States Attorney: Hearing Before the Subcommittee on the Judiciary, 93rd Congress 1974, 65.

9 "J. Response to Criticism," 142.

ally about gathering campaign intelligence and therefore would have questioned the obvious inference that high White House officials might have been behind it. But the public received exactly the opposite sense from the *Post*—that is, that the wiretapping was in fact about political intelligence gathering, without any discussion targeting tawdry conversations.

As of late September 1972, curiously, no *Post* article had identified Baldwin as the wiretap monitor, nor had the *Post* reported sexual talk. The *Los Angeles Times* published the first Baldwin interview, amid great fanfare, on October 5, 1972, over three months after the burglary. But the fact that the FBI had Baldwin's first statement in early July 1972 led astute analysts to conclude that Deep Throat could not possibly have been an FBI agent. This was so because the timing suggests that this key source seemingly had not told his friend Woodward of this key witness and his three weeks of monitoring prior to the burglary arrests, a huge scoop.[10] Hougan states the consensus regarding Deep Throat not being with the FBI:

> *There were sources he did not have, and contrary to what Woodward tells us, one of the sources that he seems to have lacked was someone in the FBI. For example, one of the most critical and newsworthy developments in the Watergate affair was Alfred Baldwin's blockbuster confession concerning the electronic eavesdropping that he had conducted, the earlier May break-in and much more, but, like everyone else, Woodward and Bernstein did not learn about Baldwin until the Democrats held a press conference on the subject in September...*
>
> *For Throat to have known about Baldwin and not to have mentioned the matter to Woodward would have been an unconscionable breach of faith. The Post reporters risked their careers with every article they wrote, and much of what they*

10 Oddly, in a scandal with numerous oddities, reporter Tom Condon of the *Hartford Courant* published a short piece on September 25, 1972, with quotes from Baldwin casually admitting his role. Like other seminal stories, this one was not picked up by other papers and certainly not by the *Washington Post*. What this also shows is that Baldwin was available for a *Post* interview, which could have been obtained without any unethical payment to Baldwin.

> *wrote was falling on deaf ears, in part because the burglars were thought to have been ineffectual...*
>
> *Why, then, didn't Throat tell Woodward about Baldwin? The simplest explanation is best: he didn't know about him....*
>
> *The FBI's top echelon and many of its agents can be eliminated from consideration, since it was they who first developed the lines of investigation leading to Baldwin....*
>
> *Contrary to what Woodward says, therefore, Throat did not have sources in the FBI...*[11]

But, of course, while his logic was impeccable, we now know that Hougan was wrong, but why? Was it really the case that Deep Throat did not tell Woodward about Baldwin? Likely not. Hougan was correct that a Deep Throat from the FBI would likely have told Woodward of Baldwin.[12] And the broader question might be asked, given that Woodward likely knew of Baldwin: Why would the *Post* not print the scoop? Put differently, Woodward and Bernstein had numerous FBI sources, as well as Democratic legal sources connected to the DNC suit against CRP, all of whom knew of Baldwin and his role. Indeed, the DNC's lawyers were Williams, Connolly & Califano, and partner Joseph Califano was general counsel not only of the DNC but also of the *Post*. The DNC lawyers had access to Baldwin and interviewed him in August. Yet *Post* reporters never attempted to interview him and never reported his name (even then not identifying him as the monitor) until October 3, a day before the *Los Angeles Times* piece was about to break.

Of course, as I have noted, it is highly likely, to the point of metaphysical certitude, that the *Post* knew early on about Baldwin. In fact, likely before the *Post* knew what Baldwin would say, it gave strong indication in

11 Hougan, *Secret Agenda*, 284–285.

12 In fact, as Woodward and Bernstein wrote in *All the President's Men*, the two reporters had contacts deep and wide throughout the FBI, getting numerous tidbits from a number of agents. This disclosure was likely meant to throw analysts off the scent of Deep Throat's likely FBI employment by explaining how the reporters got some FBI-sourced information. It is true, though, that the reporters were well connected to a number of investigating agents, as shown by the erroneous tip from an FBI agent, likely Special Agent Angelo Lano, that Haldeman had been named by Hugh Sloan in grand jury testimony as a slush fund signatory.

an article on June 27, 1972, that the DNC had already gained access to Baldwin's lawyers, who would represent the only party who knew of the first wiretapping and who was talking:

> *The Democrats believe their party headquarters may have been under surveillance for several weeks before the arrests were made.*[13]

It is reasonable to infer that the *Post* never published a story featuring Baldwin as the monitor, prior to the *Los Angeles Times* report, precisely because the *Post* had in its files vivid descriptions of what Baldwin overheard, which the paper had obtained from DNC lawyers, Baldwin's own Democratic-friendly lawyers, and the FBI. Let me explain.

There were pending both the civil suit and the criminal trial in which the parties had subpoena power, so any printed piece naming Baldwin might "win" the *Post* the duty to turn over its presumably red-hot notes. And if it did, the Watergate spotlight would shift away from the Republican White House's possible guilt in a "third-rate" burglary to a sleazy Democratic National Committee that arranged call girls for its bigwigs.

Each step that the *Post* took to avoid a Baldwin subpoena, ironically, is proof that it had much embarrassing material to offer in response to such a subpoena.

Circumstances suggest that the *Post* selected the *Los Angeles Times* as its cutout to break the Baldwin story. The *LA Times* was not a true competitor of the *Post*, whereas the *New York Times* and *Boston Globe* were. So it made sense that a West Coast paper would break the Baldwin interview. This allowed the *Post* to be the first East Coast paper to publish the reprint of the *Los Angeles Times* article of October 5,[14] as well as Baldwin's first-person account. Given that the DNC and Califano seemingly controlled Baldwin's lawyer, John Cassidento, and therefore Baldwin, yet did not give the story to the *Post* (which was so intimate with the DNC and its general counsel Califano) is highly suspicious, albeit not conclusively probative.

---

13 James Mann, "O'Brien Suit Is Heard," *Washington Post*, June 27, 1972, C1–C2.

14 The *Times* may have published a late-edition Baldwin story on October 4, by Bernstein's account in *All the President's Men*.

But it is beyond doubt that the *Post* scooped the *Los Angeles Times* by publishing all the key facts before October 5. And the *Post* did so by isolating itself from Baldwin in ways that in hindsight can only be viewed as showing the *Post*'s guilty institutional mind.

The *Post*, for example, made sure it let all readers know it received its earlier, pre-*Times* facts not from Baldwin directly but from the DNC, much of it from a public DNC press conference of September 6, such that there would be no basis for a court to believe the *Post* had hidden information that called for a subpoena. Even at that, the DNC did not even call Baldwin by name but called him an "unimpeachable source" who was, according to the *Post*, a "self-described participant."

But wait–isn't it odd that the DNC would not call Baldwin by his name, which it knew? The only reason for this failure would be that the *Post* and the DNC had a deal with the *Los Angeles Times* that the *Times* would be the first to name Baldwin as a monitor.

The *Post* further isolated itself from a Baldwin subpoena by claiming in its September 11 article that "the *Post* could not learn the name of the person who provided the Democrats with the purported account of the operation." This most certainly was a lie, but one designed for even more protection against a subpoena of Baldwin notes, especially since the statement implied, falsely as well, that the paper had no other information about the unnamed participant.

How did the DNC protect itself from subpoena? Many observers have scratched their heads at the strange non-interview interview of Baldwin by a WCC lawyer on August 26, 1972, at Cassidento's Hartford, Connecticut, office. Rather than question Baldwin, Alan Galbraith, the WCC lawyer, representing the DNC, asked Cassidento and his associate, Robert Mirto, a question, whereupon one lawyer would leave the room, seemingly to ask Baldwin in another room outside the view of the WCC lawyer, then return with an answer.

This odd procedure ensured that no subpoena could ever require production of any embarrassing answer. If the WCC attorney had asked the questions directly to Baldwin, the answers would not be protected by attorney-client privilege but only by the qualified immunity of the "work product" doctrine.[15]

WCC's odd questioning ensured against this because WCC did not receive answers from the witness but only from the lawyer outside the presence of the witness, which would therefore remain protected by privilege.[16] And the *Post* could say, we assume, that it had not interviewed Baldwin, and thereby could fight a subpoena, even though, we also assume, it had information in its files about Baldwin relayed through WCC, as a June 27, 1972 article suggests.

Both the *Post* and the DNC thereby protected themselves from disclosure of dirty secrets. But if they so much wanted protection, why the monthlong (in September 1972) publicity campaign by both, generally revealing all of the facts subsequently printed in the supposed *Los Angeles Times* "scoop"? Because there was much in Baldwin's knowledge that, if separated from sex talk, could be used to point at the Nixon administration, material consistent with at least part of what the FBI was finding.

To be sure, a few political conversations, quite minor, were overheard, but they were important for McCord to use to fool Liddy that this was political espionage. And Baldwin knew by hearsay of Republican authorization supposedly going up the chain to Mitchell. Perhaps because of this need to show a political connection, but purpose still unclear, McCord, when out of town June 7–8, had Baldwin rush to the CRP with an envelope of recent logs.[17] McCord did bring Baldwin with a group on a senseless mission one night to case the McGovern headquarters, being sure to include Liddy, all for "political spying" show for Liddy.

---

15 Under this doctrine, if a witness, for example, said in court that she could not remember the speed of the auto before the accident but did remember when Attorney Jones questioned her shortly after the incident, the court would normally find "good cause" or "necessity" and order production of interview notes from Attorney Jones.

16 Certainly the DNC was briefed on Baldwin's knowledge before Galbraith's non-interview interview, one instance being Edward Bennett Williams briefing of Larry O'Brien on August 15. We assume that with this foreknowledge, Galbraith stayed away from explicit details of Baldwin's overhearings.

17 McCord refused to name the guard who was to receive this package, perhaps Lou Russell, and claimed before the Ervin Committee it had nothing to do with Watergate. It may well have had sensitive "take," which, as in other CIA operations using White House cover, the CIA wished to keep out of White House hands.

So if Baldwin would refuse to detail sex conversations and simply state he was listening to both political and personal talk, his account could be used to support a largely false narrative that the operation was targeting political espionage. That is precisely what the *Post* did in September 1972 to suggest political targets of the monitoring.

Contrary to journalistic legend, it was not the October 5, 1972, *LA Times* article that first broke the story of the prior wiretaps. It was the September 6 DNC press conference, reported by the *Post*, albeit not referring to Baldwin by name or referring to a monitor. The *Post* had no admitted knowledge of whether there really had been such a tap,[18] on O'Brien's line, but it quoted O'Brien's suggestion that the wiretaps had overheard him, or had attempted to hear him, discussing confidential campaign strategy:

> *O'Brien, now national campaign director for Sen. McGovern, said that during the time his phone was tapped he "had conversations with perhaps every prominent Democrat in America, including every candidate for the Democratic presidential nomination."*
>
> *From the phone tap and information revealed last week to have been photocopied from his files, "People could–out of context–develop some ideas that might be useful or helpful in the campaign," O'Brien said.*[19]

The *Post* here knew that it was creating a false impression. By uncritically reporting O'Brien's claims, it omitted far more than simply the lack of a provable tap on O'Brien. It omitted its knowledge that O'Brien had not been in town for several weeks when he was on these supposedly strategic calls, and that all the key players, including the Republicans, knew it. So O'Brien could not possibly have been a target, faulty tap or no.

Of course, by noting O'Brien's present position as "a national campaign director" for McGovern (likely a ceremonial, overblown title), the *Post* suggested that O'Brien had confidential information in June about the not

18 Even if the Post had knowledge of an FBI or DNC interview of Baldwin, which was likely, it would have known that McCord told Baldwin that the O'Brien bug did not work and would have also learned that Baldwin had been listening only to Oliver's phone.

19 Bernstein and Woodward, "Watergate Called Part of Big GOP Plan–More Phone Taps Charged," *Washington Post*, September 8, 1972, A6.

yet nominated McGovern's campaign strategies, when in fact he had none. And the *Post* headline called the Watergate taps "Part of Big GOP plan," a claim with no basis.

Finally, the article sets up its subsequent articles by noting the names of Glenn Sedam and Robert Odle of the CRP, among others, as potential witnesses to be called, both suggesting and foreshadowing the future false claim that these officials received the June 7–8 wiretap logs from Baldwin, or at least were part of the illegal operation:

> *The following eight persons associated with the Committee for the Re-election of the President will also be summoned: Clark MacGregor, the head of the committee; Jeb Magruder, Fred LaRue, Robert C. Odle, Jr., Robert Mardian, a former assistant attorney general in charge of internal security; J. Glenn Sedam, John J. Caulfield and Sally H. Harmony, the secretary to G. Gordon Liddy, the former finance counsel to the committee.*[20]

The next day, Woodstein inserted yet another deceptive assertion to prove the theme of political spying by distorting FBI conclusions:

> *Handicapped by the absence of an insider's account of how and why and for whom the Democratic offices were invaded, FBI agents were not able to learn positively the exact objective of the Watergate break-in–but there is no question that intelligence gathering was at least a major part of it.*
> *"All I know is the evidence," one person with access to FBI files said. "And on that score we've pretty much come to the end of it...without any of it making too much sense."*[21]

This article is cleverly constructed to say that, while federal authorities couldn't make complete sense of the objectives of the wiretapping, clearly "intelligence" (connotation: overhearing political strategy) was one of them. No FBI official actually said that, which is precisely the point: the

20 Bernstein and Woodward, "Watergate Called Part of Big GOP Plan."

21 Bernstein and Woodward, "Justice Completes Watergate Probe," *Washington Post*, September 9, 1972, A6.

agents, in fact, *couldn't* say that *political* conversation was the target, but the *Post* inserted its own word "intelligence" to give that false impression. (Clearly, any wiretap seeks some form of intelligence.) Because of this willful suppression of what it knew, the *Post* created the long-enduring "mystery" of why the astute Nixon would wish to burgle such an odd target. So let's clear up the mystery now: Nixon did not wish to do so, and there was never a target of political intelligence.

In the next article, designed to pave the way for the *Los Angeles Times* Baldwin interview (and to disclose even more of the coming *Times* scoop), Woodstein revealed more new details. First, they identified on September 11 the source of the allegations as a "self-described participant" in the buggings. Then it claimed "the *Post* could not learn the name of the person who provided the Democrats with the purported account of the operation."

When Baldwin was set up for this *Los Angeles Times* interview on September 28, 1972, his lawyers had provided him with a valid legal excuse for not telling all to the interviewer:

> *On the advice of his lawyers, Baldwin declined to give specifics on the conversations he monitored. The attorneys told him that he would be violating the federal wiretapping statute if he disclosed the contents of those conversations.*[22]

The Baldwin story was reprinted in the *Post* on October 6, 1972, with two other lengthy accompanying articles: Baldwin's first-person statement, reprinted from the *Times*; and the *Post*'s own "advance" on the *Times* story, inaccurately naming the CRP's Robert Odle and Glenn Sedam, as well as William Timmons, a White House aide, as likely wiretap log recipients. In *All the President's Men*, Woodstein admitted their highly damaging mistake. But falsely naming these men helped to firmly establish the *Post*'s narrative because these innocent men connected the wiretapping to CRP and White House political designs.

Almost all of the three lengthy stories carefully culled the details showing seeming political purpose for the wiretaps. Buried deep in Baldwin's

22 Jack Nelson and Ronald J. Ostrow, "Bugging Witness Tells Inside Story on Incident at Watergate," *Los Angeles Times*, October 5, 1972, 31.

first-person account (page 38 of the October 6 *Post*) was his revelation of racy talk, perhaps confusing secretaries with other professional ladies:

> *But a number of persons besides Oliver used his phone, too. Over the next three weeks I would monitor approximately 200 telephone conversations. Some dealing with political strategy and others concerning personal matters...*
>
> *...with several secretaries and others using the phone, apparently in the belief it was one of the more private lines in the Democratic offices, some conversations were explicitly intimate.*
>
> *"We can talk," a secretary would say, "I'm on Spencer Oliver's phone."*[23]

Of course, there was not a word printed thereafter by the otherwise aggressive *Post* reporters delving into the "explicitly intimate" conversations, Oliver's marital issues, or the sex lives of the DNC officials.

The *Post* and the DNC, as planned, successfully avoided subpoena, while, as suspected, the *Los Angeles Times* interview tape and its reporters were dragooned into Sirica's court to nobly lose its fight against production, giving them their Watergate badges of honor.

But in hindsight, Woodstein and the *Post* realized that history would view their September 11 denials of knowing Baldwin's name, and their claims of being scooped, with great skepticism. So in *All the President's Men*, Woodstein bravely attempted to explain the inexplicable–why they missed the scoop–by casting Ben Bradlee as a noble editor:

> *On September 11, Bernstein and Woodward had written a story about the participation of such a former FBI agent.*
>
> *A week later, with help from the Bookkeeper, they had identified him as Baldwin, a 35-year-old law-school graduate... He seemed to have unimaginable secrets to tell, and reporters were in line to hear them. Woodward had joined the queue. He began making regular phone calls to Baldwin's lawyer,*

23 "Phone Monitored for 3 Weeks," *Washington Post*, October 6, 1972, A1, A38.

> *John Cassidento, a Democratic state legislator from New Haven, Connecticut.*
>
> *"We've got hundreds of requests for interviews, hundreds," Cassidento had told Woodward. "Everyone wants to talk to Al. There are two* Los Angeles Times *reporters camped out there. Al is getting no peace..."*
>
> *Several days later, Cassidento called Woodward back. "Hey, Al needs some money...Everyone is offering him money for his story. Just want to let you know in case you want to enter the bidding." It was rumored that a major magazine had offered $5000 for Baldwin's first-person account.*
>
> *Woodward explained that the Post never paid for news.*
>
> *"Okay, okay, I'm sorry you don't care about the story," said Cassidento. "We have other offers."*
>
> *Woodward started to say that the Post cared very much about the story, but Cassidento had hung up.*
>
> *Woodward and Bernstein told the editors about the invitation to bid on Baldwin's story. "I bid this..." Bradlee said, and raised the middle finger of his right hand.*
>
> *Two weeks later, and without paying a penny, the* Los Angeles Times *had gotten the story that brought Woodward back to his desk the night of October 4...*
>
> *Woodward and Bernstein were aced out...*
>
> *"I would like to have had that one," Bradlee said the next day...*[24]

All of this is obviously arrant nonsense. It does not explain how all these other "camped out" newspapers knew of Baldwin before the *Post* did. Since these apocryphal papers were supposedly eager to interview Baldwin, they had to have known why it would have been a scoop. If they did know it, they could still publish the story about Baldwin and what he'd allegedly heard even without an interview.[25] And so could have the *Post*! And if the *Post* didn't

24 Bernstein and Woodward, *All the President's Men*, 109–110.

25 Belying all that Woodstein put forth in their lame defense regarding Baldwin, a young *Hartford Courant* reporter, Tom Condon, called up Baldwin, spoke with him, and published a nice piece confirming Baldwin's role on September 25, 1972! Perhaps Woodstein could have done the same.

get the interview because it wouldn't pay, how did the *Times* get it without paying? If the *Post* did not know Baldwin's name until around September 18 as claimed, why had its close ally, the DNC, not given it to them previously? And why would the DNC itself not reveal the name in its press conference, unless it was honoring a *Post/Times/*DNC deal?

In the narrative above, note that Woodstein got Baldwin's name not from one of its many street-level FBI sources, from Deep Throat, from the DNC, from the WCC law firm, or from its general counsel, but from...the CRP bookkeeper! This occurred per this account around September 18.

Yet, just a page later in their book, they talked about their "advance" on the Baldwin story, which they obtained from the DNC investigator (read: WCC) confirmed by a Justice Department source (read: FBI) two weeks before the *Times* interview (which occurred on September 28). So their sources finally leaked as to Baldwin, by this account, on September 14, four days before the bookkeeper! But they waited weeks to print this "advance" until *after* the *Times* printed its scoop:

> *But two weeks before the* Los Angeles Times *interview, Bernstein had been told by a Democratic Party investigator that Baldwin had named two persons he thought had received them: Robert Odle, Jeb Magruder's intensely nervous aide-de-camp at both the White House and CRP; and William E. Timmons, Assistant to the President for congressional relations and chief White House liaison to CRP for the Republican national convention. Baldwin had seen McCord addressing the memos...*
>
> *...Bernstein suggested to Woodward that they write a story saying that Baldwin had named Odle and Timmons, and describing how he picked Sedam's name. Bernstein called a Justice Department source who confirmed the details. Woodward agreed to go ahead.*
>
> *The story would be a significant advance on the Los Angeles Times account. It ran on October 6. There were no denunciations from CRP or the White House.*[26]

26 Bernstein and Woodward, *All the President's Men*, 111–112.

All of this is too big a pill to swallow, and we do not need to try. The *Post* was deeply dishonest in all things Baldwin and went to acrobatic lengths to avoid revealing what we now know to have occurred on the phone lines of an otherwise unimportant Democratic official. Of course, Woodstein here soft-soaps the tremendous damage done to Odle, Timmons, and Sedam, whom they later acknowledged in their book had been falsely accused, seriously defaming them.

Following the *Times* article, the *Post* unleashed its series of October 1972 articles, beginning October 10, inspired by Deep Throat, on the Segretti campaign, the slush fund, and the overall campaign of electoral "spying and sabotage." All of this combined to make an explosive political scandal out of what had been a strange and inexplicable "third-rate burglary." Much of the import of the explosive October 10 Segretti article was set up by the building Baldwin story throughout the preceding month, all of which was slanted toward the political and away from the meretricious.

It was fine and dandy for the *Post*, the DNC, and the CIA (through McCord's assistant Baldwin) all to suggest that the burglary was about spying for political intelligence and the later Segretti story to put the alleged political spying in a larger narrative context. But looming ahead was a burglary trial in which Baldwin would be forced to testify, presumably about what he had overheard. There the political spying narrative would face a serious challenge, where the stern, no-nonsense Judge Sirica had been forcefully demanding that the prosecution prove the motive of the burglary, including the persons authorizing it. And what better way to prove motive than to show the sexual fruits being harvested?

Once again, at trial the DNC and its lawyers would successfully cover up the truth about Watergate, and once again, the *Post*, in partisan collaboration with the DNC, would successfully conceal the truth from the public. But the challenge they all faced was stiff, and the story of how they overcame it highly intriguing. To that we will now proceed.

Chapter Fifteen

THE BURGLARY TRIAL CONCEALMENT

By the end of October 1972, the narrative about the Watergate burglary had both changed dramatically and become overwhelmingly dominant in public discourse. No longer was the burglary a puzzling, isolated episode of minor criminality, provenance unclear, but rather had become a nasty conspiracy of political spying and sabotage directed from the highest parts of the White House and CRP, through use of a secret "slush fund." This advancement in the narrative came at least partially as a result of blatantly dishonest reporting by a paper that had posed convincingly as courageously independent but in reality was the house organ of the Democratic National Committee. Clear evidence of CIA sponsorship was actively hidden, as was the intimate nature of what was overheard. The journalism was very successful nonetheless, and the *Post* only grew in stature as a result.[1]

1 To be sure, the White House *did* engage in a sabotage program through Segretti, but Watergate was not part of it. Watergate was rather a detour that was likely the brainchild of Dean (which he denies) and Hunt–likely Hunt inveigling, for CIA purposes, the overly ambitious counsel to get dirt on the Democrats. But because of the connection of Segretti to Hunt and Liddy, Segretti's nominal supervisors, the Segretti program should have been, to be sure, explored as part of the Watergate investigation, as Deep Throat sought. Because the Segretti program originated in the White House with Nixon aide Dwight Chapin, and Segretti had been paid by Nixon's personal lawyer Herbert Kalmbach, it was a logical, but ultimately incorrect, inference that the burglary was also hatched in the higher echelons of the White House. The reporting was true about Segretti, but it omitted, as we have noted, other parts of the "spying and sabotage" narrative, specifically that Watergate was only superficially similar.

If this was indeed a *Post* cover-up, however, the paper–and the DNC–were not yet out of the woods as trial began in January of 1973. Both the CIA's involvement and the naughty girl theme were still looming as threats to the *Post*'s neat, compelling story of an amoral presidency.

With the January 1973 trial on the horizon in fall 1972, several key players were vulnerable to potentially devastating harm. If it were to surface that there had been a call girl referral operation at the DNC, the Democrats, now riding high on offense, might soon lose both their lawsuit and their increasing political capital. The CIA, after claiming adamantly that it had nothing to do with Watergate, might see its top officials fired, deprived of pensions, and perhaps put in jail. The *Post*, after fending off brutal attacks from the White House and winning increasing public confidence, faced a fall from grace back to its local-rag past. And John Dean, if exposed as perhaps the highest official authorizing Liddy's operation (which he denies), would face not only loss of his prestigious job but his freedom as well.

Several developments threatened all these players. It was not a secret amongst the lawyers in the criminal case that Howard Hunt was planning a CIA defense. Hunt's case would not be far off that planned by the prosecution. Lead government assistant US attorney Earl Silbert, or "Earl the Pearl," was an excellent, dynamic trial prosecutor who saw both the CIA connection of the burglars and the lewd calls monitored by Baldwin as providing Hunt's motive. Fortunately for the entities at risk here, Silbert was also meticulously ethical about not leaking harmful evidence, so he sought no pretrial publicity about his intentions.

Also fortunately for the CIA, DNC, and *Washington Post*, and unfortunately for both Hunt and Silbert, Dean hid the Hermès notebooks he had pulled from Hunt's safe, denying knowledge of them to the inquiring prosecutors in December 1972, after Hunt sought them in discovery. This seeming treachery kept valuable evidence from Hunt, from the prosecution, and from the public.

Coincidentally, if one believes in coincidence, Hunt's wife and former CIA agent Dorothy Hunt's plane crashed near Chicago on December 8, 1972, killing her as she carried hush money for the bug fabricator, as Hunt was continuing, even without the notebooks, to forge his defense–

perhaps not a defense with which the CIA was happy. It is theoretically possible that the CIA did not cause the plane crash, but if it did not, it was supernaturally lucky. Eventually, the combination of no wife and no notebooks sucked the fight from Hunt, who finally gave into Dean's imprecations to plead guilty in January 1973.

It was in December 1972 that the DNC, along with its attorneys and the *Post*, revealed its desperate need to keep the CIA and the girl talks out of evidence. Their main challenge was limiting the testimony of Baldwin, who had already told the FBI of the intimate conversations he'd overheard. Their answer was Charles O. Morgan Jr.

In December 1972, burglary prosecutor Silbert and his assistant Seymour Glanzer received a lunch invitation from Morgan, a prominent civil rights litigator long associated with the ACLU. The Democrats, through Morgan, sought to quash even the general *characterization* of the overheard conversations (which they knew Silbert would adduce), as well as the substance of the conversations themselves, with the genteel Morgan clothed in the garb of a noble civil rights protector. His theory: it was illegal to disclose the contents of illegally overheard conversations, even in trial, or even any general characterization of them, which, if not illegal in itself, could lead on cross-examination to a fuller, and allegedly illegal, specification of what had been actually overheard. Morgan represented not only Oliver's Democratic group, the Association of Democratic Chairmen (ADC)[2], but also Oliver and his secretary, Maxie Wells, so that he could point to specific individual victims of the threatened disclosures.[3] Interestingly, the likelihood was small that either of these two individuals themselves had meretricious conversations, and for Oliver the worst phone conversations would likely have been dialogue between him and a legitimate girlfriend.

The DNC's (and likely the *Post*'s) worst nightmares were confirmed at the lunch. Silbert gave Morgan and his associate a very frank overview of

2 While Watergate lore has the Nixonites wiretapping the DNC, in fact Oliver's group, the ADC, was not a formal part of the DNC, albeit closely associated, but likely obtaining separate funding. Perhaps for this reason, the ADC phones were separately owned, did not go through the DNC switchboard, and therefore were secure phones ideal for intimate conversations.

3 There was a very impressive list of Democratic officials from throughout the country overheard on Oliver's line. It is not clear if they were speaking from Oliver's office.

his case: Hunt, according to Silbert, was monitoring these naughty conversations precisely because of his position within the CIA front organization Mullen and Company. It seems, truly coincidentally, that Hunt's rival for the ascendency in the company, with its fat government contracts, was one Spencer Oliver Sr., the father of Spencer Oliver Jr.! And Oliver Sr. had tried to bring Oliver Jr. aboard over Hunt's objection. Silbert, connecting the dots in a reasonable but not perfectly accurate way, concluded that Hunt must have been seeking girly dirt for purposes of extorting Oliver Sr. so that Hunt could become the lead Mullen dog. Clearly, Silbert's theory fit broadly with the evidence and would have caused a stir. Moreover, it would have raised the topics both of the naughty girl conversations and the CIA's involvement in monitoring same. And it would also, not incidentally, have absolved the Nixon administration of high-level responsibility for the burglaries. To Silbert, this was a rogue operation not authorized by the CRP, and the only political party deserving of shame was Democratic.

Parenthetically, Silbert's team reacted venomously to any suggestion that a CIA defense was anything other than "spurious" or "phony." They were worried because they clearly knew that the facts supported such a defense, which would result in embarrassing acquittals.

"Hunt was trying to blackmail Spencer," Silbert told Morgan, emphatically pounding the table, "and I'm going to prove it!" With that statement also witnessed by his associate Hope Eastman, Morgan had what he needed at least to put on a prima facie showing, however weak, of potential illegal disclosure of personally embarrassing overheard conversations, and hopefully to quash the anticipated Baldwin testimony characterizing the naughty talk.

There were three big stumbling blocks, however, to Morgan's admittedly "unprecedented longshot" initiative, which any criminal lawyer would immediately see. First, the ADC, Oliver, and Wells had no standing in a criminal case to object to anything because they weren't parties. A criminal case is brought by the government–of the federal, state, county, or smaller governmental entity–against the individual defendant. Morgan's clients, in short, were not parties and could not object to evidence. Today, many states give criminal victims "rights" to limited participation, usually at sentencing. But there were not even these limited rights in 1973.

Secondly, as suggested above, Morgan's legal argument, which sounds good at first hearing, made no sense. What if, in order to prove illegal wiretapping, the prosecution needed to have testimony that the defendant had repeated certain conversations to a particular witness, which conversations had been said only in private on a telephone line and thus inferentially proved the illegal wiretap? Is the prosecution barred from introducing the contents of that conversation, which would be needed to prove the crime? That would make no sense, yet that is what Morgan was arguing. What if, more to the point, the crime charged was the illegal disclosure itself? Is the prosecutor barred from presenting evidence on the very crime charged, on the theory that it is illegal to disclose (in court) illegally overheard conversations? Of course not. According to Morgan, if a defendant overheard electronically the statement by John Doe that "Socrates is a man," a witness could not testify that the defendant told him that Doe had said, "Socrates is a man." If so, the prosecution could never prove such a crime. Criminal libel is proved, for example, by repeating the libelous statement in court, which is not illegal if for purposes of proof. In short, otherwise illegal statements are often repeated in court as a part of a criminal prosecution.

Thirdly, the prosecution was not even attempting to introduce the overheard conversations themselves but only a general *characterization* of the conversations. That is, that they were explicitly intimate and dealt with sexual assignations. Morgan's retort, noted above, was that such general characterization could lead to more explicit disclosures on cross-examination. This was a legitimate argument, if one accepts that disclosure in court was illegal, but presupposed that specific conversations would be both relevant and admissible, a questionable premise.[4] Why would it make a difference what the nature of the sexual act discussed was? Or the price? Courts deal with these issues every day, and could have done so here, restricting witnesses from repeating the unnecessary specifics of embarrassing conversations. So, in short, the move by Morgan was an admitted long shot, unless he got help from a friendly judiciary.

---

4 Courts often find fair ways to restrict scurrilous testimony, where the prejudicial value outweighs the probative value, while allowing into evidence the probative parts of the proposal testimony.

In each of the following public hearings, the colloquy about blackmail was anything but incidental. On January 3, 1973, five days before the burglary trial was to begin, Charles O. Morgan Jr. filed his motion to suppress the conversations overheard by Baldwin. After the clerk denied them that day, Morgan readied for an emergency appeal to be filed the next day. But Sirica had a change of heart, had Morgan into chambers, and set the motion for hearing on January 5. But the primary focus of that hearing was never reported.

Rather than report on Silbert's intentions to emphasize the explosive theme of blackmail, the *Post* avoided altogether this intriguing dialogue, both before Sirica and David Bazelon, chief judge of the Court of Appeals for the District of Columbia. Before the motion and later appeals were argued, the *Post* published a deceptively vanilla description of the motion, concealing the central content:

> *The American Civil Liberties Union, acting on behalf of several officials and employees of the Democratic Party, asked the presiding judge in the Watergate bugging trial yesterday to suppress any evidence or testimony that would reveal the substance of illegally wiretapped telephone conversations.*
>
> *The motion, set for a hearing today, asks Chief U.S. District Judge John J. Sirica to order 18 officials from the Nixon administration, the White House and the Committee to Re-Election of the President to testify secretly under oath whether they received any logs, memorandums or other communications describing conversations that may have been monitored in the Democratic National Committee's Watergate headquarters....*
>
> *The motion was filed after reportedly unsuccessful attempts were made to receive assurances from the prosecution that neither the participants, nor the substance of allegedly bugged conversations would be revealed in testimony or submitted as evidence. The motion contends that disclosure "of all or any part of the contents" is unnecessary to establish the guilt of the seven persons charged in the case....*

> *The motion asserts that any further disclosure "of any part of the contents or answers at trial or otherwise" would violate federal law and the "rights of privacy and political and private speech and association" guaranteed under the Bill of Rights.*[5]

During the open court hearing that day, January 5, 1973, Morgan came right out to deliver what should have been a stunning headline in the *Post*. He quickly told Sirica that the prosecutors intended to prove "the motive in this case was blackmail, not politics."

Sirica asked Morgan, "You say the motive the government expects to show is blackmail?"

"Yes," Morgan replied.

"That is the first time I heard that," Sirica rejoined.

In his book *One Man, One Voice*, Morgan quipped, "Actually, it was the second time in ten minutes that he had heard that, for McCord's lawyer, Gerald Alch, had told him 'hypothetically' that was what the prosecution might do." Morgan then launched into a discussion of what he knew, but the court did not, was one of the few "political" calls that the operation netted. A Republican official named Harry Flemming had been overheard talking to Oliver, causing his demotion. Later it was discovered that the call was innocent, part of a bipartisan activity of a club to which Flemming and Oliver both belonged. Now, of course, by revealing this call, Morgan was violating the law, at least according to his own argument!

But this call gave Morgan an opportunity to claim that the electronic monitoring was for a "political use rather than blackmail as a use." Notwithstanding Morgan's argument, Sirica ruled in favor of the prosecution. The fact that blackmail evidence was seemingly forthcoming should have been newsworthy, but the *Post* deemed it otherwise. The paper reported nothing about the blackmail argument, which would have raised the question: blackmail threatening revelation of what dark secrets?

At the appellate hearing one week later, Morgan repeated Silbert's dramatic statement made to Morgan at their December lunch: "Hunt was trying to blackmail Spencer, and I'm going to prove it!" Morgan then made

5 Lawrence Meyer, "Evidence Suppression Asked in Bug Case," *Washington Post*, January 5, 1973, A4.

a show of speaking with Hope Eastman at counsel table, who assured him that he repeated the words exactly, then telling the three judges, "I find no attempt at blackmail. The only purpose for it is it looks mighty good. Mr. Hunt went off on his own adventure and nobody else knew anything about it."

Apparently persuaded that the blackmail motive was a ruse to embarrass Democrats and unnecessary to prove the prosecution's case, the court of appeals overturned Sirica.

It is of note that there was no detailed *Post* coverage of the arguments before both Sirica and Bazelon. In both arguments, Morgan explicitly noted Silbert's planned blackmail motive, indeed dwelled on it at hearing. An incredulous Bazelon, not understanding the tight-lipped Silbert's intended evidence, questioned whether it made sense for anyone to blackmail Oliver Jr., a man with presumably modest wealth. One would think that these musings by Bazelon would invoke at least a modest headline. My point here, of course, is that the blackmail motive was not even hinted at by the *Post* for its readers' consideration. Not a word about "blackmail" or "extortion," indeed, was published by the *Post*, even after this second public discussion before the DC appellate court.

Certainly, the *Washington Star-News*, the only other major local DC paper, thought the blackmail ruling was highly significant. The paper gave the story a front-page headline [6] with a report emphasizing the scrutiny the topic should be afforded:

> *Charles Morgan, Jr., an American Civil Liberties Union attorney, who has filed a motion relating to the Watergate case, told the U.S. Court of Appeals today that on December 22 a prosecutor told him "Hunt was trying to blackmail Spencer and I'm going to prove it."*
>
> *Asked by an appellate Judge which prosecutor this was, Morgan replied, "It was Mr. Silbert." Silbert, arguing after Morgan had finished, said that he "must disagree with Mr. Morgan as to the conclusion he draws" about the two men's conversation that Friday before Christmas. As on Friday*

6 *Washington Star-News*, January 12, 1973, 1.

> *Morgan said today he did not believe that blackmail was the motive behind the bugging plot for which seven men were finally charged.*
>
> *"I find no attempt at blackmail," Morgan told the Judges. "The only purpose I can find for it (attempting to show blackmail was the motive) is that it looks mighty good. Mr. Hunt went off on his own adventure and nobody else knew anything about it."*
>
> *Morgan was implying that Silbert might be taking this tack at trial in order to counter suspicion that Hunt and the six men indicted with him were, in fact, working for high-ranking Nixon administration or Nixon campaign officials.*

Of course, the story, printed by DC's second-fiddle newspaper, was picked up nowhere. At the very least, the *Post* could have reprinted the story, giving it widespread circulation, just like it had reprinted the *Los Angeles Times* Baldwin piece. But to report on the story, the *Post* need not even reprint the *Star-Times* article since its own reporters were in court and able to cover it through its own original journalism.

Having mischaracterized Morgan's motion, and staying mum on the arguments about a blackmail motive, the *Post* continued to claim, as it had in earlier articles–and as did Sirica from the bench–that the prosecution was not proving the motive for the burglaries, thus implying that the Nixon administration, not the *Post* and the DNC, was still covering up the true burglary motivation as the *Post* and others had documented in a spate of earlier articles:

> *"Judge Asks Broader 'Bug' Trial,"* Washington Post, *December 5, 1972;*
>
> *"Judge Wants Prosecution to Widen Watergate Case,"* Washington Post, *A14, cols. 1–3; "Watergate Judge Hints at Wider Trial,"* New York Times, *December 5, 1972; "Watergate Motives Sought,"* Washington Star-News, *December 6, 1972.*

The *Post*, even after the blackmail arguments began, retreated to its narrative gift from Deep Throat, to wit, the logical assessment that the burglaries were likely a part of the Segretti "dirty tricks" program, lobbying for this motive and intent evidence to be adduced at trial, while ignoring the quite immediate motive and intent evidence of a sexual target:

> *Chief U.S. District Court Judge John J. Sirica, who is presiding over the Watergate trial, has said he wants the trial to explore fully the motives, sponsorship and financing of the alleged bugging.*
>
> *But the chief prosecutor, Assistant U.S. Attorney Earl J. Silbert, has indicated that the trial will focus on the alleged bugging and not other incidents of spying and sabotage. Silbert said in several pretrial hearings that the evidence and testimony will allow the jury to only draw "inferences" about the broader questions.*
>
> *The prosecution witness list as originally drafted included the name of California attorney Donald H. Segretti, who according to numerous accounts was hired and paid to disrupt the campaigns of various Democratic presidential candidates.*
>
> *Segretti was a witness before the federal grand jury that investigated the Watergate bugging, but his name was not read as a prosecution witness by Silbert in court yesterday.*[7]

By emphasizing Deep Throat's "spying and sabotage" theme,[8] the *Post* was focusing its readers on a political motive for the eavesdropping, thus implicating high levels of the Nixon administration, and away from whatever would be the basis for extortion, blackmail, or Hunt's personal financial gain. By noting that Segretti would not be a witness, the paper falsely suggested a cover-up by the prosecution, and certainly not one by the defense. In fact, the real cover-up was run by the *Post*.

---

7 Woodward and Bernstein, "GOP Aides Listed as 'Bug' Witnesses," *Washington Post*, January 9, 1973, A6.

8 Mark Felt's pushing in October 1972 of the Segretti story was a means of keeping the Watergate investigation open in response to the September 15, 1972, indictments of the seven burglaries–the seeming conclusion of the investigation.

As of the end of January 1973, after Hunt's guilty plea, the danger of publicizing his CIA defense and his Hermès notebooks had passed. With the *Post*'s clever assignment of the Baldwin interview to the *Los Angeles Times*[9] and Bazelon's crucial grant of Morgan's "desperation" motion, the previously strong likelihood of the public learning of the DNC girly referral operation had for the time vanished. Silbert's trial theme would also have revealed Mullen's coveted CIA cover contract, over which Hunt and Oliver Sr. were purportedly fighting.

I note parenthetically that the *Los Angeles Times* had avoided exposing the CIA in its reporting, perhaps in concert with the *Post*, which had most likely thrown the scoop its way. The tape of Baldwin's interview with the *Times*, put under seal by Sirica, contained Baldwin's casual reference to his lawyer's conclusion and several related facts showing that the CIA was behind Watergate, as well as opinions held by Baldwin himself, according to none other than Morgan, who was allowed to hear the tape and read the transcript. However, the *Times* printed nothing about the CIA, nor did the *Post*, which likely had access to the *Times* interview and to Morgan as well.

Because it appeared to him from the transcript that Baldwin was working for the CIA, Morgan made an unsuccessful in-camera motion to Sirica that the prosecution prove "they were not Government [meaning: CIA] wiretaps." So the trial exposed neither the lurid sex talk nor seeming CIA sponsorship of the burglary.

In any case, at this point the odd participation in the burglary of recently "retired" James McCord had not yet been deeply explored. And John Dean's devious acts beyond his superiors' authorization had not been put under spotlight.

What was to be called the Ervin Committee was formed on October 12, 1972, in response to the *Post*'s sensational Segretti reporting beginning October 10. Would this Democratic-majority committee, with full subpoe-

9 As WCC indubitably foresaw, Sirica did in fact order the production of the tape of the *Times* Baldwin interview. Because Baldwin had been prepared to avoid revealing the girl talk issue, the tape revealed nothing to worry any Democrat, other than its brief reference to "explicitly intimate" conversations. While Morgan was evangelical about his wish to expose the CIA, he tied his own hands, ironically, by successfully requesting Sirica to seal the 161-page transcript of Baldwin's interview, which strongly indicted the CIA.

na power, later set to begin hearings in May 1973, stumble into sensitive subjects that the DNC, the CIA, and the *Post* had so skillfully avoided? And if so, could the *Post* continue a successful cover-up? To respond, we must focus on the strange figure of James McCord.

Chapter Sixteen

JAMES MCCORD

We begin with Woodward's description of the appearance of burglar James McCord at his arraignment the morning of the arrests before Judge James Belson in the DC courthouse:

> *The Judge asked his occupation.*
>
> *"Security consultant," he replied.*
>
> *The Judge asked where.*
>
> *McCord, in a soft drawl, said that he had recently retired from government service. Woodward moved to the front row and leaned forward.*
>
> *"Where in government?" asked the Judge.*
>
> *"CIA," McCord whispered.*
>
> *The Judge flinched slightly.*
>
> ***"Holy shit," Woodward said half aloud, "the CIA."***[1]

Involvement of James McCord in this burglary, to any thinking person, should have raised serious questions immediately. McCord was an individual recently retired from the CIA, who, by his own admission, was not hired by the CRP for cloak-and-dagger operations, as Hunt presumably was by the White House. Rather, Mitchell's CRP was looking for a retired Secret Service agent, mainly for technical security duties. To White House detective Jack Caulfield's chagrin, all that the CRP got from the Secret Service's Alfred Wong, after his supposed "exhaustive search," was McCord, who had no personal security experience. Was Wong's help a personal fa-

---

1 Bernstein and Woodward. *All the President's Men*, 18.

vor to McCord, whom Wong knew well, or a favor to the CIA, with whom Wong had a long relationship by "borrowing," (through McCord) CIA technicians for White House duty?[2]

The main point here is that McCord was not hired by the CRP for purposes of mischief (as was Hunt by the White House), nor was McCord ostensibly seeking the same. How did this straitlaced Baptist immediately tumble to criminality, if that is what McCord thought this was? We will get to his frail explanation later, but there is no good answer that does not involve the CIA, and his thoughts that this was, as the CIA intended, a plausibly lawful national security operation, with an undercover McCord participating and curating any fruits for the benefit of the CIA.

Liddy later described McCord's first meeting with Hunt, in Liddy's presence, in which they both feigned not having known one another. Yet both Hunt and McCord had probably worked together on the CIA's big fiasco, the Bay of Pigs, and certainly by 1963 were working together closely on the Second Naval Guerilla operation, the CIA's program to again invade Cuba. Both Hunt and McCord had later worked with the CIA's OS Security Research Service, the ultimate dark ops section of the CIA, which reported directly to Helms. This feint of not having known one another, of course, bespeaks undercover intelligence protocol and itself is some evidence of CIA infiltration.

So was it just coincidental that this former OS man and Second Naval Guerilla veteran "retired" and then was quickly pushed to the CRP, just after his former colleague Hunt had been hired by the White House and had recruited CIA-connected Cubans? And that McCord would soon be reunited with this anti-Castro team? Yet, according to McCord, he had no knowledge of being hired by the CRP for any hijinks, nor did he know Cubans were being recruited by Hunt.

Originally, beginning September 1971, McCord worked at CRP part-time; he began full-time in January 1972. His part-time employment had started shortly after Hunt was retained by the White House in July 1971. His date of full-time employment is also coincidental, if one, again, be-

2 Hougan brilliantly posits that the CIA, through this McCord-Wong arrangement, had been spying on the White House through these technicians, who likely had planted listening devices throughout. From today's vantage point, there can be no doubt that the White House was infiltrated by intelligence operatives.

lieves in coincidence. That is when Liddy came over from his minor White House post to be the full-time CRP general counsel, and both McCord and Liddy began work for the November Group, an influential group of PR and ad executives centered in New York, which itself had strong intelligence connections. As Liddy later wrote, he made the switch only because Dean had promised him a big-budget ("How's a half a million for openers?") intelligence operation, maneuvering that occurred in November and December 1971. So McCord did not commit himself full-time to the CRP until it was clear that the unguided missile Liddy, with his intelligence ambitions, began work with a campaign organization that would be flush with campaign funds.

There is another oddity about the use of McCord on the burglary team, as opposed to his hiring by the CRP. Liddy was quite conscious of the need for the team to be "double-blind," that is, the team was not to know who ultimately hired them, and there was to be no one on the team who could be traced back to the CRP. Yet here was McCord, front and center on the burglary team, while holding the position of Director of Security of the CRP!

Liddy knew at once following the arrests that he had made a big mistake, and that because of McCord's presence, he would, as he told his wife that night, likely go to jail. But why was it that McCord was there at all? Liddy had given Hunt the responsibility of hiring a "wireman," of which there would be hundreds in the DC area, where lived countless retirees with intelligence experience. So just as Jack Caulfield was frustrated that he was given McCord when he asked for a retired Secret Service agent, Liddy was frustrated by Hunt's not seemingly being able to retain a double-blind retiree. From these facts alone, we may infer that Liddy was the victim of a hidden CIA agenda that foisted McCord upon him.

The timing of McCord's CRP hookup looks especially suspicious when one also considers covert White House detective Tony Ulasewicz's testimony that he was sent on a casing mission by Dean via Caulfield, in October or November 1971,[3] to stroll through DNC headquarters. Puzzled by the assignment, the rumpled detective reported to Dean that the DNC headquarters office looked like any regular office, with desks, file cabinets, and

3 Ulasewicz cited the incorrect date of April 1972, after Caulfield had left the White House; Caulfield put the date per the above, consistent with other evidence.

the like. This casing mission took place shortly after Dean, through Caulfield, had Ulasewicz look into the "Happy Hooker" ring in New York.[4]

As Dean was pushing Liddy into the CRP in November and December 1971, McCord had just come on board part-time, and Ulasewicz had made his odd casing trip, strong specific rumors began circulating in the intelligence underground in New York: the Republican campaign was planning to burglarize and wiretap the DNC headquarters. This rumor began several weeks before Liddy hatched his fatuous Gemstone Plan and many months before the DNC was allegedly targeted by Mitchell. The inference is, of course, that the CIA had already been planning this and that Hunt had lured Dean into White House approval of the DNC mission, likely convincing the ambitious Dean that he could feather his own intelligence nest by harvesting dirt on opponents–thus, Dean's assigning of the October/November 1971 mission for Ulasewicz. There is solid circumstantial evidence that Dean (who denies all), through his own sources should have known then of the recently begun DNC prostitution referral program brokered by Phillip Bailley, and at the least it is uncontradicted that Dean knew Bailley.

These rumors of a future wiretap were so strong that A. J. Woolston-Smith, a New York gumshoe with strong intelligence connections (he had been a private intelligence-connected detective working with Hunt and McCord on the Second Naval Guerilla operation), relayed them to a small-time Manhattan muckraker, William Haddad, who thereafter, as the rumors grew even stronger, in March 1972 relayed them in turn to syndicated columnist Jack Anderson. So it would appear that the DNC operation was hatched quite apart from anything Liddy, or for that matter the wrongly accused John Mitchell, had or did not have in mind in the fall of 1971.

Interestingly, as Jack Anderson was receiving these rumors, the CIA began overt harassment of Anderson, dubbed Operation Mud Hen,[5] with visible observation posts outside his house. Hunt brought Liddy to meet with the CIA poison expert, Edward Gunn, about ways to disable or kill Anderson. At the same time, the "retired" McCord was preparing a report

4 Ulasewicz found plenty of Democrats using the prostitution ring, but, alas, also many Republicans.

5 Far and away the best reference for this and related subjects is the excellent seminal work *Secret Agenda* by Jim Hougan.

on Anderson for the CIA, delivered to his apparent CIA handler Lee Pennington. Only after a sit-down between Anderson and CIA director Richard Helms was the operation ended. Did Anderson agree to keep silent on the upcoming DNC burglary? All of this, again, occurred before Mitchell supposedly told Magruder on March 30 to break into the DNC.

Another significant development was occurring around this same time period, beginning in fall 1971. A high-class bordello was being run out of the Columbia Plaza apartments two blocks from the DNC headquarters on Virginia Avenue. The madam had a small-time lawyer/boyfriend, Phillip Bailley, who bragged about his Democratic Party connections, which included a girlfriend working at the DNC. Seeking new business, the madam asked Bailley to set up a referral network at the DNC, in which out-of-town high rollers would be sent to her operation for dates. This arrangement was instituted around October 1971.

The request to get a referral source in the DNC may not have been the madam's brainchild. Her group was already being protected by CIA operatives, who, in return, were taping, with the ladies' consent, the prostitutes and their johns, an illegal operation unless approved by the White House. Whether drugging was involved is unknown but suspected. In any event, the CIA may well have put up the madam to making the DNC initiative via Bailley.

If there was a CIA taping operation in place at the Columbia Plaza, there would be very good reason, first, for the prostitutes to get a DNC referral network and, second, for the CIA to get seeming, and necessary for its protection, White House authorization to burglarize and tape the operation, using DNC "dirt" as bait to get the White House (Dean) approval.

Thus, if it at some later date the CIA's prostitution taping program were discovered, the Agency could point to White House authorization, coming ostensibly from the attorney general, who conveniently for the CIA was soon to run the CRP, where both Liddy and plenty of dark money were also to be made available. That there was in fact a CIA taping program involving prostitutes seems at this present remove not to be doubted. Bailley later told researchers that on a visit to the madam's apartment, he observed a man sitting in a hall closet listening electronically to the intimate activities in the next room. A burly former minor league baseball player "bouncer" was around, described as sounding much like McCord associate Lou Russell, a former minor league player.[6] A similar CIA taping program was run in San Francisco in the 1950s by a Colonel Harry White. The shadowy Russell was heard by reliable witnesses to brag, well prior to the first burglary, about the DC taping program, replete with colorful anecdotes of what he overheard.

Certainly, this information about the prior Russell taping program was not likely known by the *Post* at the time of the burglary arrests, so we cannot fault the paper on this score. However, as noted in Chapter Twelve on Mullen and Hunt, the *Post* reported the questions about the CIA connections of the burglars in its early articles, soon to discontinue the exploration. Obviously, had the *Post* reported its knowledge of the Mullen/CIA cover status, which it did not, suspicion would have been cast not only on Mullen's employment of Hunt but also on McCord and the Cubans as being possible covert CIA operatives working under CRP cover.

But there was nothing publicly known at the time of the arrests, other than McCord's conspiratorial whisper at the arraignment, to suggest McCord had an ongoing CIA connection. And as the investigation hurtled toward indictment, trial, and conviction, McCord's stoicism did little to attract public attention. To be sure, the curious intervention by civil rights attorney Charles O. Morgan Jr. at trial prevented the prosecution from introducing evidence of the contents of the wiretapped conversations by Alfred Baldwin, who was hired by McCord and had been on McCord's payroll. This quashing of testimony, we have shown, kept any light from being shone on prostitution, and thus vicariously on the CIA.

As suggested in Chapter Fourteen, *Post* reporters likely discovered the prosecution's thwarted plans for Baldwin's testimony and knew of the intimate nature of the calls he overheard, but they published nothing on the subject. My point here is that until March 1973, there was very little published that should have given rise to suspicions about McCord's sponsorship.

It wasn't until McCord's dramatic letter delivered to Judge Sirica on March 20, 1973, that this opaque spook was thrust into the spotlight. The *Post*, appropriately, trumpeted the content of McCord's letter: there was

6 See Stanford, *White House Call Girl*.

perjury in the trial; higher-ups were involved; the White House had tried to hush him up, offering him money and clemency; his life was threatened; the White House tried falsely to blame the burglary on the CIA.

In subsequent interviews with the *Post*, McCord made a point of naming Mitchell, albeit through hearsay, as the author of the burglary plot:

> *James W. McCord, Jr. testified under oath yesterday that he was told by his principal superior in the Watergate conspiracy that former Attorney General John N. Mitchell had personally approved plans to bug the Democrats' headquarters, according to Senate sources.*
>
> *McCord testified that his coconspirator and former White House aide, G. Gordon Liddy, told him that Mitchell was still serving as attorney general in February 1972, the sources said.*[7]

McCord also later offered his reasons for thinking the burglary was lawful as a national security operation, consistent with the theory I offer, because it had been approved by Mitchell:

> *Convicted Watergate conspirator James W. McCord Jr. has sworn that he considered the Watergate break-in and bugging legal because he had received assurance that the operation had been cleared by then-Attorney General John N. Mitchell and then-presidential counsel John W. Dean III....*
>
> *McCord said he thought that the bugging operation was legal because Liddy told him Mitchell, as attorney general had authority on his own signature to authorize wiretapping either for domestic security or national security purposes. (The Supreme Court last year ruled domestic wire-taps illegal without prior court approval.)*[8]

---

7 Woodward and Bernstein, "Mitchell is Linked to Bugging Plans," *Washington Post*, March 29, 1973, A1.

8 John Hanrahan, "McCord Felt Mitchell Made Bugging Legal," *Washington Post*, May 12, 1973, A15.

The *Post* also reported on McCord's interview with the Senate Select Committee, performed in advance of the public testimony, in which he again pointed to Mitchell:

> *After about three hours of listening to him, Sen. Daniel Inouye (D-Hawaii) made a mild stab at challenging McCord. Why was it, he asked, that a man with such an enviable record as a law-enforcement officer would have taken part in an act of political sabotage?*
>
> *McCord had an answer for that, too: because he was told the Attorney General (John N. Mitchell) and the counsel to the President (John W. Dean III) had approved it, with what McCord surmised was the blessing of the President himself.*[9]

Then, beginning on May 24, 1973, McCord testified publicly before the Ervin Committee. He explained further why he claimed to think that the burglary was legal as a national security operation. Not only was the direction given by the attorney general, McCord explained, but very importantly to him, Mitchell continued to authorize the burglary after a thirty-day waiting period, which suggested to McCord that Mitchell had thoroughly vetted the idea. McCord, as he had stated to *Post* reporters earlier, named Dean, Magruder, and Mitchell as sponsors, again conceding that his basis for naming them was hearsay.

McCord's justification of the burglary on national security grounds echoes the rationale that the CIA was likely planning to claim should the operation have been discovered in future years. What his defense was missing, and not explored by his questioners, was the actual national security purpose of the wiretapping. In fact, since Liddy thought the burglary was political, only a hidden CIA agenda would give it a national security purpose. Indeed, the only targets to which McCord admitted were political.

He explained that his charge was to wiretap DNC chairman Larry O'Brien and one other prominent Democrat, who could be chosen by the burglars at their discretion. The burglars chose the phone of one Spencer Oliver Jr., although McCord did not specify what had caused them to

9 Jules Witcover, "McCord Testimony: TNT in a Plain Brown Bag," *Washington Post*, May 19, 1973, A10.

choose the non-prominent Oliver's phone. The taps, according to McCord, were put on O'Brien's phone by tapping the "call director" on a phone in a room adjoining Oliver's, in testimony not challenged by the *Post*.

A call director, as described by McCord, was simply a line from the main switchboard to another's phone, which may have had between two to eighteen lines coming to it. One of these lines from the switchboard, McCord testified, might from that phone be dedicated as an extension to O'Brien, who presumably had on his phone a multitude of lines extended from phones throughout the office. So, yes, it was possible to bug this line, but the fruits would be limited to conversations routed through that line. McCord expressed ignorance as to whose phone the extension belonged, so it was unclear to him if any meaningful conversations would be overheard, or how many. In any case, McCord knew that O'Brien would be out of town for months, and that any tap would be worthless if the burglars wished to overhear O'Brien. My point is that this testimony alone showed, with appropriate analysis, that O'Brien was not a true target of the first burglary.

Of course, I doubt that any such line was tapped, a view confirmed by Liddy's later book averring that McCord told him he had put a room bug in O'Brien's office, which did not work because of concrete and steel "shielding" of the signal. But even if McCord's testimony was honest, it belied that O'Brien was the true target, an inference left unexplored by the *Post*.

Indeed, Baldwin had publicly claimed that a week before the second burglary McCord did not even know where O'Brien's office was located, thus his visit to the DNC around June 12, 1972. We hasten to add that this was also nonsense. Recall that the burglars had a diagram of the offices of DNC officials and had claimed to have photographed documents found in O'Brien's office during the first burglary. So at least one of these stories is false. It is more likely that Baldwin was locating Maxie Wells's desk on his visit, not O'Brien's office.

In any case, McCord noted that he was looking for political gossip and that wiretap summaries were given to the CRP. This contradicts Baldwin's testimony that he was to tape both political and personal calls, and that during this week of June 12 Baldwin was sent to the notorious (known hooker haven) Watergate Lounge, apparently to look for DNC-connected bigshots hooking up.

McCord detailed the White House efforts not only to pay him hush money but also to shut him up with clemency offers relayed from the Oval Office through White House detective Jack Caulfield. As reported by the *Post*, McCord was insistent that the White House had attempted falsely to blame the burglary on the CIA. He also angrily recounted the attempt by Hunt's lawyer to get him interested in a CIA defense.

So the sum of McCord's testimony, as reported and supplemented by the *Post*, was that the burglary was a White House operation, run by the former attorney general; that its intention was campaign-related gossip; that the tap on Oliver was simply incidental to that of the main target of Larry O'Brien; and that the White House tried falsely to blame the operation on the CIA while trying to hush the burglars with support money and clemency offers. How was the *Post* supposed to know better? What, we must ask, was missing from the *Post* reporting? How can we say that these reports were not reflective of the *Post's* state of knowledge at the time of its reporting? Let us look at the evidence.

We have discussed already Mark Felt's initial suspicion of CIA participation and his later apparent leak to Sandy Smith in February 1973, revealing Mullen and Company's cover contract, of which the FBI had learned days after the burglary arrests. Did the *Post* also gain evidence early on relating to McCord's connection to the CIA? The *Post* has long touted its wide range of contacts in the DC police department. Woodstein boasted in *All the President's Men* that reporter Alfred Lewis, with whom both collaborated, was "half cop, half reporter," and that reporter Eugene Bachinski was also wired into the DC police. The book also touts their receipt from the police of an inventory of evidence gathered from the burglary suspects. So if a noteworthy event occurred at the jail, the *Post* most likely would have learned of it.

One item that the *Post* clearly would have gained in the weeks after the arrests was the jailhouse record showing that McCord was picked up at jail after making bail by someone named "Pennington." Mark Felt quickly learned of this and immediately suspected that this unidentified man might be McCord's CIA handler or supervisor. The FBI tried in vain to determine Pennington's identity, finally sending a formal request to the CIA on August 18, 1972, seeking to identify and locate a CIA agent with that surname. Finding this "Pennington" was very much on Mark Felt's mind in the summer of 1972, as he later related in *The FBI Pyramid*. It is hard to believe that he would have hidden this from Woodward.

The *Post* had made much in other reporting of missing or unidentified burglary team members. For instance, when Hunt went missing right after the burglary arrests, *Post* headlines blared his absence. When Douglas Caddy would not name his client "Mister X" (Liddy likely), the *Post* likewise jumped on this. Did they ever publish McCord's pickup by "Pennington"? Or the FBI hunt for him? The answer is a definite no.

Would the *Post* think this person significant? Certainly Felt and the FBI thought so. Just raising the fact of the FBI search for Pennington would have been important, because it might have borne significantly on the sponsorship of the burglary and kept alive the question of the CIA's role. After all, this is why the FBI sought out Pennington. But not a word was published by the *Post* about Pennington until Nixon was about to resign in July 1974. When the paper finally mentioned him, forced to do so by the Senate minority's Baker Report, the treatment was muffled, dismissive, and inaccurate, as we will later see.

Moreover, Felt and other FBI sources had known after some months' delay that the CIA had provided the FBI with what turned out to be a Pennington–Cecil Pennington–with no connection to DC, McCord, or his jail pickup. The FBI, including Felt, was quite aware it had been sent on a wild goose chase, a CIA obstruction.

Yet it is difficult to believe that the vaunted *Post* jailhouse sources, its FBI agent sources, or gold-plated source Deep Throat would not have told Woodstein far earlier of Pennington's pickup of McCord, or the FBI's search for him, or later of the CIA's deception. So we must conclude the high likelihood that the *Post* knew "Pennington" picked up McCord and knew of his importance pertaining to the CIA but deliberately suppressed reporting about him.

Had the *Post* published Pennington's name and investigated his employment, the paper eventually would have discovered that he was likely a CIA contractor involved in highly sensitive operations, with connections to the secretive OS. But again, whether the *Post* should have reached a conclusion as to Pennington's status can be argued, at least up to the Baker Report of July 3, 1974. (More on the Baker Report in Chapter Twenty.) But it is inarguable that it should have at least reported known facts about him, about his pickup of McCord, and the FBI's frustrated search for him.

We know now, of course, that McCord did not claim in Ervin Committee testimony to have planted a room bug in O'Brien's office, as he told Liddy, but he did claim that a "call director" bug was planted but "shielded" by concrete and steel. We also know from Liddy's memoir that he related no direction to the burglars to wiretap a second phone line in the first burglary. But if in fact two lines were to be tapped, as McCord testified, how was one human monitor–Baldwin–to overhear both lines at once? None of this was explained by McCord, nor did he explain why the burglars would pick a seeming nobody like Oliver to tap at their discretion, who was not even directly employed by the DNC but by the Association of Democratic Chairmen. Why not tap, if indeed a second tap was ordered, an official engaged at least in fund-raising, if not in political strategy? Why this unprepossessing minor official?

Pointing even more directly to the Agency, a DC police intelligence officer, Garey Bittenbender, had encountered McCord in the DC jail on the morning of McCord's arraignment on June 17, 1972. We should note, as Woodward did so astutely, that the burglars had not made any calls that night. So when McCord was going into court that morning, he likely thought that the CIA would claim, as per the thinking he expressed to the Senate and the *Post*, that because the CIA operation was approved by the attorney general, it was legal. In other words, he was not likely thinking that the CIA would deny the burglary was one of its own operations, as it later would, and blame it all on the White House.

According to Bittenbender, he had known McCord for a number of years by virtue of their coordination on intelligence matters. When Bittenbender, encountering McCord in the jail as he headed to court, asked him what had occurred, McCord told him that he had been on a CIA operation. Bittenbender gave his statement to the FBI shortly after the conversation had occurred. Given the *Post* "jailhouse sources," it would have been highly likely that leaks of Bittenbender's statements would have made it to the *Post* from the DC police.

Also, Woodward and Bernstein not only had Deep Throat as a source, but they also had numerous FBI sources within the local DC field office, which had interviewed Bittenbender. And if they had not learned of Bittenbender earlier, the FBI 302 report of July 18, 1972, reflecting the Bittenbender statement was given to defense counsel in the fall of 1972. The *Post* clearly had relationships with defense lawyers for the burglars, each of whom received Bittenbender's statement in discovery. It is difficult to believe, then, that Woodstein did not know of the Bittenbender statement within days or weeks of the burglary, and in any case, should have heard of it by December 1972.

In his May 1973 Ervin Committee testimony, McCord admitted that Bittenbender claimed McCord had told him that McCord had been on a CIA operation. McCord offered that Bittenbender had known him previously as a CIA agent, and therefore must have been confused.

But how likely is it, we must ask, that this highly qualified intelligence officer, with many years of experience, was so badly mistaken? Simply reporting his full FBI statement would have raised a serious question about the CIA's participation. However, in treating this issue, the Post deliberately refrained from mentioning Bittenbender's detailed FBI interview:

> *McCord testified that Alch mentioned during the Dec. 21 lunch that metropolitan police Intelligence Officer Gary Bittenvender [sic] had "purportedly claimed" that McCord told him the break-in was a CIA operation.*
>
> *Insp. Albert Ferguson, chief of intelligence for the metropolitan police, said yesterday that Bittenvender's [sic] notes indicate only that he knew that McCord was a former CIA agent, not that he had been told the break-in was a CIA operation.*[10]

A reader would have, from this article, inaccurately concluded that Bittenbender did not say that McCord had admitted to him that this had been a CIA operation.

---

10 Edwards, "McCord Disputed on Idea of Linking Burglary to CIA," *Washington Post*, May 23, 1973, A12.

The Ervin Committee seemingly accepted at face value McCord's lame explanation without reading Bittenbender's FBI statement into the record. We now know that, not only did the Post know of the FBI statement and conceal it, but also that it deliberately threw sand in the public's eyes by referring to Inspector Ferguson's notes, provenance unclear. Because of this failure alone, we must conclude that the Post deliberately concealed a key fact about the Watergate burglary in an effort to deflect attention away from the CIA and toward the White House.

Around this same time, as Mark Felt was being pushed out of the FBI by Ruckelshaus for the Ellsberg leak, FBI agents were interviewing one Miriam Furbershaw, a retired CIA senior clerk, who had rented a small "in-law" apartment to McCord at some undetermined time before Watergate for his occasional use.

Furbershaw had a "no women" rule and evicted McCord after numerous young women had visited. Anyone knowing McCord, an active Baptist, would know the girls were not for his pleasure. Hunt also had visited.

Of greater significance is that Furbershaw was told by a telephone technician that McCord had a significant store of bugging equipment in the apartment. In short, the combination of the CIA, girls, and bugging did not begin with Watergate.

Even though Woodstein was tight with numerous FBI agents by May 1973, and Felt was a loose cannon on his way out, we cannot say with certainty that they would have learned of the Furbershaw tableau. But good reporters should have.

Additionally, early in the investigation, around July 1, 1972, the FBI interviewed McCord's Assistant Security Officer, Penny Gleason. She told investigators of a signed picture of Richard Helms that McCord hung in his CRP office, quickly removed after the arrests. It was inscribed, "To Jim, with deep appreciation." The word "deep" was twice underlined, hardly the best "deep" cover procedure! This photo was but one more indication that McCord was falsely retired at the time of Watergate, as he had once before in his CIA career.

Gleason was well known as McCord's Assistant Security Officer and should have been an obvious source for the *Post*. Whether the reporters sought her out or actually interviewed her is not clear, but we know they published no statement from her. Felt of course knew of Gleason's 302 statement, as would have the agents working with him. All of these men were friendly with the reporters, such that we can confidently conclude that Gleason's name was known to them, as was most likely her description of the photo. Indeed, throughout the Watergate investigation, the reporters appeared to "tailgate" the FBI, questioning most witnesses shortly after the feds did, even boasting that they often received more candid statements than did the FBI.

Gleason also witnessed that McCord's assistant, Robert Houston, cleared out McCord's files immediately after the arrests, which included some cassette tapes. McCord likely had some bits of evidence in his file pertaining to Watergate, perhaps copies of logs. That everything was taken away suggests a rich cache of evidence of his clandestine activities. It is likely that he was concerned about evidence of his CIA undercover status and activity other than in Watergate.

Gleason's FBI interview, the substance of which was likely available to Woodstein through their many agent sources, contained widely overlooked nuggets regarding Bittenbender. Gleason detailed McCord's regular contacts with Bittenbender in April and May 1972, when McCord was supposedly employed only by the CRP. Bittenbender was so friendly toward McCord that he visited the CRP the afternoon of the arraignment, where he unburdened to Gleason his concern for McCord. So we know that Bittenbender was likely not confused, as McCord later hypothesized to the Ervin Committee, about the identity of McCord's ostensible employer. If Bittenbender heard McCord say that the burglary was a CIA operation, he was not so testifying under the confused belief that McCord was still an ostensible CIA employee.

Finally, in the Ervin hearings, it became known that before the burglaries, McCord had sent to the CIA a report on columnist Jack Anderson, with whom the Agency was engaged in a silent war over an undisclosed issue—perhaps, as I suggested earlier, Anderson's knowledge of the planned burglary. McCord claimed that this report—sent to the CIA via Pennington—was simply independent research he had voluntarily undertaken, an absurd contention. If done at the behest of the CIA, it would have been considered an illegal domestic operation and also would have shown his

CIA agency. But the *Post* did not disclose this report, so clearly evidence of McCord's ongoing employment with the CIA.

The *Post* also failed to report in any meaningful detail the five confidential letters McCord wrote to the Agency, first via Pennington, later directly to Gaynor, during the key months of December 1972 and January 1973, updating the Agency on his fears that the CIA would be implicated at trial. These letters were mentioned in the Ervin hearings, without deep interpretation, several times in May through July 1973, but again, not with description in the *Post*. As I mentioned previously in Chapter Thirteen, these letters, originally routed through chain of command, show McCord acting as a loyal undercover agent.

The *Post*, in short, suppressed facts about Pennington, Gleason, Bittenbender, and perhaps Furbershaw, as well as McCord's continuing Agency communications. These are clear, set-in-stone markers of *Washington Post* dishonesty.

To be sure, the *Post*'s reporting, or lack of same, about McCord could be criticized for plenty of other reasons. There was beyond question absurd or vulnerable testimony of McCord that the *Post* ignored but should have critiqued. For instance, the paper did not question the contradictory testimony about McCord's professed thinking that the burglary was legal as a national security operation, while at the same time he testified that the burglars were (supposedly) looking for political gossip, which clearly is not a national security matter. Nor did anyone question why he would tap not O'Brien's phone but a "call director" extension line to overhear O'Brien, at least with the relatively pedestrian bugs they had.

McCord, in short, has never satisfactorily explained this evidence, while consistently denying any intent to pursue a CIA agenda. Helping to shield this spook, the *Post* never directed any of its vaunted investigative reporting to the issue of McCord's continuing CIA affiliation, while repeating his sensational allegations uncritically and ignoring glaringly vulnerable aspects of his testimony.

If we ignore the *Post*'s failings as to Mullen, Hunt, and Baldwin and focus solely on the failures we have documented in this chapter regarding McCord, the newspaper must stand not only indicted, but also convicted, on its outright concealments. After all, even if, for two examples, the credulous among us would believe McCord's weak explanations about Bittenbender, or about tapping the call director to O'Brien's line, the latter should have been explored and the former reported with due significance attached. A third example is its repeated failures to report about Pennington.

But even if the credulous could believe McCord as pertains to Bittenbender (he was not asked about Pennington), there would have been no room for McCord to deny the story about his interactions with Michael Stevens.

Chapter Seventeen

MICHAEL STEVENS

It appears that by March 23, 1973, after McCord wrote his dramatic letter to Judge Sirica and the latter read it in open court, McCord and the CIA thought they were home free.

Mullen had enjoined the DNC and the *Post* to keep silent about its cover status, an easy sell because the DNC wished to avoid embarrassing questions about what would interest the Agency in Spencer Oliver Jr.'s phone. The Baldwin reporting and Baldwin trial testimony had been handled by the *Post* spectacularly skillfully, if dishonestly, avoiding publication of the naughty phone calls, and the prosecution's proposed blackmail theme. And with Judge Bazelon's ban on testimony characterizing the overheard conversations, Prosecutor Earl Silbert's zeal for showing motive based on Hunt's extortion waned, thereby silencing talk of Mullen's fat CIA contract as part of Hunt's motive. And, of course, with Dean's destruction of Hunt's notebooks and Dorothy Hunt's death, much evidence of a CIA connection was also destroyed, along with Hunt's desire to plead his CIA defense. Finally, Gonzalez and Martinez had stayed silent through trial on their own version of the CIA defense.

So as McCord was about to be sentenced, he fired his highly competent criminal defense lawyer Gerald Alch and hired CIA-connected lawyer Bernard Fensterwald, not an experienced defense lawyer, to unleash on the White House. With beloved former CIA director Richard Helms shipped off to Iran, McCord could make good on his December 1972 threat by letter to Caulfield that "every tree in the forest will fall" (if Helms was fired). McCord's sentencing hearing was an ideal opportunity to point sensationally to the White House, in a diatribe certain to be lapped up by the public, taking away any potential focus on the CIA.

The *Post*, the DNC, and the CIA, each having avoided embarrassment, were now all on board for a roaring campaign against an increasingly vulnerable White House. But there were still lingering dangers posed by CIA contractors who might spill the beans. CIA threats in order to keep one certain contractor silent, however, had the reverse effect, driving him in from the cold and into the arms of the FBI. Thereby ensued perhaps the most frightening tableau in our nation's most explosive scandal, one so consequential that our Pulitzer Prizewinning reporters did not dare report it at the time, doing so only later, after the danger had passed, in their bestselling book.

Recall both in the book and the movie version of *All the President's Men* a highly dramatic garage meeting between Deep Throat and Woodward on the night of May 16–17, 1973. In that meeting, Deep Throat hysterically warned the reporter that "everyone's life is in danger!" Deep Throat also tipped off Woodward of the likelihood that he and others would be overheard electronically by the CIA. The motive, according to Deep Throat, was that the CIA was not worried so much about Watergate as about other CIA operations to which an investigation of Watergate would lead. But according to Woodward's book, after weeks of wariness following the warning, nothing occurred of note, implying that Deep Throat may have been unnecessarily worried. Deep Throat, in short, appeared to have been clearly mistaken about the allegedly murderous intelligence community, alarmed without cause:

> *For several days after Woodward's meeting with Deep Throat, Bernstein and Woodward behaved cautiously. They conferred on street corners, passed notes in the office, avoided telephone communications. But it all seemed rather foolish and melodramatic, so they soon went back to their normal routines. They never found any evidence that their telephones had been tapped or that anyone's life had been in danger.*[1]

1 Bernstein and Woodward, *All the President's Men*, 321–322.

We know now that Deep Throat was no White House amateur but a career FBI senior official, a crack agent with significant intelligence experience. From this vantage point, it is hard to believe that his warnings were unwarranted by the evidence. In fact, on May 14 and May 16, 1973, *Chicago Today* published reports about one Michael Stevens (assumed name), who had put himself under the protection of the FBI. His statements were likely to have been at least part of the source of Deep Throat's warnings to Woodward, since the FBI had interviewed Stevens on May 12 and 14, 1973.

Stevens had apparently come to the FBI fearing for his safety after getting threatening anonymous calls, presumably from the CIA. On May 14, *Chicago Today* reported:

> *Stevens, who is married and the father of a 3-year-old girl, now says that his life may be in danger. "I may go down the tubes any time," he told investigators, CHICAGO TODAY learned.*[2]

One of the first significant revelations of Stevens (likely relayed to the paper by Deep Throat) was that when Hunt's wife Dorothy was traveling in December 1972 to Chicago, where she died in the United Airlines crash, she was doing so to bring what may be interpreted as hush money to Stevens. Indeed, $10,000 in cash was found in her possession at the site of the crash. This earlier death, as well as death threats to Stevens, may have been part of the reason why Deep Throat thought lives were in danger at the hands of the CIA.[3]

McCord in his later Ervin Committee testimony named Dorothy Hunt as a hush money courier. As wife of burglar Howard Hunt, her role in the cover-up, even if she was a CIA agent herself, did not suggest by itself that this was a CIA operation she was covering up. But if it were known

2 Howard S. Marks, "CIA Linked to Watergate," *Chicago Today*, May 14, 1973, 1.

3 Well-known conspiracy theorist Sherman Skolnick claimed that the plane crash was caused by foul play, a claim largely ignored on the "boy who cried wolf" basis. The crash was investigated by the FAA, soon headed by Colonel Alexander Butterfield, late of the White House, long regarded to himself be a deep-cover CIA or DIA (Defense Intelligence Agency) operative. Butterfield's investigation found no foul play, even though the crash was never satisfactorily explained.

that she was paying Stevens hush money, an entirely new inference would have been raised, to wit, that the Watergate burglary was at least in part a CIA operation. After all, no one in the White House inner circle knew of Stevens' existence, nor did Liddy. By October 1972, it had become obvious that the burglars had been wiretapping and had been caught with bugs in their possession. So why would any White House official care to hide that the burglars had purchased these bugs from a particular source? He wouldn't. Guilt and innocence, for the White House and CRP, did not hinge on identification of the bug supplier. But it did for the CIA.

No one in the White House, including those who turned prosecution witnesses, had known of payoffs to Stevens–not Dean, not Magruder, not Nixon aide Fred LaRue or anyone else. Nor had anyone testified as to knowledge of Stevens. So hushing Stevens would have been only for CIA purposes, not for those of the White House. But what about Stevens' knowledge would suggest CIA involvement and thus necessitate his hushing?

As *Chicago Today* reported, likely based on Deep Throat leaks, Stevens was a specialty bug fabricator who did much work for the various national intelligence agencies, and he therefore needed verification that these bugs were being ordered by a legitimate governmental intelligence agency. McCord had presented to Stevens a letter on CIA stationery attesting that his purchases were for a CIA operation. Stevens then called his CIA contacts, relating McCord's operational alias, and was assured that McCord was on a CIA operation. All of this was reported by *Chicago Today*.

All of the foregoing could be contended to be subject to interpretation in some form or fashion. Perhaps, it could be argued, McCord was helping the White House by using his CIA connections to obtain bugs. But that could not be so because of the items that McCord sought from Stevens. He ordered, in addition to simple bugs already delivered to McCord, two highly sophisticated and expensive room bugs and one phone bug, for a total of $18,000. These devices could uplink to a satellite, meaning that the taps could be monitored without a human, like Baldwin, near the site. Moreover, Stevens noted that the bugs were to be set to the frequency of the satellite used by the CIA to monitor double agents in Vietnam:

> *Bugging devices capable of reaching top-secret spy satellites were ordered by Watergate conspirator James W. McCord, Jr., investigators have told CHICAGO TODAY...*
>
> *...Investigators were reported to be startled by the news that McCord, a former Central Intelligence Agency (CIA) agent, had ordered two room bugs and one phone bug capable of feeding into the nation's highly classified satellite communications network.*
>
> *Stevens is said to have close ties to the intelligence community...*
>
> *...The bugging device can pick up all conversations in the room where it is planted and transmit it as high as a fixed orbiting satellite parked 22,300 miles above the earth in a synchronous orbit.*
>
> *The signal is then retransmitted to a ground receiving station and relayed to such places as CIA headquarters in Langley, Va., a suburb of Washington.*
>
> *Stevens told investigators that the bugs were set to transmit on the frequency used by the CIA to track suspected double agents in Viet Nam [sic].*[4]

Neither the White House nor the CRP had a satellite, and certainly not one that could link up with any electronic bugs. This was explosive stuff, strongly showing any information gathered using these bugs would be for a CIA-sponsored operation. And the money trail would suggest, again, White House approval of these bugs, which the CIA could later use to justify their use.

To be sure, the *Post*'s republishing of this information would have raised at the least two questions: first, was this a CIA operation, and second, what information was the Agency seeking that was important enough to send to its satellite on an ongoing basis?

The *Post* did not report on this explosive Stevens story, even though it had been reported in *Chicago Today*, a credible paper with good circulation, albeit confined to its Chicago locality. As we have seen, when other

4 Marks, "McCord Sought Secret Sky Spy Devices Here," *Chicago Today*, May 14, 1973, 3.

papers printed Watergate stories the *Post* wished to adopt, such as the *Los Angeles Times* story on Alfred Baldwin, it published them.

Not only that, in *All the President's Men*, Woodstein omitted any mention of the Stevens story and in fact stated deceptively, but clearly, that there turned out to have been no basis for Deep Throat's agitated warnings. So we can conclude that the *Post* reporting was deeply deceptive and intentionally so, by concealing the *Chicago Today* story and its underlying facts, facts that fit neatly into the highly dramatic garage meeting of Woodward and Deep Throat in May. The paper also concealed credible information, from the head of the FBI's investigation, that the CIA was threatening lives and reportedly conducting electronic surveillance to keep hidden its covert activities somehow connected to Watergate, all part of the May 16–17 garage meeting.

In what must be termed an epilogue, but a confirmatory one, Liddy detailed his dealings with McCord in his 1980 memoir, *Will*. McCord knew, when testifying in 1973 before the Ervin Committee, that Liddy was remaining silent. In 1980, Liddy broke his silence after the statute of limitations expired and revealed that McCord had hustled Liddy for $30,000 for what he described to Liddy as a super-sophisticated "room bug." It was not to be put on O'Brien's phone but in his office to record conversations, as Liddy put it, "as if we were there." Liddy, to his frustration, wrote that this room bug did not work because, according to McCord, it was "shielded" by concrete and steel intervening between the monitoring station and O'Brien's office.

So today we know that McCord was lying to Liddy, first, about having purchased and planted the $30,000 room bug, or any room bug, and, second, by concealing his $18,000 order for three satellite-uplinking bugs, clearly coming out of the $30,000. It seemingly had been the plan of the CIA and McCord that, in the future should these bugs (likely set for overhearing prostitutes) be discovered, White House payment could be shown, thus implying White House approval of the operation.

It would seem that the *Chicago Today* stories came to the paper directly from an FBI agent since they noted Stevens' refusal to be interviewed by the paper. Moreover, the article purported to detail what Stevens had told "investigators." If the FBI source was not Mark Felt, certainly Felt knew the story and could have put Woodward on the scent. One sound inference is that Felt planted the stories in the Chicago paper because Woodward and the *Post* would not publish them. His purpose would have been to protect Stevens.

But even if Felt or one of Woodstein's many FBI agent sources did not inform the *Post* reporters of Stevens' story, certainly the *Post* could have republished the *Chicago Today* article, as it did with other significant stories. But it did not.

We know the matter had come to the attention of the reporters and the *Post* at least by virtue of Deep Throat's dire warning to Woodward in the May 16–17, 1973, garage meeting, since as the reporters described in the book, both Bernstein and Bradlee became deeply involved and frightened as they huddled in the dark in Bradlee's yard in the early morning hours following the meeting.

At the very least, as the book proves, the editor in chief and his star reporters knew that night that the CIA was so concerned about potential revelations that it was threatening murder, with a credibility that impressed the most astute and experienced of FBI agents. If so, why wouldn't this fact alone have warranted an article about CIA threats, or deep CIA concerns? If the warnings were good enough for the book and movie, and good enough to scare Deep Throat, why weren't they publishable in some form in the paper? This concealment of the threats revealed to Woodward by Deep Throat, putting Stevens' story aside for the moment, seems to prove a *Post* cover-up of the CIA's involvement.

We know now that the reporters' book covered up for the CIA by claiming that the threats never bore fruit and no one was harmed. But the book, it also seemed, helped the CIA by noting that the Agency was concerned not about Watergate so much as what else might be revealed as a result of Watergate. Certainly, there was some truth in this statement, since the CIA likely feared exposure of its long-ongoing program of using prostitutes to tape and/or drug prominent johns, whereas the CIA had an arguable White House approval for Watergate.

But let's pause for a moment to ponder this statement, true as it likely is. The fact is that the broader drug and taping program could only be revealed during the Watergate investigation if Watergate itself was part of it. Certainly, a Watergate bugging by the CIA, with its tincture of White House approval and no evidence of drugging, would be among the most innocent of CIA chapters. But the point here is that this CIA fear was rational only if it was similarly engaged in Watergate, since that is how Watergate would lead to other sensitive operations. Put differently, if the CIA was not involved in Watergate, there would have been no reason for Deep Throat to be so frightened in May of 1973, and no reason for the CIA to fear exposure.

Surely from the satellite uplinking capability of the bugs on order, the involvement of Dorothy Hunt in couriering seeming hush money, and the threats on Stevens' life, one may reasonably infer a sensitive CIA operation. But a quote from one of the *Chicago Today* articles appears to show Stevens' understandable conclusion that McCord was not merely using his CIA connections to aid the White House. Rather, Stevens, skeptical as to what McCord was up to, apparently confirmed through his own Agency contacts that McCord was at the time a CIA employee acting on a CIA operation:

> *The Central Intelligence Agency (CIA) and the Defense Intelligence Agency (DIA) have been linked by Stevens to the Watergate bugging.*
>
> *Stevens told investigators that McCord, using an assumed name, identified himself as an employe [sic] of the CIA.*
>
> ***Stevens claims that confidential sources within the CIA, told him that McCord was an active agency employee.***[5]

So the *Post*'s deliberate decision not to publish the *Chicago Today* stories on Stevens, and not to write about CIA threats aimed at suppressing the Agency's exposure, strongly indicts the *Post* and its star reporters.

McCord's new lawyer Fensterwald offered very lame rebuttals to Stevens' claims in *Chicago Today*. Stevens was not a CIA contractor, Fensterwald implied, since McCord simply "picked him out of the phone book." Dorothy Hunt was carrying cash partly to pay off McCord's debt to Stevens for the bugs, according to Fensterwald, but mainly to buy a motel to launder Hunt's future support money. Not greatly convincing, to be sure.

5 Marks, "How bugging foulups tipped off Watergate," *Chicago Today*, May 15, 1973, 3.

Honest debts can be paid by check, and one normally does not buy a motel with cash while lacking any written contract.

If Stevens' story would implicate McCord and the CIA in the planning and procuring end of the operation, there was another individual on the operations end whose participation, unlike that of Stevens, could not even be weakly explained away. That person was Lou Russell.

Chapter Eighteen

LOU RUSSELL

To those who deeply study Watergate, whether Lou Russell was involved in the burglary remains one of the most meaningful of the ongoing mysteries. To the extent considered proven, it dramatically upends all Watergate orthodoxy. And it helps answer every other major unresolved Watergate question, from the CIA's possible involvement, to the alleged monitoring of prostitutes, to the tapping of a seemingly useless political target, to McCord's puzzling failure to remove the tape on the door after all the burglars had entered.

As I discussed above, the involvement in the burglary of the other key actors–McCord, Hunt, Magruder, Dean, Baldwin–is clear and, but for Dean, admitted. Their motives, identity of their true principals, and nature of their actions all can be subject to good-faith debate, since all have testified inconsistently with evidence we have shown here.

But Russell stands apart. Any involvement whatsoever of Russell in the burglary has earthshaking import. If he was involved, it would be only in his role as McCord's own independent contractor, on McCord's tab, and unreimbursed by the CRP. It would be one thing if McCord had made a buck from Russell's labor for services provided to other McCord clients, if there were any prior to June 1972. But it would be quite another if the payments made to Russell by the allegedly financially strapped McCord were for Russell's services on Watergate. Such would strongly implicate a hidden agenda, in all likelihood one of the CIA. If Russell were needed for Liddy's operation, as Liddy understood it, Liddy would have known and would have paid him. Surely Russell's only possible role in Watergate would be as an off-the-books CIA contractor, hidden from Liddy. Simply put, if Russell was involved in Watergate, so was the CIA–secretly.

Who was Lou Russell? He had a long history in the shadowy venues of DC detective work, starting out as an investigator in the early 1950s for the infamous House Un-American Activities Committee (HUAC), which sought to root out communists in government. A beefy former minor league baseball player, Russell was a heavy drinker as well as a frequent consort of prostitutes. Since February 1972, he was a part-time contractor for McCord and Associates, ostensibly to provide security for CRP headquarters. Russell did not have his own bank account and cashed his checks through his intelligence community friends, one of whom, Bernard "Bud" Fensterwald, eventually became McCord's criminal lawyer in March 1973 to implement the post-trial strategy of lashing out at the Nixon administration. Significantly, prior to the Watergate burglary, Russell told several acquaintances, including Fensterwald, Fensterwald associate Bob Smith, and former Treasury agent Kennard Smith[1] that he had been taping prostitutes and their johns with the apparent cooperation of the prostitutes. In *White House Call Girl*,[2] Stanford describes the observation of a lawyer for the Columbia Plaza call girl ring, Phillip Mackin Bailley, as having observed in the madam's apartment a burly man, seemingly acting as security, who had been a former professional baseball player.

But in perhaps the oddest and most telling note of all, Russell had worked for General Security Services Inc. (GSS) for less than a year, ending in April 1972. His resignation occurred shortly before the first Watergate burglary and right after Jeb Magruder claimed he had the go-ahead to begin break-ins, soon to direct Liddy to DNC headquarters. His employment with the GSS in security had begun shortly after Hunt was in Florida recruiting his Cuban Bay of Pigs veterans and around the time McCord came on board with the CRP.

What is so interesting about this GSS job is that part of Russell's duties was as a security guard for the Watergate office building housing the DNC headquarters. This is likely more than a stunning coincidence. As a securi-

1 See Hougan, *Secret Agenda*, at note 118.

2 Stanford, *White House Call Girl*.

ty guard he would have had a key to the DNC offices and the opportunity to get an impression or copy of any desk key.

In Baldwin's statement, published in October 1972 in the *Los Angeles Times*, he mentions seeing, from his Howard Johnson's hotel room, McCord in the DNC office suite on May 26, 1972. Baldwin claimed to have been occupying room 419 at the time, which on May 26 was well before the first break-in, by which later time Baldwin had been moved to room 723 for improved monitoring. Perhaps Baldwin was mistaken as to then occupying room 419, but if he is correct, McCord, likely through Russell's security keys, already had access to the office suite. Moreover, on May 26, before the first break-in, McCord had Baldwin listen to an eavesdropped conversation of the talks to be monitored. This would imply, as suggested by Hougan, that the CIA was already eavesdropping, having no connection to the first burglary to be carried out several days later.

In the hubbub during the June 17 arrests, a man entered the Watergate lobby from the stairwell, chatted up the guards, and departed before the guards thought to tell the police. If Russell was involved that night as the "sixth burglar," who quickly exited the lobby post-arrest, such meant that the CIA was part of the operation and that the eavesdropping was targeted at prostitution calls. And unlike the Stevens scenario, no analyst can claim that the CIA was merely aiding a solely White House operation as a favor to its former agents. If Russell was involved, then McCord was an active undercover agent at the time, acting for the CIA. So merely raising the issue of Russell's participation would be to suggest a plausible revisionist narrative of the Watergate burglary directly at odds with the conventional version published by Watergate's paper of record, the *Washington Post*.

Early on in its reporting, on June 20, 1972, before the *Post* became palpably dishonest, it published a note that the police were investigating a sixth participant:

> *Police sources say they were still looking for a sixth person believed to have been involved in the incident.*[3]

3 Woodward and Bernstein, "Bug Suspects' White House Tie Hinted," *Washington Post*, June 20, 1972, A4.

Strangely, after this intriguing note, the *Post* thereafter went radio silent on the question of the sixth burglar.

If Russell was involved, he was most likely the sixth burglar of Watergate lore, unknown to his fellow burglars other than McCord, and the fellow who quickly disappeared from the Watergate lobby post-arrest.[4] His participation would explain the tape that McCord allowed to remain on the basement door lock, even after all the known burglars were in the building, kept on to allow Russell his covert entrance.

It would also clarify not only why McCord lied to others about having removed this tape but also would explain his false statements to Liddy that the DNC continued to occupy the office from 12:00 a.m. to 12:45 a.m., a critical delay given the frequency and timing of security rounds. Russell, it seemed, likely to establish an alibi, had earlier departed from the Watergate vicinity to his daughter's house in Benedict, Maryland, and was late driving back, causing McCord to delay the break-in. And it would explain McCord's frequent unexplained absences before the break-in, likely to confer with Russell, leading Liddy to later compare McCord to the fictional "Shadow," Lamont Cranston. Finally, of course, it would all but confirm the so-called "call girl" theory of motive, since Russell had been, prior to the break-in, seemingly immersed in taping and protecting a certain Columbia Plaza prostitution ring, and, if in the Watergate building that night, was doing so operationally for the CIA.

While there was much circumstantial evidence of Russell's involvement in the burglary at the time of Watergate, an additional intriguing fact pattern emerged years after. In the case of *Dean v. St. Martin's Press*, which John Dean brought against *Silent Coup* author Len Colodny and his publisher for defamation, certainly Dean's and Russell's finances were examined for any scent of the call girl narrative. Dean, you will recall, according to Colodny, may be inferred to have ordered the second break-in after reading with alarm the June 9, 1972, *Washington Star-News* article about a call girl ring involving "one lawyer at the White House."

---

4 Warren L. "Bud" Love, an officer of the bank where Russell frequently cashed his checks from McCord, related to the FBI that Russell volunteered to him, shortly after the burglary arrests, "I guess you're wondering who the sixth man was. Well, it wasn't me." FBI interview of July 3, 1972, FBI serial 139-4089-744.

In that case, lawyers explored an interesting set of seemingly corresponding financial transactions involving Dean and Russell. Russell was, as always, needful of cash after the burglary. Yet, without apparent meaningful employment that could justify it, he deposited amounts of $4,570 and $20,895 on November 15, 1972, and in March of 1973, respectively.

Likely not coincidentally, Dean withdrew $4,850 shortly before November 15, 1972, and approximately $22,000 from the White House safe around the time of the second Russell deposit.[5] These amounts, of course, neatly match up with the unexplained receipts of Russell. Accounting records show that the withdrawals from the White House safe were unaccounted for, and Haldeman has pointed toward Dean as the culprit, who has explained weakly that the first withdrawal was for his honeymoon, which apparently cannot be corroborated. In any case, the comparisons of dates and amounts make a compelling circumstantial case that Dean quietly paid hush money to Russell, while as cover-up counsel he was also making payments to the known burglars from hush money that White House conspirators had raised.

If, of course, Dean was paying Russell, that would be game, set, match in favor of the burglary's call girl/CIA-related motivation. Russell would only be involved in Watergate if call girls were also involved, and Dean would only personally pay Russell if he was hushing up this aspect of the case, which would damn Dean as well as the CIA, but perhaps mitigate the guilt of the unwitting Nixon higher-ups—Dean's get-out-of-jail card. But this evidence, while intriguing, is not ironclad.

Prior to Watergate, Russell had boasted to three separate witnesses that he had been taping prostitutes, replete with amusing anecdotes, according to Jim Hougan. Phil Stanford's book, *White House Call Girl*, describing the prostitution ring of one "Cathy Dieter," which he claims is an alias for Heidi Rikan, also implicates Russell, through Bailley's statements, as part of the covert taping program at the Heidi Rikan/Cathy Dieter Columbia Plaza apartment. Hougan documents Russell's work with an attractive blonde madam who appears, per Colodny's work, to have been

5 For a recapitulation of this evidence, see Stanford, *White House Call Girl*, page 135, footnote 102, a letter from the lawyers for Stanford to Dean, dated September 3, 2013, and included in the aforementioned book.

Heidi/Cathy. If true, this would explain Russell's interest in the DNC wiretapping, which would have monitored the call girl operation he had been protecting and taping with the girls' consent.

We are not certain how Russell's possible involvement first came to the attention of the FBI, but it did quite early on. In his initial July 9, 1972, FBI interview, Russell stated to agents that he ate at the Howard Johnson's restaurant but had done so the night *before* the burglary, and had visited the Watergate area that night only because he was nostalgic for an old girlfriend (a prostitute), who used a hairdresser in the area. However, in his FBI interview of October 10, 1972, he admitted that he had eaten at the HoJo on the night of the burglary but continued to deny that he had entered the office building that night. After it appeared that the FBI agents did not buy his story, Russell reportedly told them to "shove off."

Did Woodward recognize that there was a potential story about Russell? Apparently so, because he interviewed him twice, having drinks with Russell and his benefactor, CIA-connected stockbroker William Birely.

Let us stop right there. Woodward has made a point for forty years that the Nixon administration and CRP witnesses were often more forthcoming with *Post* reporters than when interviewed by the FBI in the presence of White House or CRP lawyers. The psychology is clear: witnesses are often fearful of retaliation or disapproval by their employers or coworkers when they suspect their words might get back to their employers or coworkers.

With this commonsense notion in mind, why would Woodward choose to talk to Russell in the presence of Birely, obviously some form of a CIA sponsor, sitting right next to him? Did Woodward really expect candor from this witness?

In any case, a refusal by Russell to admit to Woodward his participation in the burglary should not mean that no report should have been published. A denial is part of the story, just as it is part of a lawsuit. Indeed, many Woodstein stories reported various denials of administration officials. It is not the reporter's job to determine who is telling the truth but, rather, to lay out the facts and let the reader decide. Woodward, Bernstein, and the *Post* did not do that in Russell's case. A defensive Woodward told Hougan he saw no evidence that Russell was at the Watergate that night, adding, "He was just an old drunk, nearly as I could tell." So while Woodward often reported on administration denials and evasions, he chose not to print denials of an apparent CIA contractor.

Was the Russell story newsworthy? The other Washington, DC, paper, the *Washington Star-News*, certainly determined it acceptable for publication. On October 11, 1972, a young *Star-News* reporter, Patrick Collins, bylined an excellent piece on Russell, writing this after Russell's October 10, 1972, FBI interview:

> *A former congressional investigator was employed by a Watergate bugging suspect and by the security firm guarding the building which houses the Democratic National Committee, the FBI says.*
>
> *Louis James Russell, 54, has told FBI agents he was across the street from the Watergate a few hours before his boss, James McCord, then chief security adviser for the Nixon campaign, and four others were arrested inside the Democratic headquarters.*
>
> *Russell, chief investigator for the House Un-American Activities Committee when Richard Nixon was a member two decades ago, said he was having a late-night snack at Howard Johnson's Restaurant because he had a "sentimental" attachment to the place. Russell said he once went with a girl who used the Watergate beauty salon.*
>
> *"We often ate lunch there at the Howard Johnson's," Russell said, "and I went back that night to think about the good times we had."*
>
> *In an interview last night, Russell said FBI agents have "tried to get me to say I was a lookout that night, but I don't know anything about what McCord was doing in the Watergate." (McCord allegedly used a room on the fourth floor of the motel to monitor bugging devices on the phones at Democratic headquarters.)*
>
> *Russell said FBI agents told him "they didn't believe my story." However, Russell said, he was never called before a grand jury.*

> *He worked for the General Security Services Co., whose clients include the Watergate office building...Chamberlain said Russell worked for General Security for about a year before leaving last April.*
>
> *Russell first went to work part-time for James McCord last February, running security checks on personnel hired by the Nixon re-election committee...*
>
> *Beginning in June, Russell worked full-time at Nixon campaign headquarters at 1701 Pennsylvania Ave, N.W., as the night security manager. He said the committee decided to beef up its security after a building guard was discovered asleep on the job.*
>
> *Russell said he guarded the second floor. His main duty was to check out the closed-circuit TV bought by McCord.*
>
> *A spokesman for Nixon's re-election committee said last night he did not know whether Russell was ever employed directly by the committee.*
>
> *Since the break-in June 17, Russell has moved from a one-room $15-a-week flat in a rooming house in the 1700 block of Q St., N.W. to a $185-a-month furnished apartment in suburban Silver Spring, Md.*
>
> *Russell says a benefactor has not only allowed him use of the apartment but has provided him with a car and often takes him out to dinner at expensive restaurants.*
>
> *Russell said he is working part-time, doing freelance investigations.*[6]

Although Collins did not state the name of Russell's "benefactor" directly, Woodward certainly knew Birely's name because he admittedly met at least twice with him. So the combination of circumstances known to Woodward was compelling: Russell was a private eye working for McCord; he was outside Watergate before the arrests; he was possibly the "sixth burglar" at the time of the arrest; the FBI didn't believe his story about nostalgia for his girlfriend; and he was now being housed in luxury by a

6 Patrick Collins and Joseph Volz, "Lou Russell's Dual Hats," *Washington Star-News*, October 11, 1972, A-1.

stockbroker with strong connection to the intelligence community. Yet, unlike the *Star-News* reporters, Woodward, who worked for a paper that eventually published three thousand Watergate-related articles, did not find this newsworthy.

On May 9, 1973, the Senate minority staff of the Ervin Committee issued a subpoena to Russell, seeking his bank deposits, checks, phone records, and the like, obviously preparatory to his testimony. Russell claimed in response on May 11 that he had no such records, on its face an absurd claim, suggesting suppression of evidence since Russell had been working for McCord and paid regularly by check.

So we know with near certainty that Woodward, Bernstein, and the *Post* knew of Russell and his significance. Collins' article alone gave Woodstein sufficient material for publication. There would have been no reason for Deep Throat to withhold from his reporter friend information about Russell, including the Bureau's suspicions that he was the sixth burglar. And the various local FBI agents whom the reporters used as sources would have known of Russell and his significance, since Russell was interviewed by their DC field office. Certainly, Collins' article had to have been sourced through an interviewing FBI agent or supervisor. Finally, Woodward's friend Scott Armstrong, working for the Ervin Committee's majority, had access to the minority staff subpoena to Russell.

Woodstein often used the issuance of a subpoena as a factual premise for a story to state the purpose of the subpoena. For instance, when the DNC issued subpoenas for various CRP employees such as Robert Odle and Glenn Sedam, the *Post* featured these subpoenas in a front-page story, suggesting (falsely) that these officials had received wiretapping logs from McCord via Baldwin.

But the Ervin Committee (minority) subpoena of Russell, which Russell stiff-armed, did not draw even a blurb in the middle of the paper. This subpoena, at the least, should have given rise to an exciting story about a search for the sixth burglar.

Shortly after Russell rebuffed the minority staff on May 11, there soon followed the dramatic May 16–17, 1973, garage meeting with Deep Throat, followed the next day, May 18, by Russell's heart attack and his death six weeks later. Russell, who had been heard to talk about writing a tell-all book, claimed he had a heart attack after someone switched his heart medication. Again, however, Woodward saw nothing to report regarding Russell, even though these ominous events, including the subpoena, the Stevens articles, the heart attack, and then Russell's ultimate death, were each events around which a reporter could build a sensational story–backed up by his deep background source. Certainly, this tableau gives the lie to Woodstein's claim in their book that nothing ever came of Deep Throat's dire garage warnings.[7]

The questions surrounding Russell were serious, central, and indeed critical to the Watergate reporting. Although we should not expect Woodstein to resolve competing inferences (which they seemed to do when Nixon could be hurt), simply their reporting of the mysteries swirling about Russell would have been the minimum the public should have received.

That a young reporter, Collins, with the lowly *Star-News,* wrote such a fine piece while Woodward and Bernstein, with far more resources, deliberately failed to do so, is striking, and it strongly suggests protection by the *Post* of the CIA in order to focus all blame for Watergate on the Nixon White House.

Years later, Woodward justified his ignoring Russell's CIA and burglary connections by pointing to the detective's obvious alcoholism. But if that is the reporter's weak defense for overlooking Russell, how did he report on another burglar with an admittedly ongoing CIA employment? The *Post*'s treatment of Eugenio Martinez provides additional telling detail about the paper's motive and intent.

7 A good friend of Russell's, John Leon, deeply stunned by Russell's death, himself died mysteriously right before his planned July 7, 1973 press conference with Republican National Committee director George H. W. Bush, where Leon was set to reveal prior CIA bugging programs.

Chapter Nineteen

EUGENIO MARTINEZ AND THE KEY TO WATERGATE

I have pointed to solid evidence that James McCord and Howard Hunt were falsely retired, ongoing CIA agents at the time of Watergate, a status designed to be subject to plausible deniability. But what if, in addition to these two spooks, one of the soldiers had been an active CIA agent for over ten years? What if the soldier was reporting to a case agent at the time of Watergate and considered Watergate a legitimate CIA mission? And what if he had a role in the burglary hidden from Liddy, the team supervisor, proving a hidden CIA agenda involving sexual targets? And, finally, what if, for the two years of Watergate journalism, the *Post* printed only slim fragments of this information?

This is precisely what the case was with burglar Eugenio Martinez, a veteran of the CIA's 1961 Bay of Pigs operation who stayed with the Agency thereafter.

On January 14, 1973, famed *New York Times* reporter Seymour Hersh broke the story that Martinez had been on the CIA payroll for over ten years, was nicknamed "El Practico" by his CIA colleagues, and kept a diary. The *Post* was forced to summarize Hersh's article, using a similarly inapt headline as did the *Times*, "4 in Bug Trial Still Paid, Paper Says." The *Post* version downplayed his interaction with CIA colleagues and omitted his ten-year tenure and his diary–highly important facts.

A week earlier, on January 7, 1973, reporter Martin Schram of the *Post* wrote an article[1] on the suspected break-in by the Watergate team of

1 Martin Schram. "Watergate Case Called Broad Plot." *Washington Post*. January 7, 1973. A-19.

the Chilean Embassy, in which he mentioned the Martinez diary "written without the knowledge of the codefendants, indicates that the [CIA] – or at least a CIA case officer – may have been monitoring the activities of the Watergate team." The article also cites a source close to the defendants that they were wiretapping "liberal Democratic Senators" Mansfield, Church, and Fulbright, with Watergate "part of a widespread project."

This article deliberately muffles the profound implications of the Martinez diary. A CIA agent keeping a diary is necessarily an operational agent reporting to a case officer, as the article weakly implies, but does not emphasize. This in turn means Martinez was something other than a mere CIA informant for Cuban activities in Miami, as the Agency claimed, but, rather, an operational agent. And, if so, he would not keep a diary for the Watergate burglary if this was not a CIA operation. Indeed, it would make no sense for the CIA to "monitor" a political operation. The Chilean Embassy would most likely have been of interest to the CIA, and the named senators also of interest because they were powerful in foreign policy and intelligence matters. In short, Nixon's re-election had nothing to do with these operations, but Schram connected them to the presumably political Watergate burglary.

Although Hersh reported that an operational diary had been found in Martinez's car at the Miami airport, in fact the CIA had delayed reporting the car to the FBI for several days, when it was, as hypothesized by investigators, cleansed of the incriminating diary, leaving two meaningless calendar and address notebooks. This was such a big issue as of October 1973 that Deputy Special Prosecutor Henry Ruth commissioned an FBI investigation on the seemingly removed operational diary.

On June 28, 1973, Martinez's probation officer reported Martinez's belief that Watergate was a "national security" operation "sanctioned by the government." That same day, Hunt testified in the House Nedzi Hearings[2] that he was "shocked" that Martinez had kept a diary which meant Martinez was reporting to his case officer and "the fact that it was seized was even worse."

---

2 United States. Cong. House. *Hearing of House of Representatives, Committee of Armed Services, Special Subcommittee on Intelligence*. Washington, D.C., Thursday, June 28, 1973. (Testimony of E. Howard Hunt). 543.

The *Post* never reported the FBI's investigation of the missing diary, or the apparent cleansing of the car, nor the profound implications of the diary, in fact casting the matter in a deceptive light in January 1973.

For many months, from March 1973 through at least November 1973, Martinez contended that he thought he had been on a legitimate CIA mission in Watergate, a claim the probation office found credible. I have cited the *Post* article treating this assertion, the lame November 6, 1973, article of Timothy Robinson, who, while describing Martinez's claims of a "legitimate national security" mission, did not bring himself to mention "CIA" in connection with the item.

Finally, the Martinez dam broke in the Senate minority Baker Report, detailing Martinez's case officer's concern with Hunt's activities using Martinez and the Miami station chief's elevation of this alarm to Langley. The report also revealed that upon Martinez's arrest, his regular case officer was reassigned to a foreign post, while his new case officer was ordered to drive to DC in an untraceable manner, not using credit cards, thereafter staying two years.

All these facts, as probative as they were, would have even more conclusively proved a secret CIA agenda had the *Post* reported immediately following the arrests the most significant piece of evidence in the nation's most significant scandal, evidence I believe that *Post* reporters literally held in their hands. But the *Post* never told the public about this evidence.

I have talked about the great lengths to which the *Post* went to conceal Baldwin's overheard phone calls, Russell's presence, Mullen's CIA status, McCord's admissions, Hunt's notebooks, Dean's falsehoods, and Martinez's employment. Let's now talk about what connects the CIA, Baldwin, Hunt, Dean, McCord, Russell, and Martinez: the key to a desk in the DNC office.

The "key" to the Watergate case was, beyond a doubt, the Maxie Wells desk key. Baldwin had visited the Watergate offices the week of the second burglary, using the pretense of being the absent Oliver's friend, to gain a tour of the Oliver area by Wells herself. Although Baldwin at trial contended the visit, ordered by McCord, was to locate O'Brien's office and get his current Miami phone number, both of these were either already known to them or available to them without a visit. After all, the burglars claimed, falsely to be sure, to have already entered the DNC and O'Brien's office earlier and had photographed documents supposedly arrayed on O'Brien's carpet. And they had a diagram of the offices depicting where O'Brien worked. Anyone wishing to reach O'Brien in Miami could have called the DNC for his new number. It was not a secret, nor was his office location.

It appears that the visit was instead designed to locate Wells's desk, the main target of the burglary, and perhaps get an impression of its lock to make a key,[3] although perhaps Russell had made one already. When the burglars were arrested, photographic equipment was found affixed to the top of the Wells desk. The *Post* reported that "two file drawers" were open, but it was not clear from the article whether those were the two file drawers in Wells's desk or were drawers of a separate file cabinet. In fact, at least one of the open drawers was in Wells's desk, as affirmed in a later court opinion in the Wells defamation case. But the *Post* did not report the location of the open drawers or the desk[4] on which the photographic equipment was placed, either of which would have identified a burglary target.

More significantly, arresting officer Carl Shoffler came close to shooting Eugenio Martinez as he furtively reached into his suit breast pocket, then tried to dispose of an object, later discovered to be Wells's desk key (attached to a small notebook). Since Magruder, we know now from Liddy's book *Will*, had told Liddy the object of the second burglary was what "they" had in the lower left desk drawer (the one the Republicans used for dirt on opponents), the centrality of the desk key is obvious. Liddy, to be sure, thought the targeted desk would be O'Brien's, and was not told about Wells's desk. The burglars wanted what was in the desk, reflecting the presumed dirt the Democrats had on their Republican opponents.

---

3 FBI reports indicate that there were only two known keys to the desk, accounted for by Wells and Barbara Kennedy. However, we note that Lou Russell had worked for months as a GSS security guard in the Watergate office building. Well before the first burglary, Baldwin observed, from across the street, McCord enter the DNC offices. So between Russell and McCord, there was access to Wells's desk before the second burglary even if Baldwin did not take an impressions during his June 12 visit.

4 In a later interview with Colodny, Martinez stated that the equipment was on Wells's desk and that Hunt had given him a marked floor plan designating the Wells/Oliver area. Shoffler told him camera equipment was on the desk.

We know from several sources, some from the *Wells v. Liddy* trial, that there was evidence that the desk may have had logs of customers or pictures of prostitutes that their potential clients could view while setting up assignations. If the desk key was found on a burglar, this would suggest to us now that the objective of the burglary was salacious information.

The United States Court of Appeals for the Fourth Circuit in its opinion in *Wells v. Liddy* noted something intriguing about the documentary target[5] of the burglars:

> *Additionally, a drawer of Wells'[s] desk was opened during the break-in. As a result, she was questioned by the FBI. Although there is some factual dispute between the parties over whether the FBI informed Wells of the discovery, the FBI also determined that a key found in a burglar's possession fit the lock on Wells's desk...*
>
> *...Unknown to Liddy at the time, one of the burglars carried a key to Wells'[s] desk.*[6]

But even without any indication of possible prostitution documents or photographs, simply a disclosure by the *Post* that a burglar was caught with a desk key would have been highly significant. Such a fact would have led observers to question the purpose of the key and the desk it fit. Since it was the only key seized, that lone key would logically be seen as suggesting that its use was a "key" purpose of the burglary. When coupled with photographic equipment on the very desk to which the key fit, and the nearby open drawer, inquiry would be redoubled and answers demanded as to what it was in this desk that was the clear object of the burglary. So ordinary journalism discussing the desk key and its significance would have addressed the key question that has puzzled observers ever since: What were the burglars after?

Since there was no evidence that O'Brien's or Oliver's desks were to be searched in the burglary, this fact alone would seem to negate a political spying motive. Wells, after all, was a mere secretary. Why, it would have

5 It is not altogether clear that the open drawer was part of Wells's desk as opposed to a file cabinet near the desk.

6 *Wells v. Liddy*, 98-1962, US Court of Appeals, Fourth District, 1999.

been asked, would the burglars be looking in her desk and not those of high political officials?

In short, the desk key can be viewed as the most important piece of evidence uncovered in the Watergate investigation. Once Baldwin's trial testimony was quashed as to the intimate personal conversations he had overheard, any evidentiary value to the prosecutors of the key, or its desk, to corroborate its extortion theme was lost. Thus it is not surprising that the key was not put into evidence at trial. In fact, if the prosecution cared about a *wiretapping* conspiracy, the key would perhaps hurt that claim, since the key, standing alone without a nexus to the prostitution phone calls, suggested a document target for the burglary, not a wiretap.

I have been through thousands of *Post* Watergate articles, filling seven bankers boxes and covering what seems like every conceivable corner of the investigation. But I could find no mention in the *Post* of the key. Does this prove an intentional suppression of this "key" evidence? It does if any *Post* reporter knew of the seizure of the key.

So, we should ask, what evidence is there that the *Post* likely knew of the key? First, Woodstein boasts in *All the President's Men* about the *Post*'s jailhouse sources. These would include not only Woodward's local sources developed as a neophyte local crime reporter but also those of experienced police reporter Eugene Bachinski. Perhaps more impressively, the *Post* employed a legendary jailhouse reporter, Alfred E. Lewis, according to Woodstein a "half cop, half reporter," with thirty-five years of police reporting experience. And, yes, Lewis did get, apparently from local police sources, an inventory of what was seized. In *All the President's Men*, Woodstein describes some of the items the police seized (they don't claim these were *all* the items), which they apparently gained from a list obtained from Lewis:

> *The five men arrested at 2:30 A.M. had been dressed in business suits and had all worn platex rubber surgical gloves. Police had seized a walkie-talkie, 40 rolls of unexposed film, two 35-millimeter cameras, lock picks, pen-size tear-gas guns, and bugging devices that apparently were capable of picking up both telephone and room conversations.*[7]

7 Bernstein and Woodward, *All the President's Men*, 15–16.

Woodstein then quotes part of Lewis's oral report verbatim, albeit with ellipses:

> *"One of the men had $814, one $800, one $215, one $234, one $230," Lewis had dictated. "Most of it was in $100 bills, in sequence.... They seemed to know their way around; at least one of them must have been familiar with the layout."*[8]

Lewis also noted in his dictation: "One wore a suit bought at Raleigh's. Somebody got a look at the breast pocket."[9]

We now know that the key was seized by the police. Either Lewis failed to tell Woodstein or Woodstein deliberately left the key out of the list of items in evidence. From the description of items noted, it appears to have been a detailed accounting of what was in evidence. The initial newspaper reports were less detailed and did not purport to be exhaustive. But this account in *All the President's Men* does give the reader the sense that all seized items, or the important ones at least, were included. But no key was mentioned.

This lack of mention, one could counter, may have been inadvertent. The suspects had on their persons miscellaneous pieces of paper and "pocket litter," we know, and Martinez had a slim metal "pop-up" address book. These were not mentioned in Woodstein's listing of items on pages 15–16 of their book, or in the immediate reporting of Lewis, likely written by Bernstein or another scrivener for Lewis:

> *All wearing rubber surgical gloves, the five suspects were captured inside a small office within the committee's headquarters suite.*
>
> *Police said the men had with them at least two sophisticated devices capable of picking up and transmitting all talk, including telephone conversations. In addition, police found lock-picks and door jimmies, almost $2,300 in cash, most of it in $100 bills with the serial numbers in sequence.*

---

8 Bernstein and Woodward, *All the President's Men*, 16.

9 Bernstein and Woodward, *All the President's Men*, 16.

> *The men also had with them one walkie-talkie, a short wave receiver that could pick up police calls, 40 rolls of unexposed film, two 35 millimeter cameras and three pen-sized tear gas guns.*[10]

So perhaps one might think, if the pocket litter and address book were not mentioned, the omission of the key was not intentional, since it may have been inventoried as attached to the pocket notebook. To be sure, because of the ellipses, we don't know what was omitted from the book's Lewis quote of the seized items. And one would think a desk key, if one was seized, would have been inventoried by Lewis. But if we look only at the newspaper reporting and the initial description in *All the President's Men*, a reader would conclude nothing was seized other than the mentioned items.

However, later in *All the President's Men*, Woodstein mentions the yellow-lined paper containing phone numbers of Hunt and an envelope with a Hunt check found on one of the burglars:

> *But the first priority on that Monday was Hunt. The Miami suspects' belongings were listed in a confidential police inventory that Bachinski had obtained. There were "two pieces of yellow-lined paper, one addressed to 'Dear Friend Mr. Howard,' and another to 'Dear Mr. H.H.,'" and an unmailed envelope containing Hunt's personal check for $6.36 made out to the Lakewood Country Club in Rockville, along with a bill for the same amount.*[11]

At this point in the book, Woodstein has described all the items found on the burglars...except the address book and the attached key!

Former *Post* editor Barry Sussman claimed in a July 2005 article that the *Post* reporters were given the actual seized items themselves for examination, including two address books, inferentially one of which was the small pocket notebook to which the key had been attached by tape:

---

10 Alfred E. Lewis, "5 Held in Plot to Bug Democrats' Office Here," *Washington Post*, June 18, 1972, A01.

11 Bernstein and Woodward, *All the President's Men*, 23.

> *Also that Sunday, Larry Fox, our night city editor, told me that D.C. cops might let a Post reporter look over some of the burglars' possessions. They did, and E.J. Bachinski, a police reporter, found two address books with the name Howard Hunt in them, and the notation "WH" in one and "W. House" in the other. He also found a check for $6.36 from Hunt to a local country club. So it was that the Post, hardly 48 hours after the arrests–and through the work of its White House correspondent and a night police reporter–was able to tie the break-in to both the Nixon re-election campaign and the White House.*[12]

Thus, from Sussman's account we learn that the reporters did review the address books, although, interestingly, Sussman does not mention an attached key.[13] So the key is the only evidence not mentioned by *Post* reporters or editors. We can be sure that the following week, Deep Throat gave Woodward significant tips about what was in the seized evidence. For instance, Deep Throat gave Woodward Hunt's initials and the phone number listed for him, seemingly before Bachinski got them. This came from the seized address books. We also know that the FBI was well aware of the key and did extensive work to match it to a desk, in turn generating two FBI 302 reports,[14] both of which necessarily went to Mark Felt's desk. So it is of some interest that no article of Woodward or Bernstein mentions the key that was seized. Did someone decide it was less important than, say, the tiny tear gas guns?

But, most significantly, the key figured prominently in the most dramatic incident occurring during the arrests. According to Detective Shoffler, Martinez did not easily give up the key, causing a scuffle, a fact that Woodstein would know. The following are excerpts from Colodny's later interview of Shoffler:

---

12 Barry Sussman, "Why Deep Throat was an Unimportant Source and Other Reflections on Watergate," *Nieman Watchdog*, July 29, 2005, http://www.niemanwatchdog.org/index.cfm?fuseaction=background.view&backgroundid=51.

13 Colodny featured a police picture of an address book seized from the burglars with a key attached by tape.

14 See FBI 302 reports of interviews of Maxie Wells and DNC secretary Barbara Kennedy Rhoden, June 27, 1972, Reports 139-166-356, -358, and -359.

SHOFFLER: He went inside his, uh, coat pocket three times, I had to slam him into the wall to get him away from the key.

COLODNY: Was it, was it attached to the book?

SHOFFLER: Yes, it was.

COLODNY: And what did he do, try to rip it away from the book to–

SHOFFLER: He tried to reach inside his coat to get the key and he was gonna chuck it.

COLODNY: Did he ever get it out of his pocket?

SHOFFLER: Uh, I, first when I saw him reaching for it.

COLODNY: You must've thought it was a gun, for Christ sake.

SHOFFLER: Yeah, I was upset.

COLODNY: [LAUGHTER]

SHOFFLER: So I slammed his hand on the wall, I said don't do it, and I kicked his feet back. Uh, while, because of the circumstances, we knew that we had to be very detailed with our search and all.

COLODNY: Yeah.

SHOFFLER: Okay, cause we knew we had something more than a typewriter thief, okay.

COLODNY: [LAUGHTER]

SHOFFLER: So we said what we would do is one person would search him and one person would log, and I was logging and Barrett was searching.

COLODNY: Right.

SHOFFLER: Okay. So I didn't wanna take the stuff out of his pocket, I wanted Barrett to seize it, you see what I'm saying?

COLODNY: Right.

SHOFFLER: So, he went to that pocket–I just felt, I didn't feel a gun, slammed his hands up and told him not to do it again. I turned my head, uh, logging stuff with Barrett and I glanced back and he's going back in his pocket.

COLODNY: Was he ever able to detach the key from the book?

SHOFFLER: No, we just took it and threw it in and logged it that way.

COLODNY: In other words, he, he, although he was gonna try and swallow it, he had not detached–

SHOFFLER: He wasn't [INAUDIBLE] swallowing it. I–

COLODNY: You mean, he was trying to get rid of it.

SHOFFLER: He was trying to get rid of it?

COLODNY: Okay, he wasn't actually trying to eat the key.

SHOFFLER: No, he didn't put the key in his mouth [INAUDIBLE].

COLODNY: But he didn't want you to find the key on him?

SHOFFLER: He was trying to get rid of that key, yes.

COLODNY: Which means, he knew–see when we asked him that question, about did you get any special instructions to go with the key, you know what he told us, the key was to the target. So, you know, that wasn't the problem. The problem was, well, what did Hunt tell you to do when you got inside the target. But, just from the reaction that you're saying is, he didn't want you to know that he had that key. He wanted to ditch it somewhere so that–

SHOFFLER: Well, his intelligence training would've told him to get rid of the key. It would've identified the target.[15]

Though the interview is not a model of clarity, it reveals that, even in 1990, the struggle of Shoffler with Martinez was still memorable for the detective. At one point in the interview, describing his struggle with Martinez, Shoffler told Colodny, "I almost had to break his arm off."

It also defies common sense that Deep Throat would not have told Woodward of the key and why the FBI thought it significant, leading to its interrogation of Maxie Wells and Barbara Kennedy. After all, it held the clue as to what was already deemed a true curiosity in the matter: the target of this strange break-in. And we know from Woodward's quote of FBI agents in the Baldwin pieces that the Bureau was furiously probing for what the burglars were after. Deep Throat and Woodstein's other FBI sources would likely have disclosed to the reporters the criticality of the desk key.

In Lewis's earlier description, he noted that one officer got a look at one suspect's breast pocket, which he noted had a Raleigh's tag. This bit was likely gained from Shoffler, who should have seen the breast pocket of Martinez, where he apparently had the key initially strapped to the address book. So Shoffler, it appears, likely spoke to Lewis immediately and we presume told Lewis of the dramatic seizure of the key. Wouldn't that be the occasion where the Raleigh's tag was observed? But when Woodstein and others reported under Lewis's byline on June 18, 1972, the key was not

15 Len Colodny, Shoffler interview, August 8, 1990, tape P-97, 18–20.

mentioned, nor was a violent struggle. Why would this dramatic encounter, almost leading to a shooting, not have been reported?

We know that Shoffler was quite friendly with Maxine Cheshire of the *Post* and in any event was known to be extremely talkative. It is difficult to believe that this arresting officer would have been reluctant to talk to Woodstein about his dramatic encounter, at least without attribution.

Intriguingly, at the burglary trial in January 1973, the pocket notebook with the key attached by tape was routinely verified by officer Barrett, and admitted into evidence. Silbert breezed right through the seizure of the notebook, omitting any mention of struggle in its seizure as he took Shoffler's direct testimony following Barrett's. Clearly, in a case of wiretapping, Silbert had little use for establishment of a documentary target. But for a paper which was rabidly investigating the scandal, it is difficult to believe that *Post* reporters did not understand the significance of a desk key seized from a burglar identified as an active CIA agent keeping an operational diary.

In spite of all these sources, it is theoretically *possible* that Woodward and Bernstein innocently overlooked reporting on one item, and one item only–the key–in their otherwise energetic investigation. And it is possible that all of Woodstein's sources innocently omitted mention of the key, the camera equipment on Wells's desk, Wells's open desk or file drawer, and the Shoffler-Martinez wrestling match. But odds are that, if the two were 10 percent as good as advertised, they deliberately chose to conceal the key's existence when they wrote *All the President's Men* in late 1973 and early 1974, and did so as well in their earlier newspaper reporting.

Only when Colodny uncovered the key's existence years later, after the prostitution angle became obvious, did anyone publicize its possession by the burglars. Since the *Post* was the only paper with a vigorous local DC reporting capability[16] and the only one to hop on this local burglary case, the paper and its reporters in 1972 through 1974 could be fairly confident no one else would raise the issue of the key. The *Post* was likely the only paper, in short, with knowledge of the seizure of the key, incidentally cor-

16 The *Washington Star-News*, the other DC paper, was on its last legs financially, faced a declining circulation, and simply could not allocate great resources to the scandal's journalism. In any case, it did not have jailhouse reporting capability like the *Post.*

responding to the placement of the document camera. Please recall that during Woodward and Bernstein's visit to the Felt residence in December 2008, it was my discussion of the key that caused Woodward's immediate and palpable alarm.

Because the key did not play into the burglary trial, nor did Wells, there was no occasion for any public disclosure in court in January 1973. The opportunity did arise for public disclosure in the summer of 1973, when the Ervin Committee questioned Wells. But no question was apparently asked of her by the committee about the key, or her desk, or of the FBI demonstrating the key fitting her desk, or of who had copies of the key.

The senators, to be fair, may not have been aware of any relevant issue or even of the seizure of the key, and it appears that they had not been given the two FBI reports on the key, or any FBI interview reports for that matter. But the committee interfaced with, indeed relied on, Woodward for information and as well his close associate, the majority's chief investigator, Scott Armstrong. Apparently, we must conclude either that Woodward provided nothing to the committee on that topic or that the committee majority deliberately avoided such inquiry.[17] Certainly, the minority staff of the committee had not a clue about the key, one would think, because nothing was said of it in the minority Baker Report, its final Watergate report supplementing the lengthy report of the majority. Indeed, there is no evidence that the Ervin Committee knew of the key.

Finally, putting aside focus on the key for a moment, in my review of Woodstein's reporting, I queried whether the *Post* reported on the location of the photographic equipment as being set up seemingly on Wells's desk. Again, I can find no mention in the paper of the location of this equipment. The closest I saw to any relevant item was mentioned in the first burglary article, credited to Lewis (but written by Bernstein and others) that "there were two open file drawers." There was nothing else mentioned after that in subsequent articles about what may have been the object of photography. We know that Lewis never wrote his own articles but merely funneled information to the newsroom and that Woodstein collaborated on

---

17 Both are likely true. Robert Bennett, Hunt's superior at Mullen and the son of a Utah senator, told his case officer that he could "take care of" the committee if the CIA could take care of Hunt.

the first article. If the court's opinion in *Wells v. Liddy* is to be credited and we do have our doubts, at least one of the two "file drawers" was in fact a desk drawer in Wells's desk. But we were never told the location of these "two open file drawers." Wouldn't identification of both the desk and the file drawers tell us much about the target of the burglary?

In any case, Woodward and Bernstein should have had multiple indications that a key was seized and that it was central to this story, but they never even mentioned the key, much less featured it in a story. Nor did I find any article analyzing the placement of the photographic equipment. Wouldn't the location of the cameras or camera clamps[18] have been an important fact?

We know that Detective Carl Shoffler was available and that Mark Felt had provided Woodward with significant details of other evidentiary items seized, including Hunt's phone number. Finally, witnesses Maxie Wells and Barbara Kennedy of the DNC were questioned by the FBI about the key on June 27, 1972, and may have been available for interview by the reporters. The local FBI agents conducting the interview were sources for a number of other Woodstein stories. And we know that the reporters were provided a confidential police inventory[19] of seized items, and very likely the items themselves, if Sussman is to be credited.

This key is "key" to Watergate not only because of its direct and profound probative value in and of itself. Because it quickly learned of the key's seizure, the DNC necessarily would have realized what secrets it might reveal. It would only make sense that the DNC would immediately advise the *Post* of the key's significance so that the paper could be careful not to mention it or its implications. So when in earlier chapters it is inferred that the *Post* had red-hot information in its files that needed pro-

18 There are conflicting contentions as to whether any clamps were attached to the desk at the time of the burglary arrests. Officer Barrett's trial testimony, very cursory, listed two cameras with clamps as being in Martinez's gym bag at arrest. Barrett did not testify one way or the other about what was on any desk. Author Shane O'Sullivan interprets Barrett's identification of evidence to mean that Martinez had not yet begun his document photography. In fact Martinez had testified to the Ervin Committee, at pages 293-294, that he had begun photographing documents prior to the arrests. So I tend to credit Shoffler's claim of a photography setup.

19 In my view, adding to the intrigue, I found no such inventory having been provided by the Metropolitan Police to the FBI.

tection from a Baldwin-connected subpoena, there is sound basis for the inference. The *Post*'s stunning silence on both Baldwin (before the *Times* publicized him) and the key (at all times) became mutually reinforcing proofs of *Post* concealment of the truth.

Finally, I should note that when I raised the centrality of the key in December 2008 at the Felt home, Woodward acted guilty. He did not say, "Yes, I have heard of this key, but let me tell you why I did not report it." Nor did he deny knowledge of the key. He merely questioned me aggressively for raising the issue. Very telling evidence, indeed. Unbeknownst to me at the time, the photo of the four of us–Woodward, Bernstein, Felt, and me–documented the scene of Woodward's most revealing, albeit implicit, admission: the key to the *Post* cover-up.

It is very, very difficult for us to conclude otherwise that Woodward and Bernstein, presumably on direction from their editors, deliberately concealed the seizure of the key and its significance and thereby concealed perhaps the most significant piece of evidence in our country's biggest scandal.

Chapter Twenty

THE BAKER REPORT

In June 1974, the Ervin Committee, controlled by the Democratic majority, issued a lengthy report of 1,114 pages, following the eleven thousand pages of testimony it had impressively produced. Discussed as a separate report was thirty-four pages of factual reporting, with appendices of comments and questions totaling forty-nine pages, all dealing with the issue of the CIA's involvement in Watergate. This latter effort, written by the Republican minority staff of the committee, was labeled the "Baker Report," after Republican senator Howard Baker of Tennessee.

Up to this point, there had been essentially no *Post* reporting whatsoever about CIA involvement, and what fragments the *Post* reported tended to exonerate the Agency.[1] The *Times* had done somewhat better than the *Post,* with Hersh's extensive January 14, 1973, article discussing the intelligence and CIA connection not only of Martinez but also of the other burglars. There had been some excellent reporting by the *Washington Star-News* in its October 11, 1972, Lou Russell piece and by *Chicago Today* about the Michael Stevens revelations, running on May 14 and May 16,

1 Essentially, all the *Post* had revealed, as I have described above, was the testimony of Douglas Caddy that he had "intimations" that Mullen had done work for the CIA, which disclosure was quickly followed in the *Post* by Mullen president Robert Bennett's explanation that Caddy's intimations likely were the result of Mullen's prior dealings in the 1960s with Radio Free Cuba. Later on January 14, the *Post* very briefly, and without byline, repeated from the *New York Times* the report that at the time of Watergate, Martinez was an active employee of the CIA, quickly followed by the note that the CIA had terminated him immediately after his arrest. Both of these disclosures tended more to negate the idea of CIA involvement in Watergate than to suggest it. Additionally, the *Post* portrayed Bennett as raising funds for Nixon.

1973. Both the *Washington Star-News* and *Chicago Today* drew only local attention and none by the national television or print media.

But the *Post* had by the summer of 1974 become the Watergate paper of record and had published some three thousand Watergate-related articles detailing the moral bankruptcy of the Nixon administration. More importantly, as any trial lawyer knows, it is important to establish a narrative theme, constantly reinforced, when dealing with a complex set of facts. The *Post* had done that with its narrative theme of the Nixon administration's "massive conspiracy of spying and sabotage" on and of its electoral opponents. This theme, developed as a result of Deep Throat's Segretti "dirty tricks" campaign insights and amplified by the distorted *Post* reporting about Baldwin's monitoring, had become the dominant theme of Watergate. The fragments of excellent Watergate reporting by the other papers remained exactly that–fragments–and never became integral parts of the public's received narrative.

So the Baker Report was highly important because it was the first occasion on which any widely respected institution had made an attempt to embed any additional material component into the accepted Watergate story. To be sure, the minority staff of the Ervin Committee had lacked certain information that would have been useful in considering the CIA issue. It had no testimony from Liddy, who was simply refusing to talk. Michael Stevens did not testify either, likely on Fifth Amendment or national security grounds–highly convenient excuses after the CIA had threatened his life. And as well the committee failed to show any knowledge that a desk key had been seized during the burglary and what it implied, not surprising given that the committee did not have FBI interview reports and relied for information on Woodward's pipeline to Scott Armstrong.

Indeed, there was very little attention paid by the Ervin Committee to the burglary itself, because the cover-up, not the crimes, was the focus. Moreover, much of the documentation upon which the minority staff relied in writing the Baker Report came from the CIA after public hearings had ceased, with various facts, previously withheld by the CIA, presented to the committee in late February 1974. Only confidential executive session testimony was received after the CIA produced these documents. The public, in summary, had not been prepared for a bombshell about the CIA.[2]

Attempting to overcome these limits, the Baker Report presented, for the first time in one spot, a compilation of facts showing the CIA's involvement in Watergate. The report was not written as an advocacy brief and at least attempted a just-the-facts-ma'am tone, reflecting a hope that serious observers would recognize the report's credibility.

In short, the Baker Report showed both affirmative evidence of CIA participation in Watergate and, perhaps more devastatingly, a concerted CIA campaign of cover-up and concealment of its involvement, continuing through the time of the report's issuance. In this latter regard, the CIA was still as of the issuance of the report "stonewalling" the committee on a number of directly relevant requests.

The report's thirty-four pages of facts are themselves presented as a concise summary of extensive documentation and testimony, so I will not attempt here a duplication of the effort. Instead, I will simply address a few factual areas of the report that seem both solidly proven and highly material.

The honesty with which the *Post* reported these facts when confronted with them by this reputable report should speak volumes about the honesty of its reporting throughout Watergate. If it embraced and publicized that which was clearly shown to be true in the report–or at least factually accurate enough to raise questions and stimulate further inquiry–such reporting would demonstrate honesty and good faith. On the other hand, denial, distortion, or obfuscation of the truth in response to the Baker Report would suggest that the paper had been willfully covering up pertinent issues of facts at other times as well. Let us explore a few areas highlighted by the report.

PENNINGTON

The first area of interest in the report concerns the mysterious Lee Pennington, the "Pennington" whom the FBI sought for questioning once it learned that he had picked up McCord from jail. If the *Post* claimed that

2 However, the *Post* was well aware that Baker had been on the CIA's scent since at least the fall of 1973, so the Report did not surprise the paper.

it had simply not known of Pennington or his significance prior to the report,[3] its publication gave the *Post* quite clear notice of these facts.

The most significant finding of the report about Pennington was a blockbuster, detailing Lee Pennington's visit to McCord's home before McCord made bail, where he burned documents and tapes, along with Mrs. McCord and others:

> *The results of our investigation clearly show that the CIA had in its possession, as early as June of 1972, information that one of their paid operatives, Lee R. Pennington, Jr., had entered the James McCord residence shortly after the Watergate break-in and destroyed documents which might show a link between McCord and the CIA.4*

To belabor the obvious, after the arrest everyone had known of McCord's *past* employment with the CIA. So the only possible meaning of the admission was the Agency's concealment of McCord's *present* relationship with the CIA. This of course was huge, confirming that McCord was a falsely retired CIA agent, therefore likely plying his trade in the Watergate burglary.

The second claim of the report was the furnishing by the CIA of false information about the "Pennington" who accompanied McCord from the jail, a falsity designed to conceal his identity and role, that is, the CIA's false designation to the FBI of only *Cecil* Pennington, when the CIA knew *Lee* Pennington was the witness sought. It was the CIA's false, wild-goose-chase designation of Cecil Pennington that had angered Mark Felt when he published *The FBI Pyramid* in 1980.

The third instance of obstruction shown by the report was the removal by the director of security of the CIA of certain Pennington materials from CIA files while the Agency was responding to a request in early 1974 from

3 It is highly likely that Mark Felt told Woodward of the FBI's hunt for the mysterious "Pennington" who had picked up McCord at the jail. The *Post*'s vaunted jailhouse contacts certainly told *Post* reporters of the Pennington pickup. FBI Special Agent Angelo Lano, highly knowledgeable, was also a regular source for the reporters.

4 United States Senate Select Committee, Howard H. Baker Jr., US Senator, Tenn., "Memorandum for Director of Intelligence," February 23, 1974, appendix to Baker Report, 1127. Emphasis in original.

the inspector general of the CIA for Watergate documents to produce to the various congressional committees.

The fourth significant finding in the Baker Report regarding Pennington was that Pennington was likely acting as an illegal domestic agent, citing a report prepared by McCord at Pennington's direction on columnist Jack Anderson, delivered by McCord to Pennington in May 1972 and kept as part of the CIA's file on Anderson. Interestingly, the CIA also continued to refuse to produce to the Senate parts of its Pennington file, suggesting more illegal activities would have been uncovered and showing a likely fifth area of obstruction.

The significance of these findings cannot be overstated. The report did not in the Pennington section comment *directly* on McCord's status but clearly showed that there was a continuing connection with the CIA after his supposed "retirement," which the CIA, Pennington, and McCord attempted to obscure through the destruction of documents burned in McCord's fireplace. McCord had continued after his supposed retirement to report to Pennington, and did so on the very sensitive matter of Jack Anderson. That Pennington also picked up McCord at jail suggested that Watergate was, like the Anderson assignment, a CIA mission. When McCord reported to the CIA, through five letters he wrote the Agency on the Watergate investigation, he delivered them through Pennington–presumably his case agent.

MULLEN AND BENNETT

Regarding this subject, the report first and foremost stated clearly what everyone should have suspected all along: that Mullen and Company was a CIA front organization, providing "cover" for various CIA operations throughout the world.

Secondly, the internal memos of the CIA (e.g., Bennett reporting to a case officer, who in turn reported up the chain) verified in so many words that this cover arrangement directly involved Mullen's Washington office. Indeed, CIA memos after the arrests confided that the PR firm would likely lose its contract, but also cautioned that the Agency should be careful not to blame this loss of cover on the "WH flap" and stated that it was not planning on being straight with Mullen on this planned removal of its cover contract.

Finally, the report notes that the true nature of Bennett's and Mullen's relationship to the CIA was not known by the committee until November of 1973, when at Senator Baker's request, and prodded by honest security officers, the CIA produced another volume of CIA documents. So, again, CIA guilt was shown by its withholding of inculpatory information.

Certain explosive findings were taken by minority staff directly from CIA memos that the Agency belatedly provided to the Senate. In essence, the memos show successful efforts by the CIA to team up with both the DNC and the *Post* to tell the Watergate story falsely so as to keep Mullen's CIA involvement hidden. There are two interrelated aspects to these initiatives.

First, the Baker Report found that on July 10, 1972, Bennett revealed to the CIA his detailed knowledge of Watergate and his immediate efforts to hide his company's CIA relationship:

> *Bennett reported detailed knowledge of the Watergate incident to his CIA case officer. The case officer's report at this meeting was handwritten and carried to Director Helms on or before July 14, 1972, and in this form because of the sensitivity of the information. It revealed that Bennett had established a "back door entry" to E. B. Williams, the attorney for the DNC, in order to "kill off" revelations in the Agency's relationship with the Mullen and Company in the course of the DNC lawsuit. He agreed to check with the CIA prior to contacting Williams.*[5]

Note that this finding means that the CIA had formed an alliance with the Democratic Party lawyers, who were also, of course, the *Post*'s lawyers.

Additionally, the report notes a fourth aspect of questionable CIA conduct, that is, that Bennett had withheld key information from both the FBI and the grand jury:

> *Our staff has confirmed that Bennett did funnel information to Williams via attorney Hobart Taylor and that this information was more extensive than the information Bennett had*

5 Baker Report, 1124.

> *previously provided the Grand Jury. Although Bennett was supplying information to the CIA about many aspects of the Watergate incident and was at that time serving as liaison between Hunt and Liddy, there is no indication that these facts were disclosed to the FBI.*[6]

The report also describes Bennett's participation, along with the CIA, in preventing exposure of the Agency's role in Watergate to the Ervin hearings. Specifically, the March 1, 1973, memorandum reflects that "Bennett felt he could handle the Ervin Committee if the Agency could handle Hunt."[7]

Finally, Bennett admitted that he had been feeding stories to Bob Woodward, who was "suitably grateful" and who in exchange agreed to hide the Mullen CIA connection, and that he was doing this in order to protect Bennett and Mullen and Company from exposure:

> *Mr. Bennett does not believe that company will be bothered much more by the news media which has concluded that "the company is clean and has gotten a bum wrap while the real culprits are getting scot free." Mr. Bennett said also that he has been feeding stories to Bob Woodward of the* Washington Post *with the understanding that there be no attribution to Bennett. Woodward is suitably grateful for the fine stories and bylines which he gets and protects Bennett (and the Mullen Company). Typical is the article, "Hunt Tried to Recruit Agents to Probe Senator Kennedy's Life" on Page A-16 of the Saturday, February 10, 1973* Washington Post.[8]

WIDESPREAD CIA SUPPORT

One of the intriguing aspects of my post-Watergate research had been the extent to which the entirety of the CIA had seemingly helped Hunt's White House adventurers in their various escapades. This assistance fits quite consistently with the concept of the CIA planting Hunt in the White House undercover to carry out domestic operations. Why else would multi-

6 Baker Report, 1124. Emphasis in original.

7 Baker Report, 1126. Emphasis in original.

8 Eisenstadt, "Memorandum."

ple CIA departments, encompassing a large number of employees, all work to support Hunt and his co-operatives? The report's detailing of the extensive support of Hunt cements his role as an undercover CIA operative.

For instance, the Technical Services Division provided a gait-altering disguise and voice-altering device for Hunt's Denver hospital visit to Dita Beard, an embattled International Telephone and Telegraph lobbyist; small clandestine cameras for the Fielding break-in; and false identification for Hunt, Liddy, and McCord. The Central Cover staff negotiated Hunt's deal with Mullen. The OS provided safe houses for Hunt and Liddy. The Graphics Division made Liddy's impressive Gemstone charts. The Medical Services staff developed a profile of Daniel Ellsberg. And so on.

The CIA's preemptive explanation in the Ervin hearings of this evidence was that immediately after Hunt's hiring, White House counsel John Ehrlichman had called General Robert Cushman of the CIA to ask for carte blanche assistance for Hunt. Ehrlichman had always claimed that he never called Cushman, that Cushman had called him later for an uneventful conversation, and that he did not in any case ask for "carte blanche" help. The circumstances–Ehrlichman was on his way out the door en route to the Western White House the day of Hunt's hiring–and his lack of motive to lie about the CIA, whose involvement would not exculpate him, give his story credibility. Moreover, Hunt was not being hired by Ehrlichman to work directly with him but with White House special counsel Charles Colson. Ehrlichman was merely approving the hire. What would have prompted Ehrlichman in this fictitious tableau to ask Cushman for help when Ehrlichman had no idea of Hunt's future tasks?

Suffice it to say, it was clear from the Baker Report that the widespread CIA support for Hunt did not come because Ehrlichman asked for it. Hunt received it because he was a CIA agent, not a White House agent.

In the aftermath of the arrests, the CIA took a two-step approach. First it claimed that "carte blanche" ended when it determined that Hunt had been going "too far" as he planned the Fielding break-in. Conveniently, the Agency determined that this withdrawal of support occurred around August 27, 1971, one week before the September 3, 1971, Fielding burglary. Of course, by supposedly terminating assistance prior to that break-in, the Agency could thereby deny complicity in that felony. According to the CIA, the pre-burglary "casing" photos of a smiling Liddy outside the doctor's office were never recognized by high officials as such prior to the burglary. The second part of the CIA's approach was its wholesale destruction of pertinent CIA tapes and transcripts, except for selected fragments, fabricated or otherwise, that it decided should survive, mainly to support the claimed request by Ehrlichman.

Casting doubt on the CIA's credibility, the Baker Report detailed the Agency's continued support for Hunt following its supposed August 27 withdrawal of assistance for him. One CIA technical support employee testified, the report noted, that every request of Hunt after this date was approved by the Agency. For instance, on August 27, the day on which the Agency claims it pulled support, it approved a "back stopped" telephone request by Hunt, contrary to prior CIA claims. Indeed, the report detailed a litany of Hunt/CIA contacts and assistance well after August 1971.

The Baker Report also showed that Hunt's "Mr. Edward" file[9] was deemed by the Agency to be a highly sensitive (read: incriminating) matter, demonstrated by the CIA's refusal to produce the file to the Senate. Additionally, all Hunt's activities had been placed on a "bigot list," a CIA term for treatment of especially sensitive cases that could not be disclosed. In short, the CIA had files related to Hunt's activities after he "retired," which the CIA admitted were too sensitive to produce. This tells us a lot.

At the least, then, the CIA's response tells us that Hunt was an active CIA black ops agent after his false retirement.

MARTINEZ, HUNT, AND THE CIA

The Baker Report added many details to the facts revealed by Seymour Hersh in January 1973 about Eugenio Martinez.

When Richard Helms testified before the Ervin Committee, he said that Martinez was nothing more than a hundred-dollar-per-month retainer used as an informant on Cubans of interest to the CIA. The committee learned, however, that there was much more to Martinez's involvement with the Agency, the first being that for approximately ten years, through

9 "Mr. Edward" was one of Hunt's Agency-supplied aliases, complete with falsified identification. Hunt's black ops exploits were seemingly detailed in this highly sensitive CIA file.

mid-1971, he had been a regularly employed full-time agent. It was then in 1971 that Hunt recruited him, apparently his first assignment being the Fielding burglary.

In November 1971, a month after that burglary, Martinez questioned the nature of his involvement with Hunt to his case officer. Indeed, there were some unspecified indications that Martinez had informed the case officer earlier than that of his involvement. By March 1972, the case officer began to be concerned about Hunt's activities with Martinez, to such an extent that he alerted the CIA's Miami station chief, who himself grew alarmed upon hearing of Martinez's activities with Hunt. We do not know specifics from the record, which omitted sensitive matters divulged in executive session, but certainly what Martinez revealed about Hunt's operation, we can infer, was compromising to the CIA.

What should have been of great public interest was the response to the case officer from the CIA's Assistant Deputy Director for Plans[10] in Washington. He advised the station chief not to be concerned about Hunt's travels to Miami,[11] that Hunt was on domestic White House business and the station chief should "cool it." The station chief was "infuriated" at this response, which left him uneasy, according to the report. Martinez's case officer required Martinez to prepare a report in Spanish but to write this as a "cover story" in a way that would not come back to haunt him. The written Martinez report did not contain the "alarming" innuendos suggested earlier by him in person, according to the Baker Report.

The Agency had told the committee that Martinez's first case officer was on an African safari throughout June 1972 and showed the staff a printed itinerary of the trip, a copy of which it would not leave with the staff. However, Martinez had last met with this case officer on June 6, 1972, and, interestingly, his second case officer testified that the first case officer was in Miami as late as June 19, 1972 (two days after the burglary arrests).

Following the burglary arrests, the second case officer, Robert Ritchie, was rushed to Washington and told he would need to stay there until September for matters related to Martinez. As of the date of the report, he was

10 Hunt's apparent handler was Thomas Karamessines, the deputy director for plans. The two regularly connected on tennis dates.

11 Most of the Gemstone activities were to be pursued in Miami during the conventions, both Democratic and Republican.

still a resident of DC, two years after the burglary arrests. The station chief was, according to the report, "confounded" as to why he had not been told earlier to terminate Martinez in March 1972, after his activity became known. After the arrest, the Assistant Deputy Director for Plans told the station chief that the Agency had been "uneasy" about Hunt's activities for the White House in "March or May 1972." Why would it have been "uneasy" if in fact Hunt was not working for the CIA?

The report does state that the Agency received information on June 19, 1972, that Martinez's car was at the airport and that it contained certain "compromising documents."[12] However, the FBI was not informed about the vehicle until June 21, 1972.

In short, the report suggests not only a witting relationship between the CIA and Hunt/Martinez's activities, but an intense program to cover up the Agency's knowledge.

In summary, the Baker Report established that Mullen was a CIA cover company and that Bennett and Hunt were agents working through Mullen. McCord was falsely retired and reporting to Lee Pennington. All made overt efforts to cover up the CIA's participation in Watergate, including the corruption of reporter Bob Woodward of the *Post* and the complicity of the DNC's lawyers.

The Baker Report was devastating to the Agency, as it should have been. There was no way that a critical observer could read it and not conclude that there was a high likelihood that the CIA was directly involved in the Watergate burglary and took elaborate, risky efforts to cover it up.

Because the report's findings were based directly on CIA documents, as curated by an honest senator and his capable staff, led by experienced prosecutor and future senator Fred Thompson, the *Post* could have relied on this document for a blockbuster scoop about the CIA.

The *Post* knew that the (pre-internet) public would not review the Baker Report and that the informed citizenry would rely on the newspaper for any information about it. Its candor in recounting this report, we can conclude, is a good test of whether the *Washington Post* was honest in its Watergate journalism.

---

12 These later disappeared.

Chapter Twenty-One

THE *POST* RESPONDS

On July 2, 1974, the *Washington Post*, through Laurence Stern, prepared its readers for the release that day of the Baker Report.

The report had made a number of specific allegations that, when considered as a whole, suggested strongly that the Watergate burglary was a CIA operation. Moreover, in a case where the White House was accused of a cover-up, the CIA's cover-up made that one look like child's play.

John Dean had already testified before the Ervin Committee about Nixon's attempt to use the specter of uncovering a CIA operation as a basis to keep the FBI off the Mexican money trail.[1] In his May 22, 1973, press conference, President Nixon had noted that shortly after the burglary, he had been advised of the possibility that the CIA had been involved, likely to explain his restraints on the FBI. In early July 1974, the nation was waiting for the Supreme Court's decision on sixty-four additional White House tapes, one of which would capture the CIA/Mexican money trail discussion to which Dean had alluded. So much was riding on the public reaction to the Baker Report, including impeachment.

It appears that the *Post* had obtained an advance copy of the report, and on July 2, 1974, Stern told the public what was coming. The headline for his article told the readers that the key issue was whether the

1 The Oval Office tape of June 23, 1972, produced in July 1974 by order of the US Supreme Court, corroborated Dean's testimony that Nixon plotted to use the CIA falsely to claim to the FBI operational interference if the burglars' money was traced through a Mexican bank account, but which in fact would have led the FBI to the Nixon campaign.

CIA/Helms recommended Hunt for a job with Mullen: "Baker to Say CIA Helped Hunt Get Job."

Needless to say, this was an extremely minor point in the overall discussion of Hunt's CIA agency. After discussing whether Helms recommended Hunt, the article dismisses any link between the CIA and the break-in:

> *Sources who have examined the report say it proves no conclusive links between the CIA and the original Watergate break-in such as have been hinted by former White House aide Charles Colson and by Baker.*[2]

Note that supposedly Baker and Colson only "hinted," according to Stern, at the CIA connection, whereas in fact they had both been quite pointed in that regard. We note also that this downplaying article was featured on page 1 of the paper.

Stern then frames the CIA issue, somewhat opaquely, as whether CIA officials took "efforts...to minimize its involvement in the Watergate investigation." In fact, Stern does not state more accurately that, according to the report, the CIA *obstructed the investigation to hide CIA involvement in the burglary*.

The Baker Report's accusation was devastating in that the CIA's Lee Pennington destroyed documents at McCord's home "that would show his connection to the CIA," followed by the CIA's concealing Pennington's identity from the FBI, also clear obstruction.

Yet Stern conceals these findings by referencing Pennington as a "former federal investigator," not naming him, the CIA, or his case officer status, and hiding the significance of the destroyed records:

> *The Osborn material, as presented by Baker, suggests that the former CIA security director provided misleading information to the FBI on the identity of a former federal investigator who helped Watergate burglar James W. McCord Jr.'s wife destroy*

2 Laurence Stern, "Baker to Say CIA Helped Hunt Get Job," *Washington Post*, July 2, 1974, A1.

> *CIA records at their home immediately after her husband's arrest in the Watergate break-in case.*[3]

The following day, July 3, 1974, the *Post*, again through Stern, ran both an approximately 2,500-word article purporting to summarize the key findings and questions raised by the Baker Report and a thousand-word "News Analysis" by Stern, an odd amalgam of factual reporting and editorial.

To be fair, the paper did not deliberately choose the Wednesday, July 3, publication date, which of course was the beginning of an elongated Fourth of July holiday, an excellent day to bury news. The report's prompt issuance was important, given the pendency of the impeachment proceedings and the Supreme Court tapes decision, but the delay resulting from the CIA review of the report, submitted to the CIA on June 27, 1974, caused this unpropitious timing of its release. This late-in-the-day timing, in turn, was caused because the CIA had initially obstructed the investigation for many months by not turning over documents in a timely manner, only later to be thwarted by an honest security officer. So the CIA had benefited by its obstruction.

Stern and the *Post* highlighted as the report's most serious charge that the CIA knew in advance of the Fielding break-in! I am not joking. The headline and first paragraph bear out this absurd characterization of the Baker Report:

> *Report Critical of CIA: Baker Hints Agency Knew of Break-In*
> *The Central Intelligence Agency may have known in advance of plans for break-ins at the offices of Daniel Ellsberg's psychiatrist and the Democratic National Committee's Watergate headquarters, a report released yesterday by Sen. Howard H. Baker, Jr. (R-Tenn.) suggests.*[4]

Reading Stern's article, one would not think that the CIA was being accused in the Baker Report of being a principal behind the break-in of Daniel Ellsberg's psychiatrist, or that the Agency participated in the Watergate burglary. And one would think its foreknowledge of the White House's

3 Stern, "Baker to Say CIA Helped," A8.

4 Laurence Stern, "Report Critical of CIA," *Washington Post*, July 3, 1974, A1. Unless otherwise noted, subsequent quotes are from the same source, A1, A10.

Ellsberg burglary, not its apparent participation in Watergate, was the key vulnerability of the CIA.

Both Mullen's role as a CIA *domestic* cover participating in the break-in through Hunt and Pennington's role as McCord's case officer who destroyed evidence of McCord's agent status were concealed by Stern:

> *Among other things, the report describes how the CIA used a Washington public relations firm as a cover for agents operating abroad, asserts that the CIA destroyed its own records in direct conflict with a Senate request to keep them intact, asserts that a CIA operative may have been a "domestic agent" in violation of the agency's charter and recounts how one CIA employee fought within the agency against withholding information from the Senate committee and other congressional committees.*
>
> *The report recites several instances in which it says CIA personnel whom the committee staff sought to interview were not made available by the CIA. In addition, the report lists several other instances in which it says the CIA either ignored, resisted or refused requests for information and documents by the committee.*

Certainly, noting Mullen as a "cover for agents operating abroad" implies that it was not a domestic cover for Hunt and Bennett–somewhat relevant, one would think, to Watergate.

At this point, the reader having been told what the major issues supposedly were, including the ho-hummer of CIA foreknowledge of the Fielding break-in, the article references vague "questions" that the Baker Report raised concerning the CIA's involvement in Fielding and Watergate, after which Stern implies the lack of proof implicating the CIA:

> *Although the report raises "questions" about the involvement of the CIA in the Watergate and Ellsberg break-ins, Baker said in a letter to present CIA Director William E. Colby that was also released yesterday, "Neither the select committee's decision to make this report a part of our public record nor the*

contents of the report should be viewed as any indication that either the committee or I have reached conclusions in this area of investigation."

Then Stern discusses at some length the question whether the CIA cut off aid to Hunt, as it claimed it had, in August 1971, after it received "casing" photos hinting at the planned Fielding burglary. In doing so, Stern deceptively glosses over the finding that the Agency never actually quit supporting Hunt, whether before or after the August photos, inferentially assisting Hunt knowingly in both the Fielding and Watergate burglaries. But no reader would learn that from the article, which falsely states as a fact that the Agency's assistance to Hunt was terminated at a time well in advance of Watergate:

The report asserts, and the CIA denies, that it was only when these photographs were developed that assistance to Hunt by the agency was terminated.

Contrary to this statement, the Baker Report did not concede and in fact contradicted that the Agency terminated assistance to Hunt after the photos were developed. Stern's article also suggests that the major accusation against the CIA regarding Fielding was that the Agency should have concluded that the photos it developed were casing photos, not the more sinister implication that the Fielding break-in was a CIA operation:

The blowup revealed Dr. Fielding's name in the parking lot next to his office. Another CIA official has testified that he speculated that they were "casing" photographs.

The report had documented that high headquarters CIA officials were backing Hunt's operations. Stern, however, transforms the issue into the question of whether the Agency knew that Hunt was recruiting Cubans in Miami in 1972–a very vanilla, far weaker accusation.

In response, the CIA asserts, "There is no evidence within CIA that the agency possessed any knowledge of Hunt's re-

> *cruitment of individuals to assist in the Watergate or any other break-in."*

Anyone reading the Baker Report would know that the key question was not if the CIA knew of the *recruitment* but rather whether it knew of the *various CIA operations* Hunt had been planning and, inferentially, was behind them, as demonstrated by its allowing Martinez to work with Hunt. Martinez himself, as documented by the Baker Report, had described Hunt's operations to his case officer, who informed the Miami station chief, who, alarmed, inquired of the Assistant Deputy Director for Plans in DC who responded that they should "cool it." Presumably, Martinez and his boss would only be concerned if the activities were undertaken by the CIA.

There was no record of what Martinez said to alarm his superiors so greatly, but the implications were that he revealed various arguably illegal CIA undercover operations. But Stern deceptively describes Martinez as simply warning his superiors that Hunt was in Miami:

> *The section of the report dealing with Eugenio Martinez asserts that Martinez, a CIA operative, alerted his CIA superiors that Hunt was in Miami in early 1972. The response from the CIA to Martinez's superiors, according to the report, was that Hunt was involved in domestic White House business and to "cool it."*

How does Stern handle the clear accusations that Pennington was McCord's case officer, or CIA contact, and covered up McCord's *continuing* CIA agency? And that Pennington burned documents showing McCord's *continuing* CIA connection? Through the following deceptive statement, which refers to the minor issue of whether McCord's report to Pennington on Jack Anderson was a domestic operation, which by Stern's implication was allegedly Pennington's most significant wrongdoing:

> *The report does not make clear what domestic activities Pennington may have been involved in, although the report contains a passing reference to a CIA file on columnist Jack Anderson.*

Then, to hide Woodward's unholy alliance with CIA front Mullen, Stern lies in multiple ways:

> *Mullen and Co. was used as a "front" for CIA agents overseas. Bennett, according to the report, kept his CIA contact informed of his efforts to give information to interested parties in an effort to avoid involving the Mullen firm in news stories and legal actions stemming from the Watergate break-in.*

So Stern dishonestly omits Woodward's name as one of the "interested parties" and the name of the *Post* as the "news" outlet, omits the dirty quid pro quo deal, and conceals Mullen's domestic cover for Hunt and Bennett.

Stern's cover-up of Bennett's deal with Woodward is similar to his cover-up of Bennett's "back door" entry to DNC's counsel, WCC, via attorney Hobart Taylor. Recall that this contact was for the purpose of keeping quiet Mullen's and the CIA's involvement in the burglary. Yet Stern described the purpose to be "funneled" information to WCC and not an approach to keep the CIA's involvement out of the news:

> *The report asserts that Bennett "funneled" information to Edward Bennett Williams, then a lawyer for the Democratic National Committee and The* Washington Post, *through another Washington lawyer, Hobart Taylor.*

So what was in fact an explosive blockbuster minority Senate report, Stern describes as offering nothing new beyond assertedly weak and unproven inferences that the CIA knew of the burglaries in advance:

> *Although the report is implicitly critical of the CIA, it does not radically alter what is already known about the general outlines of the planning and implementation of the Ellsberg and Watergate break-ins. Remarks by the CIA accompanying the 43-page report reject the suggestion that the agency knew in advance about either of the two burglaries.*

In the same July 3 issue of the *Post*, Stern puts all these seemingly weak suggestions to bed in his "News Analysis," entitled: "Few Conclusions Given by Baker on CIA, Watergate Tie."

So after telling his readers on July 2 what was coming (that the CIA helped Hunt get his White House job), Stern reported on July 3 a watered-down rendition of the Baker Report accusations. Then, to nail Baker's coffin shut, in his July 3 "News Analysis," buried on page 10, he purported to analyze for his readers what the report proved: hardly anything. Before receiving the damning evidence forced out of the CIA by the honest "Security Officer No. 1," Senator Baker had noted circumstantial evidence of the CIA's position in Watergate, as Stern describes in opening his analysis:

> *Sen. Howard H. Baker Jr. (R-Tenn.) once likened the role of the Central Intelligence Agency in the Watergate scandal to "animals crashing around in the forest–you can hear them but you can't see them."*[5]

But in spite of the much stronger new evidence that Baker now had in his hands, Stern instead concludes that the Baker case was still circumstantial, and weak at that:

> *This Aesopian image still fits notwithstanding Baker's release yesterday of a 43-page report which is rich in insinuation, long on footnotes but short on substantive findings.*[6]

Again, Stern claims to highlight in his analysis the most damning allegations of the report, but again did so with very watered-down renditions of what the report actually showed. His treatment of the Lee Pennington matter, which in fact incriminates the CIA, portrays a somewhat benign charge against the Agency:

> *Baker did unearth the case of Lee R. Pennington Jr., a $250-a-month CIA contract employee who acknowledged that*

5 Stern, "Few Conclusions Given by Baker on CIA, Watergate Tie," *Washington Post*, July 3, 1974, A10.

6 Stern, "Few."

> *he witnessed the destruction of Watergate burglar James W. McCord Jr.'s records by his wife at their home after McCord's arrest in Watergate.*
>
> *CIA's then-Director of Security Howard Osborn, no longer with the agency, fed files on a different Pennington to the FBI when agents made inquiries about the incident–presumably to throw the bureau off the track. Columnist Jack Anderson reported the incident several months ago.*[7]

First off, this depiction misses the larger point that Pennington was likely McCord's CIA case officer, which then implicates the CIA in the burglary. Pennington did not merely "witness" the destruction of records but participated in and likely initiated it, again concealed by Stern, to hide McCord's continuing connection to the CIA. Once again, Stern chose to miss the key damning point.

Of course, Osborn had in fact "fed" files on Cecil Pennington to the FBI, but the article ignores that the Agency at the same time was concealing files on the person they knew was involved–Lee Pennington–to hide its sponsorship of McCord.

In short, the *Post*'s treatment of the Baker Report was clever, perhaps brilliant, but in total and considered as a whole, fraudulent. Its seemingly substantive–but in fact jejune–unpacking of the Baker Report likely satisfied critical readers, few of whom would ever lay eyes on the actual report. Stern's analysis would lead such a critical reader to believe that he was faithfully recounting the major issues raised by Baker.

Soon after the *Post* quashed any effect of Baker's work, the Supreme Court ordered the release of sixty-four additional White House tapes, one of which showed Nixon ordering his aides to call the FBI off the Mexican money trail investigation by claiming possible interference with a CIA operation. The tape also implied this was being done for political–not national security–reasons, thus arguably constituting obstruction of justice. On this basis, Nixon's aides urged his resignation, and the president resigned on August 9, 1974.

---

7 Stern, "Few."

So as far as the public was concerned, given the unconvincing pablum of the Baker Report, there now was simply no basis for the question of CIA burglary participation, even though, unknown to the public, the theory of CIA involvement was first hypothesized by none other than Mark Felt soon after the arrests, and the evidence strongly supported it.

At the time there was, of course, no internet and no widespread dissemination of the Baker Report, so there was no practical vehicle for public analysis of either the report or of the *Post* reporting on it.

But we now can compare the two–the report and *Post* reporting of it–as a test of the *Post*'s honesty in its Watergate journalism, and we must conclude that the *Post* failed badly.

No occasion for the *Post* to correct the record occurred until 1980, when Gordon Liddy published his frank, painfully candid autobiography, *Will*. Because Liddy revealed facts not yet in the public domain, his book unintentionally became yet another test of how candid the *Post* had been in its earlier reporting. In other words, if any of the *Post*'s omissions were merely unintentionally wrong or incomplete, Liddy's book would give the paper and its reporters a good chance to correct the record in a graceful fashion. If the *Post*'s omissions or half-truths had involved intentional fraud, *Post* reaction to Liddy's book would inform us whether an intentional cover-up was continuing.

To Liddy's book we will now turn.

Chapter Twenty-Two

G. GORDON LIDDY

In 1980, Gordon Liddy published his candid account of Watergate, *Will*, and was the last of the scandal's main actors to do so. He waited so long to ensure that all statutes of limitation, and his term of probation, had expired. He set out to be brutally honest about both his criminality and his stupidity. His work has generally been acknowledged as the most honest of this genre of Watergate memoirs.

The salience of his book comes from his centrality in the scandal. On the one hand, Liddy was a direct eyewitness to both burglary operations, whereas there had been no other book offering candid firsthand observations of either of them. Of the other burglary team members, McCord wrote an odd, inscrutable work, *A Piece of Tape*, that cannot even be called an account. Hunt's book was only a feint at revelation, with little attempts to describe all that actually had happened during the night of the burglary.

On the other end of the operation, its administration, Liddy had direct contact with the political figures alleged to be behind the burglary and the cover-up: Mitchell, Dean, Magruder, Colson, Kleindienst, and Klein[1]. He as well dealt with financial functionaries such as Maurice Stans and Hugh Sloan of the CRP and Nixon campaign aide Herbert Porter. Liddy also briefly supervised, to a limited degree, Segretti, whose dirty tricks Deep

1 Herbert "Herb" Klein was a White House communications official who accompanied Liddy to Burning Tree Golf Club on the morning of June 17, 1972, to buttonhole Attorney General Richard Kleindienst in an unsuccessful effort to enlist him to gain release of the burglars from custody, telling Kleindienst that this was John Mitchell's request. Although he was the nation's highest law enforcement official, Kleindienst did not report this significant interaction.

Throat thought were the key to understanding the context of Watergate, and also had contact with acknowledged CIA officials, including a number of functionaries who supported Liddy and Hunt with disguises, false credentials, charts, weapons, and cameras. He was also in the middle of the first awkward cover-up discussions, including his approach along with Klein to Kleindienst at the Burning Tree Country Club. Not finally, he participated in a number of Plumbers' operations and interactions with the original Plumbers team of Young and Krogh, and also participated in numerous other shady operations, including the burglary of the Ellsberg psychiatrist, Dr. Fielding, and his Jack Anderson assassination discussions with Hunt and a CIA poison specialist, Edward Gunn.

Liddy thus had some connection to all of the unanswered questions of Watergate, even if he himself had been appropriately cast in the role of an unguided missile as to much of the scandal. While Liddy earned much grudging public admiration for his stout "stand-up" refusal to turn on any of his associates, in so doing, he deprived the public–and the various Watergate juries–of important firsthand information: Dean's sponsorship of the Gemstone Plan and likely the subsequent burglary; Dean's architecture of the cover-up; McCord's treachery during the burglary; Hunt dealings that revealed his CIA agency; and hints of the true target of the burglary (the desk drawer, which Magruder had strongly emphasized).

As a result, Liddy deprived Nixon and the White House of potentially exculpating or mitigating information, such as the identity of a key potential burglary conspirator–Dean–who was leading the White House over the cliff as a professedly innocent White House counsel. Liddy thus could have warned the White House of facts suggesting (to others) that Dean was a quisling protecting himself to the detriment of his clients. Liddy's silence, which unintentionally protected Dean, allowed Dean, according to Colodny, not only to lead Nixon into the ill-conceived attempted obstruction using the CIA but later allowed Magruder to peddle a false story to the public, suggesting former attorney general John Mitchell's responsibility for the burglary. Liddy also unintentionally deprived the public of details showing CIA involvement in White House/CRP operations that was deep and wide. The conventional Watergate story, which excluded the centrality of Dean, the targeted desk drawer, and the CIA, was firmly imbedded in the conventional narrative by the time that *Will* was released in 1980. So, Liddy's desire during the scandal to help the White House's cause actually damaged it in the eyes of history and certainly hampered the public's ability to obtain relevant information.

But whether his silence was admirable or very stupid—and it likely was both—his book amounted to a test of the bona fides of Woodward and the *Washington Post*. If Liddy in his honest account revealed facts at variance with the received narrative, would the *Post* acknowledge these newly revealed truths and revise its take on Watergate accordingly? Or would it ignore or distort *Will*'s firsthand revelations? This book, as it turned out, was a test of the hypothesis that I had developed by 2010: the *Post* was deeply and intentionally dishonest in its Watergate reporting.

Luckily, the *Post* did directly address Liddy's book. Apparently realizing that Liddy's account was an inarguable part of Watergate history that could not be ignored completely by journalists and historians, the *Post* characterized it for posterity head-on by having it reviewed by the unchallenged master of all Watergate wisdom, its managing editor, Bob Woodward himself. Because of his iconic status, Woodward's analysis of Liddy's work, rather than the work itself, was more likely to become part of the received version of Liddy's claims. While Woodward used this opportunity to cement selected observations of Liddy into Watergate lore, he also gave us from our present vantage point a direct view of Woodward's—and the *Post*'s—candor, or lack of same, about Watergate. Put differently, if Woodward concealed or distorted Liddy's revelations in the book, it is likely that he and the *Post* also did so regarding the same facts during Watergate and were continuing to cover up whatever consequential falsities it had published years earlier, or what truths it had concealed.

Making this exercise meaningful is the universal acknowledgment that Liddy's account was extraordinarily candid and truthful. Woodward himself joins this chorus in praising the book's truthfulness:

> *Liddy's account of Watergate is not only believable, but some of what he reveals is front page news...Liddy is meticulous. His story rings true, and balanced against the other evidence and testimony of the many Watergate investigations, it is cred-*

ible. A hundred little facts and inferences convince me he has been as honest as he could be.[2]

So with this acknowledgment, Woodward/*Post* cannot claim that Liddy's account was knowingly false, even if, as I recounted in several instances above, he was likely a dupe, as for example in his belief that O'Brien had been targeted and that the photos pinned to a shag carpet were taken in O'Brien's office.[3] So how faithfully Woodward recounts Liddy's observations amounts to an excellent test of good faith and of the presence or absence of intent to deceive, both on his part and that of his editors at the *Post*. Written in 1980, the review would have the added advantage of years of perspective and opportunity for reflection.

Woodward explicitly tells us what is new in Liddy's book, offering eight categories, as per the following quoted passages under each of my headings.[4] I will divide my analysis of Liddy revelations into two segments. The first will deal with these eight categories of new insights that Woodward claims Liddy made. The second will deal with the items that Liddy revealed but which Woodward did not fully address. There will necessarily be some overlap between the two because in some cases Woodward described Liddy's insights only partially.

A. Liddy giving Kleindienst a full account of the break-in on the day of the arrests:
   Richard Kleindienst, who was attorney general on the day of the break-in (Mitchell had by then become chairman of the re-election committee), was given a full account directly by Liddy the day the burglars were arrested.

B. The tape placed intentionally on the door lock so a guard could see it:

2 Woodward, "Gordon Liddy Spills His Guts," *Washington Post*, May 18, 1980.

3 To "prove" they had penetrated O'Brien's office during the first burglary, the burglars presented Liddy with photos of purported DNC documents, claimed to be taken in the office. His office did not have a shag carpet, but Baldwin's hotel room did. This is clear evidence of a secret CIA agenda necessarily duping Liddy, who never understood the targeting of the DNC and O'Brien.

4 Each of the following eight quotes are taken from Woodward's book review, "Gordon Liddy Spills His Guts."

The much-discussed piece of tape holding open a stairwell door in the Watergate office building was put there intentionally so a guard could see it. That way, Liddy reasoned, the guard would assume it had been left innocently by a janitor whereas a clandestine and inconspicuous method of holding the lock open would arouse more suspicion.

C. Liddy's lack of belief that McCord was a double agent who sabotaged the entry:
Liddy says he does not believe the speculations that James McCord, one of the burglars, was a double agent who knowingly sabotaged the illegal entry.

D. The plan to assassinate Jack Anderson:
So when he gets down to the accounts of crucial meetings, planning sessions and the actual illegal operations themselves–the Watergate break-in of June 17, 1972, or the "entry" at the office of the psychiatrist of Pentagon Papers defendant Daniel Ellsberg, or the planned assassination of columnist Jack Anderson–Liddy is meticulous. His story rings true, and balanced against the other evidence and testimony of the many Watergate investigations, it is credible.

E. Mitchell's willingness to pay organized crime for kidnapping and drugging demonstrators:
Mitchell was willing as attorney general to pay Nixon campaign funds to members of organized crime for their services in a scheme–never carried out–to kidnap, drug and ship to Mexico radical demonstration leaders. Liddy quotes Mitchell as saying in response to the proposal, "Let's not contribute any more than we have to the coffers of organized crime."

F. Liddy's telling Mitchell of the planned second break-in:
Liddy says he delivered logs of wiretapped conversations to Mitchell two days before the Watergate arrests and told him of the planned break-in by announcing that, "The problem [with one of the microphones] will be corrected this weekend, sir."

Mitchell has repeatedly denied that he knew of the June 17 break-in in advance; Liddy offers convincing evidence to the contrary.

G. The motive for the break-in:
Liddy offers his explanation of why the Nixon White House wanted to break into the Democratic National Headquarters in the first place...to find out what [Democratic National Chairman Lawrence] O'Brien had of a derogatory nature about us, not for us to get something on him or the Democrats.

H. The CIA's knowledge of the break-in:
The CIA made the expensive charts used to brief Attorney General John Mitchell in early 1972 on the planned illegal GEMSTONE break-in and bugging operations. For me, this suggests more than anything available to date that top CIA officials must have known in advance about Liddy's illegal operations. In my opinion, CIA Director Richard Helms must have been given some inkling from the men over at the CIA graphics department, but Helms has denied it.

Is Woodward being truthful in his recounting of Liddy's insights? Hardly. There is of course no defense to the claim that Liddy told all to Kleindienst on the morning of the arrest. And, yes, Woodward is mostly correct about the tape. The burglars did not *intend* that the guard see it, but if he did, in Liddy's view, the guard would think an innocent maintenance man placed it.

Liddy did not believe that McCord sabotaged the operation, but much of his description is consistent with a CIA agency. Liddy compared McCord to the fictional "Shadow" Lamont Cranston, because he slipped away so often (consistent with Lou Russell's hidden participation), conduct Woodward wished to keep hidden from the reader.

Woodward makes the discussion of assassinating Jack Anderson sound like a White House initiative, whereas any knowledgeable observer understood this to be part of the CIA's Operation Mud Hen, and that Dr. Edward Gunn, a poison specialist, was, as Liddy noted but Woodward omitted, a "retired CIA asset." So, properly understood, this meeting supports the theme of the CIA's inveigling White House dupes to legalize the Agency's otherwise illegal operations.

Woodward is directly dishonest in stating that the dry Mitchell was willing to pay organized crime. The former attorney general, rather, was wittily rejecting a fatuous scheme of Liddy, and Woodward's addition of the parenthetical microphone reference was even more deceitful, if that is even possible. A microphone was never mentioned, and Mitchell had no idea what "problem" Liddy was obliquely hinting at in a meeting attended by non-burglary team members. Mitchell did not know of the second break-in, contrary to Woodward.

By 1980, Woodward also knew that Larry O'Brien was not the true target and that Liddy was duped on this score, lacking even in 1980 knowledge of the Wells desk key. And to suggest that "more than anything" the Gemstone charts showed the CIA must have known about the planned break-in and bugging operations is to praise with faint damn. I have detailed in this book a raft of far more inculpatory facts.

Perhaps more significant are two Liddy revelations that would have revised the commonly believed narrative of Watergate but which Woodward ignored precisely for that reason, because there was no good spin possible. It was Dean, Liddy documents, who was the father of Gemstone, pushing Liddy to the CRP with a promise of an intelligence budget of "half a million for openers." Dean's sponsorship of the Mitchell presentation meetings, where Mitchell swats away Liddy's silly plans, is a key part of Liddy's account. Dean's participation in this "blind ambition" dirt gathering is consistent with his sending of Tony Ulasewicz to Watergate for a casing trip in November 1971. In short, Mitchell was not the father of Watergate but its attempted abortionist.

Woodward also ignores the $30,000 McCord pulled from Liddy for what Woodward should have known was McCord's false representation of purchasing a sophisticated room bug for O'Brien's office. This ties in nicely with the tableau of Michael Stevens and the CIA satellite-uplinking bugs that the confirmed CIA agent McCord ordered from him, using part of the $30,000. Again, Woodward omits this discussion because it devastates the false narrative he sold the public during Watergate.

In short, Bob Woodward's dishonest review, after years of reflection and discussion, buttresses the conclusion that he was similarly dishonest during the scandal and was simply continuing his cover-up of what actually occurred.

Chapter Twenty-Three

FINAL ARGUMENT

I have in this book summarized a number of facts about Watergate, or allegations of fact, that were either completely ignored or distorted through half-truth and concealment by Bob Woodward, Carl Bernstein, and the *Washington Post*. Any one of these cover-ups could be explained as simply imperfection, perhaps carelessness or cluelessness.

But given the sum total of evidence about the CIA's participation in a cover-up, Mullen's cover status as a CIA front, and phone calls Alfred Baldwin overheard, together with willfully deceitful *Post* reporting of these objective facts, we must convict the *Post* of covering up the truth about our nation's most significant political scandal. The facts presented here also support the continuation by the *Post* of this cover-up through the present, with consciousness of guilt shown by all involved. The *Post* was as highly motivated to take down the hated Nixon as it was to protect its beloved ideological brother, the DNC.

It is now clear that the only reason PublicAffairs publisher Peter Osnos was so ardent in his courtship of the Felt family was the *Post*'s desire to control Mark Felt's story. The phony "Lone Ranger" theme, stolen to no effect by Woodward, shows that PublicAffairs never had any intention of publishing a successful book that deviated from the Watergate canon.

Felt himself, when his memory was sound, likely had plenty of negative facts to unload about the *Post*, if he were ever inclined to do so. Not only did Woodward breach all of his protective promises to him, but Felt also knew where many bodies were buried about the *Post*'s suppression of the story, involving both the CIA and Baldwin.

After Woodward visited a memory-challenged Felt in 2000, he likely breathed a sigh of relief as he and the *Post* awaited their source's demise, whereupon the *Post* could shape history's final chapter on Deep Throat. The snarky *Secret Man*, in the hopper and ready to roll when Felt released his identity, was emblematic of Woodward's simultaneous plan to throw dirt on his "friend" so as to continue to cover up Watergate's truths and to use Mark's previous unread book, *The FBI Pyramid*, as Woodward's own marketable asset.

So when the Felt family surprised them all by the sudden appearance of our *Vanity Fair* article, panic likely set in for fear that a real journalist would aggressively take a new look at Watergate and at Deep Throat and expose the truth.

What better way to keep the lid on than by hiring a busy lawyer/amateur author to add to an already written book? What could go wrong? Even better, by waiting a year to publish it, Woodward's book would suck the oxygen out of interest in the Deep Throat story and out of book sales.

What could go wrong is what did go wrong. The naïve lawyer/author, yours truly, actually tried to do right by his client, as lawyers usually do, and tell the full story, however awkwardly and amateurishly I attempted to do so. When I did, even more *Post* cover-up and dishonesty resulted. Unfortunately, while many devious ploys were ambiguous and could be chalked up to PublicAffairs' incompetence, the deceitful scheme to send me to Washington, DC, to avoid *Book TV* could not be spun as anything other than outright fraud. Perhaps when I did not show at Copperfield's, PublicAffairs would assume that no filming, or at least no showing of any filming, would thereafter occur. All of this simply proves that it is highly difficult, even for the newspaper with control of a large part of the media, to commit the perfect crime.

The *Washington Post* got away with its crime for over forty-five years. Now it should be on trial. I hope that the paper and its reporters will admit to youthful indiscretions. But I do not expect candor. I expect, ironically, a Nixonian reaction–attempting to kill the messenger.

I have but one preemptive response: explain the key.

ACKNOWLEDGMENTS

Without the dedicated, energetic, and critical help of key associates, I could not have completed this project. My longtime aide-de-camp Allison Baltzersen has been my rock, contributing her advice, research, editing, and cite checking; all the while I called upon her wide array of administrative talents. My paralegal Will Rehling helped me through thousands of pages of transcripts and documents, and was a wise, steady sounding board. Lisa Kemp, while carrying a full load teaching high school history, found the time for valuable niche projects.

I as well was helped by the generosity of a number of highly accomplished authorities in all things Watergate. In writing this book, as I trust the text acknowledges, I stand on the shoulders of giants who, as it eventuated, were far more than impressive predecessors. Jim Hougan, author of Secret Agenda: Watergate, Deep Throat and the CIA, the godfather of all revisionist research on Watergate, generously responded to my inquiries. Len Colodny, co-author of *Silent Coup: The Removal of a President*, availed me both of his exceptional Colodny Collection housed at Texas A&M, and also offered his sage advice. We appreciate greatly the gracious help of Dr. Luke Nichter, co-author of The Nixon Tapes with Douglas Brinkley, today's most prominent scholarly force in the continuing research into Watergate mysteries.

Leading Watergate writers Ray Locker, Geoff Shephard, and James Rosen also provided valuable guidance. Superlawyer Kerrie Hook, who understands Watergate as well as any living human being, was brilliantly insightful.

Any shortcomings in this work have occurred in spite of, not because of, this assistance, for which I am deeply appreciative.

CAST OF CHARACTERS

BURGLARS	LAWYERS FOR BURGLARY TEAM
Eugenio Martínez	Henry Rothblatt
Bernard Baker	""
Frank (Fiorini) Sturgis	""
Virgilio Gonzalez	""
James McCord	Gerald Alch and Bernard Fensterwald
BURGLARY SUPERVISORS	**LAWYERS FOR BURGLARY SUPERVISORS**
Howard Hunt	William O. Bittman
G. Gordon Liddy	Peter Maroulis
WIRETAP MONITOR	**LAWYERS FOR WIRETAP MONITOR**
Alfred Baldwin III	John Cassidento and Robert Mirto
COMMITTEE TO RE-ELECT THE PRESIDENT (CRP)	
John Mitchell, Director	Jeb Magruder, Deputy Director
G. Gordon Liddy, Counsel	James McCord, Director of Security
Penny Gleason, Assistant Security Officer	Paul O'Brien, Outside Counsel for CRP

Glenn Sedam, General Counsel	Robert Odle, Director of Administration
CIA	
Richard Helms, Director (terminated by Pres. Nixon in January 1973)	
Gen. Robert Cushman, Deputy Director	
Howard Osborn, Director of Security, Office of Security (OS)	
Paul Gaynor, Chief of Staff, Security Research Staff (SRS), Division of OS	
Dr. Edward Gunn, retired, former Chief of Medical Division ("poisons" doctor)	
Louis Vasaly, case officer of Lee Pennington	
Lee Pennington, contact with James McCord	
Cecil Pennington, CIA agent with last name "Pennington" identified to FBI by CIA	
Martin Lukoskie, case officer for Robert Bennett of Mullen and Co.	
Rob Roy Ratliff, White House CIA liaison	
Miriam Furbershaw, retired CIA clerk, rented room to and evicted James McCord	
FBI	
J. Edgar Hoover, FBI Director, 1924–May 1972 (deceased)	
Patrick Gray, Acting FBI Director, May 1972–April 1973	
W. Mark Felt, Deputy Assistant Director, directed investigation of Watergate until June 15, 1973	
Angelo Lano, Special Agent, investigated Watergate on behalf of Washington Field Office	

William Ruckelshaus, Interim Acting Director May–June 1973, seeks Felt's resignation
William Sullivan, retired Assistant Director, rival to Felt
DEPARTMENT OF JUSTICE HEADQUARTERS ("MAIN JUSTICE")
John Mitchell, Attorney General January 1969–March 1972
Richard Kleindienst, Attorney General (acting) March 1972, (confirmed) June 1972–April 1973
Elliot Richardson, Attorney General May 1973–October 1973
William Ruckelshaus, Deputy Attorney General under Richardson
Archibald Cox, Special Prosecutor terminated in "Saturday Night Massacre
UNITED STATES ATTORNEY'S OFFICE
Earl Silbert, Assistant US Attorney in charge of Watergate burglary prosecution
Seymour Glazer, Assistant US Attorney, chief assistant to Silbert in burglary prosecution
John Rudy, Assistant US Attorney in charge of prosecution in *U.S. v Bailley*
DEMOCRATIC NATIONAL COMMITTEE (DNC)
Lawrence O'Brien, Chair
Robert Strauss, Treasurer
Spencer Oliver Jr., employed by ADC, an affiliate of DNC
Ida "Maxie" Wells, secretary to Spencer Oliver Jr.
Barbara Kennedy Rhoden, successor to Maxie Wells

<table>
<tr><th colspan="2">COUNSEL FOR DNC</th></tr>
<tr><td colspan="2">Williams, Connolly, & Califano (WCC), represented DNC and Washington Post, 1972–1973</td></tr>
<tr><td colspan="2">Joseph Califano, partner at WCC, General Counsel to Washington Post and DNC 1972–1973</td></tr>
<tr><td colspan="2">Alan Galbraith, partner at WCC, interviewed Alfred Baldwin III</td></tr>
<tr><td colspan="2">Charles O. Morgan Jr., Alabama civil rights attorney, intervened in burglary trial for DNC, Oliver, Wells Hope Eastman, associate of Charles Morgan Jr.</td></tr>
<tr><th colspan="2">WASHINGTON POST</th></tr>
<tr><td>Ben Bradlee, Editor</td><td>Bob Woodward, reporter</td></tr>
<tr><td>Barry Sussman, Assistant Editor</td><td>Carl Bernstein, reporter</td></tr>
<tr><td>Timothy Robinson, reporter</td><td>Richard Cohen, reporter</td></tr>
<tr><td>Alfred E. Lewis, reporter</td><td>Martin Schram, reporter</td></tr>
<tr><td colspan="2">Eugene Bachinski, reporter</td></tr>
<tr><th colspan="2">REPORTERS NOT WITH THE WASHINGTON POST</th></tr>
<tr><td>John Crewdson, New York Times</td><td>Jack Nelson, Los Angeles Times</td></tr>
<tr><td>Seymour Hersh, New York Times</td><td>Ronald Ostrow, Los Angeles Times</td></tr>
<tr><td>Howard Marks, Chicago Today</td><td>Tom Condon, Hartford Courant</td></tr>
<tr><td>Patrick Collins, Washington Star-News</td><td>Jack Anderson, freelance journalist</td></tr>
<tr><td colspan="2">Sandy Smith, Time Magazine</td></tr>
<tr><th colspan="2">PUBLICAFFAIRS, PUBLISHER</th></tr>
<tr><td colspan="2">Peter Osnos, President and Founder</td></tr>
</table>

MULLEN AND COMPANY
Robert Mullen, former owner
Robert Bennett, purchased Mullen and Co. in 1971
Spencer Oliver Sr., Mullen officer, father of Spencer Oliver Jr., of ADC/DNC
Howard Hunt, retired CIA agent, part-time Mullen copywriter, part-time White House contractor
Douglas Caddy, counsel for General Foods, closely associated with Mullen
Hobart Taylor, outside counsel for Mullen

WHITE HOUSE	
Richard Nixon, President	Alexander Butterfield, Deputy Assistant to Nixon
H. R. Haldeman, White House Chief of Staff	Charles Colson, Special Counsel to Nixon
John Ehrlichman, Assistant to the President	William Timmons, White House Aide
John Dean, White House Counsel	Rose Mary Woods, Nixon's personal secretary
Fred Fielding, Deputy White House Counsel	Donald Segretti, "Dirty Tricks" program operator
Henry Kissinger, National Security Advisor	Herbert Klein, Communications Director
Alexander Haig, Aide to Kissinger	Herbert Kalmbach, Nixon's private attorney

Jack Caulfield, White House detective	Alfred Wong, Supervisor of White House Secret Service detail
Tony Ulasewicz, Caulfield's covert investigator	
US SENATE	
Senator Sam Ervin, North Carolina Democrat, Chairman of Select Watergate Committee	
Senator Howard Baker, Tennessee Minority Leader, Select Watergate Committee	
DC POLICE	
Officer Carl Shoffler, burglary arresting officer, DC Police	
Officer John Barrett, burglary arresting officer, DC Police	
Garey Bittenbender, Intelligence Officer, DC Police	
COURTS	
John Sirica, Judge, *U.S. v. Liddy*	
David Bazelon, Court of Appeals Judge, *U.S. v Liddy*	
James Belson, Judge, burglary arraignment, *U.S. v. Liddy*	
OTHER CHARACTERS	
Lou Russell, contractor, McCord and Associates	
William Birely, benefactor of Lou Russell	
Maureen Biner Dean, fiancé and later wife of White House counsel John Dean	
Cathy Dieter, alleged madame of Columbia Towers call girl operation	

Phillip Mackin Bailley, lawyer for Cathy Dieter, arrested for unrelated Mann Act violation
McCord and Associates, private security firm of James McCord
Michael Stevens, supplier of surveillance equipment to James McCord
Dorothy Hunt, Howard Hunt's wife, "hush money" courier killed in United Airlines plane crash

INDEX

18 ½ minute gap 14

A

A G-Man's Life 75, 105, 107, 114, 115

A Piece of Tape See McCord, James

ACLU 129, 173

Alch, Gerald 145, 147–150, 152, 177, 200

All the President's Men xii, 1, 2, 3, 5, 15–16, 17, 20, 21–28, 46–47, 61, 63–64, 66–67, 77–78, 86, 89–90, 151–152, 166–169, 192, 201, 205, 224–226, 231

Anderson, Jack 140, 186, 197, 239, 251, 257, 260

Articles of impeachment 15

B

Bachinski, Eugene 192, 224, 226–227

Bailley, Phillip Mackin 119–121, 186–187, 210, 213

Baldwin, Alfred III 11, 122, 129, 147 fn 11, 152, 153–170, 172–173, 174, 176, 179, 181, 188, 191, 194, 198, 200, 203, 205, 209, 211, 217, 221, 222 fn 3, 224, 230, 236, 259 fn 22

Balsam, Martin 5

Baltimore Sun 157

Barker, Bernard 132, 151

Bay of Pigs 9, 127, 130–131, 184, 210, 219

Beard, Dita 242

Beckman, Chase Culeman 40
Bennett, Robert 9, 118, 123–124, 127–129, 133–140, 235 fn 1, 239–241, 252
Bernstein, Joshua 37, 40, 71
Bill of Rights 116, 177
Bittenbender, Gary 194–196, 198–199
Bittman, William 141, 145–151
Black bag jobs 77 fn 11, 101, 117, 126
Books on Tape 95–96, 106
Book TV 95–96, 104–107
Bradlee, Ben 5, 76, 84, 85, 88–89, 92–94, 98, 108, 206
Bush at War 3–4
Bush, George H. W. 218 fn 7
Bush, George W. 4
Butterfield, Alexander 14, 130, 143 fn 6, 202 fn 3

C

Caddy, Douglas 9, 131–134, 193, 235 fn 1
Califano, Joseph 137, 160–161
Call girl 111, 117–121, 154–156, 172, 210, 212–214
Campaign of spying and sabotage 10, 19
Carter, Graydon 54
Carter, James "Jimmy" 84
Carter, William "Billy" xiii fn 1
Cassidento, John 147 fn 11, 130, 167–168
Castro, Fidel 130, 184
Caulfield, Jack 120, 126, 140 fn 2, 165, 183, 185–186, 192, 200
CBS Evening News 91
Chapin, Dwight 171 fn 1
Chappaquiddick 11
Chicago Today 202–207, 235–236
CIA Central Cover 242
CIA defense 124, 141, 143, 144, 145, 147–152, 172, 181, 192, 200
CIA involvement 85–86, 118, 150, 152, 203, 235, 240, 247, 255, 257

CIA Office of Security 118, 184, 242
CIA Technical Services Division 242
Clawson, Ken 11
Clinton, Hillary 15
CNN 92
Cohen, Richard xiii fn 1, 71
Collins, Patrick 215–218
Colodny, Len 86–87, 110, 119, 120 fn 9, 122, 154–155, 212, 213, 227–230, 231
Columbia Plaza 117–118, 119, 187, 210, 212, 213
Committee to Re-elect the President 9, 10–11, 13, 17, 22, 86, 119, 122–123, 137, 140 fn 2, 160, 165, 169, 171, 174, 183–186, 187–188, 191, 196, 203–204, 209–210, 214, 217, 257
Concealment 124, 206, 237–238, 264
Condon, Tom 159 fn 10
Conein, Lucien 129 fn 3
Copperfield's Bookstore 95, 105, 106
Couric, Katie 91–92
Court of Appeals 12
Cox, Archibald 13–14
Crewdson, John 52, 67, 70 fn 5, 77, 115
C-SPAN 102
Cummings, Mark 101–102
Cushman, Robert 128, 242

D

de Diego, Felipe 129
Dean, John 12–14, 24, 27, 32, 53, 82, 85–86 fn 2, 108–111, 117, 119–123, 141–144, 146, 150–152, 157, 172–173, 181, 185–186, 187, 189–190, 200, 203, 209, 212–213, 221, 249, 256–257
Dean, Maureen 13, 121
Dementia 38, 43, 47, 50, 64, 73, 93, 101
Democratic National Committee 8, 12, 130, 133, 155, 160, 173, 176, 215, 248, 252

Department of Justice 8, 10, 25 fn 4, 27–28, 30–31, 76
Desk key 87, 100, 122, 123, 211, 221, 222–224, 226, 230, 236
Dieter, Cathy 213–214
Dirty tricks 10, 79, 102, 180, 236, 257
DNC headquarters 140 fn 2, 185–186, 187, 210
Downie, Len 54
Duke University 118

E

Ehrlichman, John 13, 14, 15, 24, 27, 30, 127–129, 141–142, 144, 154, 242–243
Eisenstadt, Eric 136 fn 13, 241 fn 8
Ellsberg, Daniel 52 fn 3, 67 fn 2, 70 fn 5, 115, 127–130, 139–140, 141, 242, 248–249, 252, 257
Ephron, Nora 71
Ervin Committee 13, 128, 147, 181, 190, 195, 202, 205, 217, 232, 235–236, 241, 243, 246
Ervin Committee hearings 14, 197, 242, See Ervin Committee
Ervin, Samuel 11, 13–14, 147, 181, 190, 194, 155, 202, 205, 217, 232, 235–236, 241, 243, 246
Everyone's life is in danger! 31, 85, 201
Explicitly intimate conversations 154–156, 167, 175

F

FBI 302 Report 66, 77, 115 fn 2, 195, 197, 227
FBI Pyramid 67, 73–75, 78–79, 85, 115 fn 2, 116, 193, 238
Felt, Audrey 38, 40
Felt, Joan 6, 37–41, 43, 45, 47–52, 55, 57–60, 63–64, 93, 96, 99–101, 104
Felt, Mark Jr. 6, 40, 48, 64, 81, 84
Felt, Wanda 48
Felt, William 58–59, 104

Fielding, Fred 53, 68, 82
Fielding, Lewis 128–129, 139, 142, 242, 244, 248–250, 257
Final Days 3
FISA xiii, 76
Fourth Estate 16
Fox News 156
Fraud 46, 106, 109, 124, 255
Friend, David 54
Furbershaw, Miriam 196, 198

G

Garage meeting 18, 31, 69, 85, 201, 205, 206, 217
Gemstone Plan 13, 120, 127, 130, 140 fn 2, 186, 242, 244 fn 11, 257
General Security Services, Inc 210
Gergen, David 5, 55
Gettings, Brian 101
Gettlin, Robert 86, 110 fn 2, 119, 155
Glanzer, Seymour 173
Gleason, Penny 196–197, 198
Globe 40
Gonzalez, Virgilio 143, 147, 150–151, 200
Gorelick Wall 77
Graham, Katharine 5
Grand Jury 29–30, 66, 71, 77, 134, 240–241
Gray, Patrick 12–13, 24, 26–27, 32, 34, 69, 74, 77, 79 fn 14, 135, 145
Greenspun, Hank 129 fn 3, 140

H

Haddad, William 140 fn 1, 186
Haig, Alexander 31–32, 87
Haldeman, H. R. 10, 13, 15, 23, 27, 29–30, 68, 94, 123, 213
Harmony, Sally 165
HarperCollins 82

Hartford Courant 159 fn 10
Helms, Richard 118, 127, 184, 187, 196, 200, 240, 243, 247, 261
Hermès notebooks 140, 145–147, 150, 151¬–152, 172, 181
Hersh, Seymour 219, 235, 243
Hippocampus 6
Hoffman, Dustin 5
Holland, Max 115 fn 2
Hoover, J. Edgar 26, 31, 72 fn 7, 74, 77–80, 116–117, 126, 130
Hougan, Jim 86–87, 109, 114 fn 1, 117–119, 147, 156–157, 159–160, 184 fn 2, 211, 213, 214
Houston, Robert 197
Howard Johnson 214, 215
Hunt, Howard 8–9, 13, 27, 31 fn 9, 72, 112–113, 118–120, 122–124, 127–135, 137–138, 139–152, 155, 172–174, 177–178, 180–181, 184–186, 188, 192–193, 198, 200, 202, 207, 209, 210, 219, 221, 226–227, 233, 241–245, 247, 250–251, 253, 256–257
Huston Plan 116–117, 126–127
Huston, Tom Charles 116, 126

J

Jones, Nick 36–38, 41, 55–57, 58, 104
Jones, Robert 58, 104

K

Kalmbach, Herbert 171 fn 1
Kennedy, Edward 11, 71, 129 fn 3, 222 fn 3, 241
Key in breast pocket 122, 222, 225, 230
King, Larry 92–94, 96
King, Martin Luther Jr. 79–80, 111–112
Kissinger wiretaps 31–32, 52 fn 3, 61, 67 fn 2, 70 fn 5, 115
Kissinger, Henry 31, 52 fn 3, 61, 67 fn 2, 70 fn 5, 115, 116 fn 3, 127
Kleindienst, Richard 13, 32, 256, 259

Koppel, Ted 5, 56
Kuhn, David 62, 83, 87

L

LaGarde, Yvette 40
Landesman, Peter 102
Lano, Angelo 238 fn 3
Lardner, George Jr. 29 fn 8
Larry King Live 92, 94, 108
Leak See Holland, Max
Leon, John 218 fn 7
Lewis, Alfred 192
Liddy, G. Gordon 9, 13, 110–112, 119–123, 127, 128–129, 140, 156, 158, 165, 172, 184–187, 189, 193–194, 203, 205, 209–210, 212, 222, 233, 236, 241–243, 255–261
Lincoln, Abraham 116
Lone Ranger 81, 84
Los Angeles Times 11, 62, 110, 129, 156, 159, 160–161, 164, 167, 168–169, 179, 181, 205, 211
Lukas, Anthony 109 fn 1, 114 fn 1, 117, 119, 154

M

Magruder, Jeb 12–13, 121–123, 140, 154, 169, 187, 190, 203, 209–210, 222, 256, 257
Mann, James 120 fn 11, 132 fn 8, 161 fn 13
Mardian, Robert 32
Mark Felt's funeral 101, 103
Martinez, Eugenio 107, 122, 130, 143, 147, 150–151, 200, 218, 219–222, 225, 227, 230–231, 235, 243–245, 251
Mayhew, Alice 47
McCord, James 8–9, 11–14, 85–86, 113, 118–119, 122–123, 129 fn 3, 130, 141, 143, 145, 147–150, 152, 154, 156, 158, 163, 169–170, 177, 181, 183–186, 188–199, 200, 202–203, 205, 207–212,

215–217, 219, 221, 222 fn 3, 237–239, 242, 245, 247, 249, 251, 254, 256, 257, 260–262
McGovern, George 72, 164–165
McManus, Eleanor 93
McNeil Lehrer Newshour 54–55
Mexican money trail 246
Miami, FL 86, 221–222, 226, 244, 250–251
Mister X 193
Mitchell, Andrea 5, 54–55
Mitchell, John 10, 12–15, 24, 32, 70 fn 5, 85–86 fn 2, 116, 122, 124, 126, 140, 183, 186, 189–190, 256, 257, 259–261
Mitchell, Martha 154
Morgan, Charles O. Jr. 129, 173–179, 181, 188
Mueller, Robert III 33, 38
Mullen and Company 9, 112, 118, 123, 127, 129 fn 3, 130–138, 139, 141, 152, 174, 188, 192, 198, 200, 221, 235 fn 1, 239–242, 247, 252
Murphy, Jerry 72 fn 7
Muskie, Edmund 11, 129 fn 3, 140

N

New York Post 82
New York Times 17–18, 52 fn 3, 67, 70 fn 5, 75 fn 10, 109 fn 1, 115, 117, 148–149, 152, 154, 161, 219, 235 fn 1
Newhouse, Si 54
Newsweek 5, 85, 108–109, 146
Nightmare 114 fn 1, 117, 119
Nixon administration 1, 15, 34, 70 fn 5, 74, 174, 179–180, 210, 214, 236
Nixon Library 108–109

O

O'Brien, Lawrence 86, 100, 115, 117, 122, 164, 190–192, 194, 198–199, 205, 221–223, 259, 261
Obstruction 123, 152, 238–239, 247, 248, 254, 257
O'Connor, Christy 36, 93
O'Connor, Janet 36, 63, 102, 104
Odle, Robert 165, 169, 217
Oliver, Spencer Jr. 100, 110, 122, 154–158, 167, 173–174, 177–178, 191, 192, 194, 200, 221, 223
Operation Mud Hen 140, 186
Operation Sandwedge 126
Osnos, Peter 81, 83–92, 95, 96, 98, 106–109, 114 fn 1

P

Parkinson, Kenneth 157–158
Patman, Wright 11
Patriot Act 76
Pennington, Cecil 85
Pennington, Lee 85, 187, 192–194, 197–199, 237–239, 247, 251, 253–254
Pentagon Papers 67 fn 2, 127, 130 fn 4
Phone bug 143, 172, 189, 191, 194, 203, 205
Plumbers 116, 127, 128, 141, 257
Politics and Prose 95–96
Pottinger, Stanley 71
Powers, Richard Gid 89–90
Prostitute monitoring 86, 118, 124
Prostitution 87, 110, 112, 119–120, 122, 181, 186–187, 188, 211–213, 223–224, 231
Public Affairs 84, 88, 89, 95, 97, 105–107
Pulitzer Prize 1, 2, 150, 201

R

Radio Free Cuba 9, 134, 235 fn 1
Rafferty, Joseph 9, 131
Reagan, Ronald 68
Redford, Robert 5, 64
Regan, Willy 101
ReganBooks 82–83
Revisionist 87, 88, 100–101, 103, 107, 108–111, 115, 123, 211
Rhoden, Barbara Kennedy 156, 227 fn 14, 233
Richardson, Elliot 14
Rikan, Heidi 213
Ritchie, Robert "Buddha" 244
Roach, Jay 102
Robinson, Timothy 150–151
Rodino Committee 15
Rosen, James 156
Rothblatt, Henry 157
Ruckelshaus, William 14, 38, 70 fn 5, 115
Rudy, John 121
Russell, Lou 119, 123, 188, 208, 209–218, 221–222, 235

S

Sachs, Stephen 26
Safer, Morley 91
Santa Rosa, CA 50, 58, 95, 96, 101, 105–107
Schanberg, Sydney 75
Secret Agenda 86, 109–110, 114 fn 1, 117–119, 147, 159–160, 186 fn 5
Secret Man 66–81, 84, 90
Sedam, J. Glenn 165, 169, 217
Segretti, Donald 10, 11, 19, 52 fn 3, 70 fn 5, 77, 79, 102, 115 fn 2, 170, 171 fn 1, 180–181, 236, 256
Shaffer, Charles 27

Sharansky, Natan 84
Shipley, Alex 102
Shoffler, Carl 122, 222, 227–231, 233
Silbert, Earl 114 fn 1, 121 fn 13, 144–145, 154–155, 158, 172–174, 176, 177–179, 200
Silent Coup 86, 108–110, 114 fn 1, 119, 154–155, 212
Simons, Howard 5
Sirica, John 11–12, 129, 144, 153–154, 170, 176–181, 188, 200
Sixth burglar 100, 107, 112, 211–212, 216–217
Sloan, Hugh 30, 68 fn 4, 94, 256
Slush fund 10, 29–30, 68 fn 4, 171
Smith, Sandy 134–136, 192
Stanford, Phil 114 fn 1, 118 fn 1, 210, 213
State of Denial 4
Stevens, Michael 143, 199, 202–208, 211, 218, 235, 236
Strachan, Gordon 123
Strasser, Steven 85–87
Strauss, Robert 155–156
Sturgis, Frank 151
Sullivan, William 31, 80, 115 fn 2, 116–117, 126–127
Supreme Court 2, 14, 189, 246, 248, 254

T

Tape on the door 209, 212
Taylor, Hobart 240–241, 252
The Brethren 2
The Killing Fields See Schanberg, Sydney
Time magazine 12, 15, 70 fn 5, 134
Timmons, William E. 169

U

Ulasewicz, Tony 120, 126, 262
Undercover 141–142

V

Vanity Fair 50, 52, 54, 55–57, 61, 63–64, 82, 114
Volz, Joseph 216 fn 6

W

Warrantless entries 116–117
Washington Star-News xii, 120–121, 178, 212, 215–216, 217–218, 231 fn 16, 235
Weather Underground Organization 55, 101–102
Wells, Maxie 87, 110–112, 114 fn 1, 122, 155–156, 173, 174, 221–223, 231–233.
White House Call Girl See Stanford, Phil
White House switchboard 132
White, George 118
White, Harry 188
Will , 114 fn 1, 119, 121, 205, 222, 255, 256, 258, See Liddy, G. Gordon
Williams, Connelly & Califano 137, 160, 181 fn 9, 252
Wiretap 11, 32, 86, 100, 116, 117, 120, 126, 152, 175, 186, 189, 190, 191, 194, 203, 214, 217, 224
Wong, Alfred 183–184
Woods, Rose Mary 14–15
Woolston-Smith, A. J. 186
Wright, Charles Alan 15

Y

Young, David 127, 128, 141, 257

Z

Ziegler, Ron 9

Vēstis no Austrālijas